ISOLATED EXPERIENCES

SUNY Series in Contemporary Continental Philosophy

Dennis J. Schmidt, Editor

ISOLATED EXPERIENCES

GILLES DELEUZE AND THE
SOLITUDES OF REVERSED PLATONISM

JAMES BRUSSEAU

STATE UNIVERSITY OF NEW YORK PRESS

Published by
State University of New York Press, Albany

© 1998 State University of New York

For information, address State University of New York Press,
State University Plaza, Albany, N.Y. 12246

Production by M. R. Mulholland
Marketing by Nancy Farrell

Library of Congress Cataloging-in-Publication Data

Brusseau, James, 1964–
    Isolated experiences : Gilles Deleuze and the solitudes of
reversed Platonism / James Brusseau.
        p.   cm. — (SUNY series in contemporary continental
philosophy)
    Includes bibliographical references and index.
    ISBN 0-7914-3671-3 (hardcover : alk. paper). — ISBN 0-7914-3672-1
(pbk. : alk. paper)
    1. Deleuze, Gilles. I. Title. II. Series.
B2430.D454B78 1997
194—dc21   97-12980
                                                                            CIP

10 9 8 7 6 5 4 3 2 1

I dedicate this book to my parents.

CONTENTS

ACKNOWLEDGMENTS

Quiero dar las gracias en especial a Rocio Fernandez.

I acknowledge and thank readers of this work: Alphonso Lingis, Salim Kemal, Carl Vaught, Anne Bowery.

An early version of "Emily, the Patient, Bliss, Deleuze" appeared in *Synthesis*, Vol. 2, No. 2, Fall 1997.

Permission to reprint material from "Archives of General Psychiatry" was granted by the American Medical Association.

INTRODUCTION

A modest number of dissident literary tracts and a sequestered collection of aberrant human moments inspired Gilles Deleuze. Never interested in normalizing, Deleuze carefully preserved the irregularities of his subjects while seeking to explain them. A restricted philosophic method resulted. It functioned along narrow bands of experience and then scrupulously refused broadening generalizations. The discipline was intellectual constraint. Two books, *Difference and Repetition* and *Logic of Sense*, delineate this constraint severely. In them, Deleuze controls a philosophy that defines itself not by its extending reach, but by its excessive desire for localization.

I am investigating the powers of localized philosophy. This book labors for the specific.[1] The first section follows Deleuze closely to determine how a theory, perhaps humanity's most generalizing invention, can enclose itself. The question leads to a specific notion of production: there are generative forces that strive not for boundless extension but for the construction of their own stoppage. Limitation is no longer a frustration and evidence of incapacity, it is an accomplishment and a triumph. Section two pushes past Deleuze's explicit writings to investigate several distinct cases of limiting theory infecting an individual. The symptoms guiding my study are the possession of a body by forces, abilities, decisions, exploits, and words that refuse incorporation into a coherent biography. These episodes appear, fill specific times and places, and vanish. As Deleuze's theory secludes itself, so too do times in these interrupted lives. The third section examines the particular and impenetrable foreignness that surrounds possessed bodies. These recluses generate their own moralities, habits, sufferings, writings, and judgments independent of the society around them and without proselytizing intentions. Their lives cannot be explained by any philosophy except one they define with, and one that ends with, their own actions—or their own death.

The theoretical route to a philosophy and to experiences and ultimately to lives that limit themselves passes through history's most inclusive and imperializing thought, it goes through the ancient and ravenous attempt to organize every book, every experience, every argument and occurrence under the glaring light of one lasting idea; it goes through Platonism. Importantly, Platonism is not Plato. Plato refuses to speak in his own dialogues, and others, including Socrates, do not speak for him. A strong case can be made that Plato did not only write to valorize Socrates and his ideas, but also to criticize them.[2] Platonism, however, helplessly worships Socrates. For that reason, in this book, I use Socrates as Platonism's principal mouthpiece. Again, Socrates cannot be said to speak for Plato, he speaks for himself. It is Socrates, not Plato, that draws the *Republic*'s divided line. It is Socrates that grovels for sun-drenched reality, for the clear truth waiting outside the cave. And it is the young Socrates in the *Parmenides* that earnestly ponders whether there exist Forms of hair and dirt. When analogies, allegories, and questions like these get accepted without suspicion, Plato reduces to Platonism.

If Platonism is so stunted, why reverse it? Because a limited philosophy brings itself into existence by entering Platonism and delicately reversing it. This does not mean reading Plato's dialogues and looking up antonyms. Deleuze writes that it is not only inevitable but desirable that "this reversal *conserves* many of the characteristics of the Platonists."[3] Instead of opposing, reversing means probing for another truth and another philosophy curled inside Platonism. Two ways to draw it out: first, cannibalize Platonic ideas. Extract fractions of thought from Plato's dialogues, twist them slightly, and then reinsert them into different theoretical constructs. For example, Socrates's idea of divine madness connects to an intuitive, intellectual leap that moves his philosophy from one region of thought to another. The leap reappears in this book on the theoretical route to a limited philosophy, but the madness has a different flavor and the leap is in a different direction. Platonism survives, but in perverted form.

The second practice of reversal uses Platonism as a guide. A limited philosophy finds openings for itself at precisely those locations where Platonism tries to apply itself and its all-incorporating rule onto an episode and fails. The failure to satisfactorily explain an incident in Shakespeare, a literary character belonging to F. Scott Fitzgerald, and an entry in Isabelle Eberhardt's notebook sharply delineates quadrants reserved for another approach. The work of confined theorizing begins in these scattered zones. This line of reversal starts by testing for isolated failures in Platonism, then it refuses the Platonic impulse to repress the problem. Instead, it uses the breakdowns to craft a particular understanding that has no pretension to explain anything more than the scene that stimulated it. Platonic routes are conserved, but only as appropriated for other, more provincial destinations.[4]

Reversed Platonism is not the opposite of Platonism, and it is not another version of Platonism. It is a different philosophy that twists out of Platonism. Deleuze gestured toward this reversal, but never wrote it all the way through. Here, I follow the trail to its end, and it is a lonely end, one embodied by the nomadic wanderings of Isabelle Eberhardt, a woman alien to everyone and everything except a thinking that establishes itself and isolates itself in the midst of Platonism's voracious idealism.

PART I

DIFFERENCE

Begin with production and limitation. Production works at the base level where unformed being, where unformed experience, emerges. The specific character experience takes, whether you see a table as gracefully carved from supple wood or as something keeping books and papers off the floor, whether you hear a gurgling scream and fearfully retreat or wait in anticipation, whether you think of Beethoven as musical elegance or shrill noise, all this is limitation. To achieve identification, a production must be limited; when limitation encircles production, we have discrete experience.

The ancient Greeks gave us form and matter. In the *Phaedo*, Socrates maintained a firm duality: when the physical body died, the material stayed with it, and the philosopher's emancipated soul floated free into the spinning metaphysical afterlife. For Deleuze, production and limitation collapse. They collapse into a mechanical operation of production imposing its own limitation. But Deleuze is no simple monist. He does not talk about the origin, he points to plural sources. Further, Deleuze has no confidence in these sources. He sees them constantly separating into pieces and reforming as different beginnings with different operations. To the degree that we have origins, what we have are raw generations and their own self-inflicted definitions. Numbers like one, two, three, and titles like monism, dualism, and dialectics, will follow subsequent to the initial action; instead of describing production and limitation, these abstractions result from it. Deleuze stays closer to his idea by using blatantly inadequate terms like 'pre-singular'[1] to express the operation of his deficient monism. As a title, Deleuze chooses Socrates's bane: difference.

1

DIFFERENCE AS PRODUCTION AND LIMITATION

> . . . in place of something which distinguishes itself from other things, imagine something which distinguishes itself—and yet in distinguishing itself it does not distinguish itself from the others.[1]
>
> —Gilles Deleuze, *Difference and Repetition*

Philosophy is crowded with notions of difference. Paul de Man's means different from something. In *Allegories of Reading*,[2] he shows how we use figurative language by establishing its difference from literal language; the figurative and literal depend on each other by each laying their foundation across the other's back. The patrons for this agitated difference are Hegel, and Kojeve's Hegel, and the master/slave dialectic.

Deleuze has his own difference, one inspired by Nietzsche. It implies self-differentiation: simple difference, not different from something. Instead of difference between things, we have a produced differentiation within something. Instead of understanding and acting through the process of tense opposition, acts and things understand themselves by unilaterally limiting and distinguishing their meaning. When Deleuze uses the term 'difference,' he is not signalling the forces of opposition to begin their struggle, he is recognizing that some things don't need struggles. And if there is a struggle, it amounts to nothing more than a mock battle constructed by difference as a medium for its own action. For Hegel, the struggle was not at all simulated; it was a life-and-death battle about slavery. In his *Genealogy of Morals*, Nietzsche responded that the master had nothing to fear from the slave; the slave reduced to a constructed stage-prop or a homemade puppet the master toyed with. Far from being a threatening outsider, Nietzsche's slave is the master's own amusing and self-serving creation. Deleuze fits into the history of philosophy right here. For him, contrast and challenge and the dialectic become props for difference. If they exist, difference manufactures them. Difference generates its own meaning, definitions, and limits.

Difference for Itself

A finger turns in light circles across your toes and the pads of your feet. Is this irritating? ticklish? erotic? relaxing? According to difference, the delineation does not usher from an exterior source, like the masseur telling you to relax or a social norm insisting that when your wife does this it is sexual and when your doctor does this it is not. Instead, let the physical action define the borders and meaning. Think of fingers curling over a foot's toes and running down toward the heel. Imagine it, and only it. Not your foot, a foot. The fingers have no arm and no identity. The entire episode takes place without a background, without any time or place or situation. This instantiates the experience difference proposes. The material produces and defines its own sensations. It itself creates the episode. Tickling? Disturbing? What the event is and what it feels like arise on the scene.

When you add things from outside the immediate site, you move to a second kind of experience. Add that the foot is yours, and that the fingers belong to a professional masseur. Everything formalizes. The scene glides into the well travelled experience of relaxing because we know a massage is supposed to relax because we read it on the sign before going in.

Two separate experiences come to be in accordance with two unrelated rules. One extends from difference in the form of unilateral distinction, it is blind and deaf to anything beyond. Another works through definitions imposed, through background noise like customs and prosaic language and socialized patterns. I use Deleuze to focus on the first experience.

Restricted Ontology

Deleuze postulates:

. . . difference is that by which the given is given.[3]

and:

Being is Difference.[4]

Normally, philosophic claims about the inauguration of experience, about being, have monstrously far-reaching effects: they stretch through all reality. The breadth is natural for the Platonic tradition, understanding everything in terms of an original condition or final destiny. Either way, the world wraps into ultimate perfection. Socrates referred to the ideas, Augustine invoked God, Kant proposed the kingdom of ends. No matter the version, fundamental claims about experience incline toward the first state or the last; they tend to cover everything by default.

Deleuze's difference makes no claims about ultimate perfections. Difference's primary claim involves experience's fluid, progressive, continuing generation. Originating is no longer one place back there in the hazy metaphysical past but a grinding process constantly staking out a claim to beginning in the present. With this distinction between origins referencing the past and working the present, the philosophy of being splits. Deleuze's difference functions only in the limited, situated event it currently produces—it inclines nowhere beyond its particular moment. Difference always works here and now. Space and time are no longer fodder for overcoming as they were for Socrates, Augustine, and Kant; they are no longer vulgar obstacles on the way to universality and eternity. Naive space and everyday time satisfy difference, they give it all the room it needs. Everything localizes. Here and now, difference makes the world without awakening Socratic monsters of generality.

Coming at the same point from the other side, difference's relentless localization implies things left out. For example, dieting eludes difference's rules. Dieting is driven by a perfect state always exterior to and always preceding the actual practice.

But exceptions cannot impinge on Deleuze. Difference still works inside the particular experiences it generates and defines. When a hand turns over a foot without the attached idea of a wife or a masseur, there is still experience. Or, when Duchamp leans a urinal against the wall of the museum's display room, there is not, at first, art, and there is not a bathroom, but there is still experience. Or, when you are very young and your best friend announces a set of unusual sexual proclivities, there is not sexuality and there is not friendship, but there is still experience. And, crucially, the questions ringing these episodes are not about which experience, not about perspectives. They are questions about experience itself. Drive deeper than epistemology, drive to the origin. Difference composes occurrences now and from inside. It joins your back and the hands of another into a slow rolling wave of skin, muscle, and bone; it creates a nervous agitation from a museum display room; it makes a social encounter into downcast eyes and the furtive search for a door.

Now we have a paradox: difference operates on the fundamental level generating discrete experiences, but it also admits some valid, right, or true being may be left outside and come to be at the hands of other rules. Philosophy's tolerance of the situation depends on a re-evaluation. Socrates started with every important experience and insisted that his philosophy stretch out to meet them—he employed a notion of the whole as global imposition. But whatever difference explains, it explains by its own standards. Thus it itself standardizes the whole of experience. The whole is generated on the spot, not imposed. Therefore, what Socrates would consider less than the perfect whole becomes perfect in the context of difference because difference recognizes nothing beyond its relatively narrow territory. It works rigorously, but only on its designated subject. When Deleuze writes "Being is Difference," he does not mean all being necessarily reduces to the production of difference. "Being is Difference" means that being as difference is that being brought into existence and saturated by difference's regulations.

The succeeding two chapters elaborate some of those regulations, but here, stay focused on difference's paradox. It can be rendered in sharper terms. Socrates imagined the whole encompassed its parts and was by definition superior. For difference, the perfect whole sits on the same shelf as its parts. It is one among many, like a part that has taken the name of the whole. It is a qualified perfection or a limited whole. It claims no priority over its own members because without the Socratic valorization of beginning or end, perfection has no necessary precedence. Deleuze seizes onto this. His difference grants us a framework wherein the part can be adequate to, even exceed, the whole.

Examples of this commonplace but still revolutionary truth

are everywhere. Take an ironic case from philosophy's history, the comparison between Alcibiades and Socrates. Plutarch wrote that Alcibiades exceeded every Greek in every imaginable category of judgment. Plato himself called Alcibiades the man who lacked nothing. He was stunningly beautiful, keenly intelligent, witty, rich, an unparalleled military commander, a leading politician. Socrates was something less: short, loathsomely ugly, a foot soldier, financially barely self-sufficient. Socrates is only a fraction of what Alcibiades is. And Alcibiades is the perfect whole. Yet Plato insists through his dialogues that Socrates is the superior. He insists that somehow Alcibiades should and even did envy that man who had in every way less. From the *Symposium*: "[Socrates] is the only person in whose presence I experience a sensation of which I might be thought incapable, a sensation of shame. . . ."[5] Alcibiades's shame is Socrates exceeding Alcibiades is the part exceeding the whole. Plato, presumably the first guru of the whole as unsurpassable, unwittingly or intentionally admits evidence that the part can be more. For another example, take an average philosophy journal article. You can make it better simply by cutting it down. Nothing needs to be added, just take words, phrases, sentences, paragraphs, and sections out. Then take the shorter article and set it next to its longer parent. The longer version has every idea contained in the shorter. It has those and more. But the shorter one is better. Better because when you read an article you do not evaluate it against some final or original whole which would be the fantastic, perfect, and complete article. You read in accordance with the rules the article itself sets up. So a shorter article with less information can be superior. This situation makes sense only if the article itself generates the measure for marking its success and failure. And this is exactly difference's stipulation. The elements difference commands distinguish and define themselves. They give themselves the value they merit. The article obeys difference's rule, so less can be more.

Return to the claim that difference is both the genesis of being and limited in its scope with respect to being. Philosophic reflection on the deepest roots of experience continues after Deleuze, but now without having to check every claim with respect to every significant occurrence. Difference is a restricted ontology.[6] If difference explains a certain event, then understand and deploy difference in that one slim place. Socrates finds this intolerable, but difference stretches out its own field and acts there.

Difference's Fields

Where does difference stretch out and work? Three romantic examples: art, love, insanity. Difference explains how you can be under the spell of a certain piece of music and declare with all sincere confidence that this is the great composition, the definition of beauty, then later have the same unshakeable certainty and make the same pronouncement about another composition. This is not simply changing your mind. You refuse to renounce the earlier judgement even while making one irreconcilable with it. Are you deranged? rash? a critic clamoring for attention even at the cost of your reputation? On occasion, no. Difference enters here by operating twice through the same subject. In one field a beauty is erected—even stronger—the possibility of beauty is erected, and in a separate field a separate construction. In both, the definition of beauty comes from the origin of being, thus it rests imperturbable. Meanwhile, from some global, Socratic perspective, the two views contradict abrasively. But difference maintains there is no global perspective, only internally generated value. This qualification is not a diminution. Difference's generated beauty is not incomplete and weak but overperfect and vigorous. The absence of Socratic Beauty allows a restricted beauty without substantial qualification, it allows an absolute one—absolute because there is nothing against which it pales.

The same in love. You swear you love somebody forever, and some night, five years later, she rolls over and you hear her waiting. Finally she gathers herself and says, "I guess you don't love me anymore." You agree it's true. Is your heart pitifully soft? Does your commitment amount to nothing more than facile convenience? Socrates makes the accusations, and he's usually right; the paradox separating what you are saying now from what you said then betrays your irresolution, your fragility, your lies. But in an isolated circumstance, in difference's circumstance, what you said then can remain true even after admitting it is no longer there. You can love somebody permanently, you can have said that, and refuse to deny it and still take responsibility for it, and still know that it is true, and also say that now, nonetheless, I don't love you anymore. Only difference can explain this by producing a certain time and its meaning from within the pronouncement and without reference to a universal temporality or even to the minutes and hours we all share. In difference, forever has nothing to do with calendars, it has to do with the slender, incorruptible world generated from lovers' words.

Finally, insanity also subscribes to a restricted ontology. After enduring and learning from a severe mental breakdown, Scott Fitzgerald wrote: ". . . the test of a first rate intelligence is the ability to hold two opposed ideas in the mind at the same time, and still retain the ability to function. One should, for example, be able to see that things are hopeless and yet be determined to make them otherwise."[7] Difference rules Fitzgerald's definition of first rate intelligence. Or, two distinct differences, but differences having nothing to do with differences between two ideas, having nothing to do with opposition. The differences each confine themselves, they turn everything in, they limit themselves while being absolute. Thus, Fitzgerald can be hopeless without qualification and determined without qualification.

Interrogating Difference

How do we think difference? Through examples, example after example after example. And in every case, not through identity. Deleuze faults the tradition for mutating difference into an indirect philosophy of static unity. Socrates began by forcing thought to align itself with the sun outside his cave. Traditional notions of difference have never broken away. In a specific case of this predicament, thinking through concepts has constrained the effort. Deleuze writes that in this case ". . . difference is only able to be a predicate in the comprehension of the concept."[8] The subject of the concept—difference—suffers enslavement to the formal conditions of conceptualization. And these conditions belong on identity's level because concepts work in important ways like Platonism's ideas: they gather up their particular members and, in the gathering, sap the members' productive force. Concepts postulate that you are what you are because you fit in this spot, because of the framework the concept has already provided and is now imposing. A static structure closes its iron fist around a producing nature. From here, a notion of internal self-differentiation can rise, but only a derivative notion, one constrained by an inimical and prior structure of conceptualization.

In his later work, notably in *What is Philosophy?*, Deleuze will come to embrace concepts, even assign to philosophy the task of actively constructing them. Deleuze does not change his mind. Instead he redefines what a concept is by understanding what it means to make concepts within the framework of difference. At this earlier stage, however, Deleuze is rallying against the specific practice of conceptualization that the Platonic tradition bequeaths the West. Platonism understands concepts following the model of metaphysical ideas; stolid frames imprison difference by always understanding it in terms of the unshakeable identities Socrates saw outside the cave. In *Difference and Repetition*, Deleuze labors to think the other way: the self-differentiating world governs prefabricated structures. Instead of thinking difference through a concept, accept concepts and all of identity's products as themselves products of a prior, internal differentiation. In other words, start from difference on its own territory.

Start from difference on its own territory by exchanging philosophy as theoretical discussion, like Socrates in the agora, for philosophy as use. What Deleuze focuses on, and what he weighs in the end, are the products of thinking. Instead of asking why and how his theory works, he asks: does difference prove its utility? What can it explain? Deleuze proposes difference and shoves it out among us. He wants to know if difference fits, does it come through when we write and when we understand? This does not reduce theoretical concerns to irrelevance, and Deleuze does not refuse to formulate responses to objections of that kind, but before taking up self-critical worries (like Socrates always wanting to know how his philosophy got started, *eros* he answered), Deleuze wants to exercise his difference. So when questions are asked of Deleuze, they should come through the world. At least initially, they should all be forms of this: how does difference work with particular experience?

Admittedly, this is nebulous. The criteria for determining whether or not difference excels philosophically have not graduated from the shifting indistinctness inherent to earthbound reality—one still does not know exactly how to grade work in Deleuze's philosophy. The problem is endemic. Because difference as philosophy starts from the midst of the changeful physical world, Deleuze chooses his metaphors from here, he likes the term 'force,' for instance. Force summons material connotations: matter in motion striking and transforming. Nothing is safe, nothing immune to being bent or melted or dropped or colored or reconstituted. Since the determination of whether or not a philosophy succeeds must establish itself at least partially on the level of its rhetoric, for someone like Socrates, the evaluating questions happen on the level akin to the metaphorics of ideas, the permanent, clear level. But for Deleuze, who prefers material, evaluating methods gravitate toward physical force's level, the impermanent and murky. Here, what we have for ends, for successes, are constantly being eroded, painted over, cut up. If any more enduring criteria for measuring difference arise, they will rise from a separate kind of philosophic ground. They are not my concern. My concern: focus on the immediate process. If difference is working, let it go, even push it along. Exercise Deleuze in the world.[9]

In the next two chapters, I develop cases of difference in experience more complex and instructive than those I have dashed through here. I am looking for cases of unilateral distinction, of being generating its own limits. To sharpen the presentation, I artificially divide the subject into two discrete aspects, first production, then limitation. The distinction violates difference by leashing it to concepts grounded in identity. But on Deleuze's thinking field, theoretical concerns always take a backseat to practical results; determine whether or not a presentation works before determining whether or not it should work. This is the route out of identity and Platonism generally. It does not run through direct attacks on Socrates, instead through betrayal. Accept identity, but only as incorporated into the work of difference.

Next, difference as production drives Nietzsche's eternal return and invigorates Shakespeare's *Titus Andronicus*. Then, difference as limitation will circumscribe Foucault's philosophic theory of transgression and define Bataille's literary presentation of perversion.

2

THE ETERNAL RETURN DOES DIFFERENCE: PRODUCTION[1]

The adventure into which I plunge them does not astonish them, but they live it out through acts, through gestures, not through thinking about it. In that way I can escape the danger of putting together a realistic narrative according to the usual methods by which each character *knows* what he's expressing at the very moment he expresses it, and knows the overtones that his expression *should* have on his protagonist and us. . . .[2]

—Jean Genet

Nietzsche, from *The Gay Science*: "Do you desire this once more and innumerable times more?"[3] He means everything: every book you read, every lover you take and every one you refuse, all the decisions, selections, all the hopes and everything you imagine and work for and avoid. You must desire them again. You must spurn them again. Experience jacked up to the Nietzschean degree lasts through the same moment recurring eternally. But what that means remains unclear.

Begin by refusing defensive measures. The eternal return will not accept some bare level of experience and then act to ward off the dangerous or the unsatisfying. It strikes, and strikes preemptively. It makes our earth. It generates experience. Only on the heels of produced experience can Nietzsche's innumerable repeating follow.

In *Nietzsche and Philosophy*, Deleuze understands production—the production he harnesses to his own philosophy of difference—in terms of affirmation. Affirming the world makes the world. To reach the affirmation of untainted production, Deleuze divides the act. The first part orients his thought, but we must wait until the second for Deleuze to unveil a generator that makes Nietzsche into a forefather of unilateral distinction. Thus, the first affirmation's central importance lies in locating the issue; it will yield a precise state requiring overcoming. The second affirmation is overcoming which transforms immediately into production unbridled. This transforms immediately into difference as production.

First Affirmation

The first affirmation is literal. Deleuze remembers Nietzsche's disdain for the habitual.[4] Under its control, experience becomes resignation to inertia. So, break the inertia. But the rule of habit means every broken propensity comes limited by the dulling understanding: only once. Breaking a habit only once fails to break a habit. The problem is not singularity in number; Nietzsche does not reduce to something like the more the better. The problem with volition qualified by the only once is the internal decay. The rotted will reasons: Yes, act now, do it *because* the break frees me to later reembrace habit. The will reduces to working against itself because the impetus for a habit-wrecking action springs from a commitment to return to the comfort of the former pattern. For the will to function properly, it must do so without the constraint of its own denial. Even the shortest hesitation immediately seizes up everything. No degrees of success exist. The will wills or the will dies.[5]

If the will is either alive or dead, then the eternal return can begin to function as a vivifying imperative, because a will doomed to recurring eternally guarantees that within each particular action the volition refuses to lean explicitly against its opposite—I cannot act now as a reaction to not acting that way again because the again never arrives. According to Deleuze, this is the eternal return's first affirmation.

Transformation and Revelation

The first affirmation forbids contradiction within the individual will but does not preclude contradiction between an individual's various wills. For Deleuze's Nietzsche, our identity is not straightjacketed singularity; we are bundles of volitions masquerading as singular, continuous selves. Nietzsche wants to unfetter each of those wills, not constrain the set. It follows that capricious individuals may live through the eternal return without a Nietzschean rebuke. I can receive the first affirmation as long as my particular action steps away from the buttress of denial. Later, another volition may surge through my body, heading it along a contradictory line, but this fails to negate the earlier act because the perception of contradiction does not exist inside either will, only outside both, from some global and therefore hypothetical and therefore irrelevant vantage point.

Another way of writing this: wills cannot cancel each other out. Everything must always be added. Along a line, the movements from zero to one and then back from one to zero count together as two. Even stronger, they do not count together at all. Because Nietzsche's wills are self-sufficient, they break off from each other. This suggests that the eternal return patronizes the isolated and incongruous events associated with transformations or revelations.

Lying

The eternal return does not preclude lying. I can plead for money from a friend, blubbering with assurances to repay within the week and know full well I never will. Nothing pejorative here, in fact, Nietzsche approves. Only one possibility worries: feelings of remorse. Guilt planted in me by an authority figure or moral code turns me back against myself. When I repent, the contamination of denial attaches retroactively. It sounds like this, "I did that once, but I wish I hadn't and I won't do it again." The eternal return insists the will be uncontaminated at a hyper level; all comparison and regret must be shunted aside. Nietzsche envisions a volition pure by virtue of its own deed. This will expresses itself entirely through immediate action, so the immaculateness it radiates is not abstract, formal, and timeless like Socrates's ideas; it is material, actual, and now, like a lie conspicuously not repented.

In the *Genealogy of Morals*, Nietzsche moves the discussion onto the ethical plane by equating the hyper-pure will with goodness. In practice, this means a will's action and the judgment of that action must be identical. Instead of referring to laws or authority figures for the good, what is acted subsequently becomes good; the good becomes just what is acted. Judgment losses its autonomy, it reduces to a simple corollary of an act's manifestation. In Nietzsche's world, as Deleuze presents it, to deny myself does not mean to misrepresent myself, like Judas at the last supper denied his traitorous intentions. To deny myself means to doubt myself, it means accepting a judgment that rises from somewhere beyond the sacrosanct and material purity of my own body's workings. Take Judas committing suicide after selling Jesus to the Romans. The sin as registered by the eternal return was the contrition, not the disloyalty.

Reaction and Nondialectical Opposition[6]

Deleuze calls the forces working to scuttle and deny the will "reactive." Wills infected by the reactive subsist only by referring to other wills. Before anything, the reactive measures itself against them, it evaluates itself in their terms, it acts in accord or discord with them. The obvious example is physical force; the will compelled by somebody else's muscle is reactive. Even when I snap to do what the brute tells me and show no sign of resistance, our agreement buzzes with tense repudiation. At the extreme, when I would have acted exactly as directed without the enforced rule of another, the fact of the rule still saps my will by refusing to grant me exclusive control over a moment that should be my own—because there exists a question about whether I am in control, I am not.

Beyond the brute's level, there are other, more surreptitious enforcers of reaction. Prodigious numbers of moral, philosophic, and social constructs serve to make wills reflect something beyond their proper stimulus: courage, intelligence, patience, originality, legality, role models. In brief, any kind of relative or social evaluation. Before I broke the law or emulated my role model, I opposed myself to them, I deferred to them. Hegel comes in here with the master/slave dialectic of need. The master needs the slave's persistent threat of rebellion to verify his dominance, the slave needs the master to define his role and life. Both need each other. More, neither the master nor the slave can even exist without having its existence confirmed through agitated contrast. This dialectic insists a will must deny others to be. I am because I am not him.[7]

Deleuze sets the master/slave dialectic, which he comes to call simply "the dialectic," at the base of Nietzsche's reactive will. Deleuze concludes that "Three ideas define the dialectic: the idea of the power of the negative as a theoretical principle manifested in opposition and contradiction; the idea that suffering and sadness have value, the valorization of the "sad passions" as a practical principle manifested in splitting and tearing apart; the idea of positivity as a theoretical and practical product of negation itself."[8] Note especially the emotional components. They will reappear as important elements in philosophically considering the simulacrum (Chapter 9). At this stage, however, stay closer to theory. Deleuze's formulation of the dialectic reduces actions and their meaning to by-products of a fundamental negation: before I act, I go counter to something, I go because of something. I oppose it. I contradict it. Everything positive starts as against. This dialectic suits reactive forces perfectly.

Deleuze's covering of distinctly Hegelian ground leads immediately to a fair question: does Deleuze (through his Nietzsche) do justice to Hegel? The nearly unanimous answer is no. Stephen Houlgate marches in the front ranks of a contemporary procession dating back to 1963 and Jean Wahl's review of *Nietzsche and Philosophy*. These authors claim, with various degrees of bluntness, that Deleuze has portrayed Hegel's philosophy carelessly. Each commentator levels a number of charges and detects several specific faults. Reviewing them comprehensively would be a book in itself. But a single accusation mingles with all the various objections: Deleuze reduces every instance of Hegel's varied dialectic to the one definition I cited above. Too crude a reading, the critics insist, and too pessimistic. Though this characterization may be adequate for the narrow dialectical stage played by the master and slave in the *Phenomenology*, they argue that Hegel also understood a positive and productive internal differentiation not entirely unlike the force of unfettered production Deleuze will find in Nietzsche's valorized will. Houlgate stakes his claim: ". . . Deleuze sees in Hegelian dialectic the product of a tired, nihilistic will which is "weary of willing," and he contrasts it with the Dionysian affirmation of the self that is celebrated in Nietzsche's philosophy. Deleuze's interpretation of Nietzsche is persuasive . . . his view of Hegel, on the other hand, is a distortion."[9]

For his part, Wahl first praises: "Right next to the most important books on Nietzsche . . . we are able to place Gilles Deleuze's book . . ."[10] But then he writes pithily: ". . . is there not in the passages of the *Phenomenology of Spirit* something more profound that can resist the Nietzschean critique?"[11]

What is a Deleuzean response? Start with Deleuze himself, not on this particular subject, but on the subject of objections in general. In his dialogues with Claire Parnet, Deleuze propounds: "Objections are even worse. Every time someone puts an objection to me, I want to say: 'OK, OK, let's go on to something else.' Objections have never contributed anything."[12] Sarcasm and flippancy, but also a serious point. First, do not read Deleuze's refusal of objections to mean he considers Hegel or the history of philosophy irrelevant. Deleuze's earliest books are devoted to careful, selective readings of diverse, canonized thinkers. To see what lies beneath Deleuze's dismissal of objection, place his sentences on a gauge of production. The question Deleuze insists we ask before we begin disputing is: Does the objection generate philosophy or simply suffocate it? Every criticism potentially reduces thinking to a chess match of minute complaints and arcane refutations having nothing to do with experience. Deleuze palpably fears this, he fears that objections drag him away from the material world and into the vacuous space inflating theoretical debate. Thus, the first response to Deleuze's critics should be: Do your questions and concerns push philosophy forward or simply bury it in itself? Weigh objections. Set some of them aside. Deleuze's attitude is pushing past flippancy and toward a larger determination to think productively. In agreement with his ontology, Deleuze wants philosophic discussion to be more than simply reactive; at each stage, it should be generative. The strategy can be particularized to the Hegelian debate—instead of asking whether Deleuze's depiction of Hegel and the dialectic is right, ask whether it is useful for reading Nietzsche. It is. Even though it may not be historically faultless, Deleuze's depiction of Hegel and the dialectic will turn Nietzsche loose, especially the Nietzsche of production and the Nietzsche of the eternal return. In his book *Gilles Deleuze*, Michael Hardt shows how.

According to Hardt, Deleuze's specification of the dialectic sets two species of philosophic opposition into relief. The second will steer us toward the eternal return. The first keeps us away. Hardt labels the first opposition dialectical and writes that "Dialectical opposition is a restrained, partial attack that seeks to preserve and maintain its enemy; it is a sort of low intensity warfare that can be prolonged indefinitely in standing negation."[13] Dialectical opposition casts everything as a proximate, not a distant enemy, an enemy first beaten down, then succored, then beaten down again, then succored, and on and on. This is exactly the process Houlgate and Wahl mechanically operate. They sense that Deleuze stands autonomously distant from their Hegel, they cannot tolerate it, so they draw him into proximity, which means they draw Deleuze into the reactive oppositions of Hegelianism. First, they reduce the speechless alienation Deleuze feels in the face of Hegel's defenders to a low-intensity warfare by disputing Deleuze's treatment of Hegel on certain points while nurturing his philosophic standing with praise on other fronts. Houlgate: "Deleuze's interpretation of Nietzsche is persuasive . . . his view of Hegel, on the other hand, is a distortion." Thus, they start up the twin and connected and always dependent motions of acceptance and rejection. Deleuze's foreignness disintegrates into agreements and disagreements tugging back and forth. Next, the two sides—Deleuze and Hegel—lose relevance. What matters is between, the relation. And the relation is negative, carried by nots, Deleuze is no longer Deleuze but not Hegel, Hegel is not Deleuze. This is what Deleuze meant when he characterized the dialectic as forming "positivity as a theoretical and practical product of negation itself." From this perspective—an opposition demanding interminable war aggravated by the priority of the relation of nots—Deleuze can be nothing but opposition to Hegel and negative agreement with Hegel: not Hegel and not not Hegel. The unilateral action requisite to pure production fizzles. The eternal return, which can only cycle in the absence of negative, reactive dependency, breaks down. To repair it, turn to the other opposition.

This one is nondialectical. Again, Hardt writes on Deleuze's philosophy: "The result of this profound opposition is a separation that prohibits the recuperation of relations. . . ."[14] According to the rule of nondialectical opposition, distinction can exist without first depending on what I am distinct from. I can be opposed to something without being reformed by it. A production remaining unmistakably separated from others even while not accruing a debt to them replaces fundamental contrast and interminable, low-intensity warfare. Under this new regime, I can oppose without first extending toward or recoiling from what I oppose. I may extend or recoil, but only after the formative action. And this might happen from only one side. Nondialectical opposition does not require balance, it is not as though pairs engaged in nondialectical opposition must be mutually autonomous. The liberty of nondialectical opposition goes beyond every restraint by staying entirely self-contained. Consequently, a single relation may feature nondialectical opposition on one side while remaining mired in dialectical opposition on the other.

The importance of this discovery cannot be overestimated. Deleuze has used Nietzsche to formulate a structure for relation as radical as any the world has seen. Simultaneously, within a duality that exceeds the definition of duality, we find an infinite unbalance and a low-intensity war. On the one side, Deleuze's productive action carries on oblivious to anything but itself, while on the other, Hegel's cycling dialectic of dependency infinitely plays. Philosophy has seen structures of quasi-relations attaining this degree of disequilibrium, but never before have they entered entirely into the world. Aquinas, for example, postulated that his God had no dependence on humanity even while humanity found itself constantly wrapped up with, and dependent upon, God. Deleuze's idea waits in here somewhere, but for Aquinas, the one side remained perpetually hidden from everything but divine revelation. Nietzsche and Deleuze want to instantiate both the God and human sides of this nondialectical opposition right here in plain experience.

Marx brought a dialectic entirely into the material and political world, but he envisioned his antithetical pairs (understood as economic classes) culminating in a final synthesis. A century later, Paul de Man invoked the earthly dialectic for his literary theory. He diverged from Marx's structural precedent by proposing that the two terms in play could never reach a final synthesis because the opposition was always lopsided.[15] But it remained for Deleuze to make the final leap. At last, the material dialectic is no longer balanced or lopsided, it is one-sided. Nondialectical opposition instantiates a paradoxical world where two sides scratch caustically at each other while one side remains wholly self-absorbed and immune to the very reactive interplay it sustains.

In the academic world, this one-sided dialectic plays out in the form of energetic and continuing critiques charging that Deleuze fails to do justice to Hegel and never gets beyond Hegel and depends on Hegel, even while Deleuze and Nietzsche have already vacated the premises. It also plays out in this book as I am elaborating difference on the one side as reversed Platonism and on the other as unilateral distinction.

Move back to the eternal return. The idea of nondialectical

opposition will prove instrumental in sympathetically following Deleuze's thought on Nietzsche. The eternal return's focal point, one Hegel's dialectic threatens to blur, has come into focus. Nietzsche wants a self-sufficient will, a volition defining its own values and limits in one swing and without denial. Hegelian dialectics, as Deleuze presents it, counters with a full-blooded ontological declaration: values and limits cannot arise without ceding some responsibility to an exterior source. Deleuze hears this, so he writes: ". . . the relation of master and slave is not, in itself, dialectical. Who is the dialectician, who dialectises the relationship? It is the slave, the slave's perspective, the way of thinking belonging to the slave's perspective."[16] Dialectics becomes the slave's proper epistemic system, even his wishful thinking. Hegel becomes the slave, his books are rationales and excuses for a resentful, slavish philosophic life. Simultaneously, because Nietzsche's master operates in productive and not reactive modes, Nietzsche remains unaffected by the slave's struggle against the world. Now, finally, Deleuze refuses to let Hegel even visit Nietzsche:

> There is no possible compromise between Hegel and Nietzsche. Nietzsche's philosophy . . . forms an absolute anti-dialectics. . . .[17]

For Deleuze, Nietzsche's volition passes through the eternal return and moves over to the master's side by cutting away the slave's perspective and thus the master/slave dialectic of reaction. The blade is called nondialectical opposition.

This severance goes a long way toward bringing the eternal return into working operation. Most importantly, the entire rhetoric of the discussion has changed. Before, the dialectic forced us to understand every objection to Nietzsche as a counterattack strafing him violently. But that characterization lends reactive oppositions more nobility than they merit and makes the particular voices of reaction more dangerous than they need to be. The rhetoric of contradiction and struggle and war plays right into the hands of dialectics because discussion couched in Hegel's opposing terms cannot resist a dialectical outcome. How are you going to win? By defeating Hegel? Here, Nietzsche is lost before he can appear. In response, Deleuze submerges Hegel by refusing to acknowledge him: no victory, no surrender, nothing. Nietzsche resurfaces.

Instead of joining the conflict between active and reactive forces, the will affirmed in the eternal return simply neglects reaction. Defeat dialectic forces by setting them aside. Let them go on, but make them fend for themselves, by themselves. Deleuze writes:

> Negation is *opposed* to affirmation but affirmation *differs* from negation.[18]

Here, Deleuze employs the term 'opposed' where he could have used 'dialectically opposes,' and he uses the term 'differs' where he could have used 'nondialectically opposes.' In either case, the negative, reactive workings of dialectic wills continue clinging to the affirmation they want desperately to spoil, even though the eternal return no longer recognizes them.

Objections to the First Affirmation

The deepest problem the eternal return now faces is itself. Insofar as I accept the eternal return, I accept something of Nietzsche and Deleuze on me—adopting the eternal return means beginning by turning my will over to the eternal return, which it precisely specifies I cannot do. Like a catch-22, acceptance leads automatically to rejection. Like the imperative, "Be spontaneous." hearing the words precludes the possibility.[19]

And there is another problem, or another refined aspect of the same problem. The eternal return backs you into a certain temporality. Take this articulation from Nietzsche's *Gay Science*: ". . . every pain and every joy and every thought and sigh and everything unutterably small or great in your life will have to return to you, all in the same succession and sequence. . . ."[20] The eternal return invokes a continuous and unidirectional temporality. Everything that is, is in continuous time because of the guarantee the eternal return gives to succession. Further, everything that is, is in unidirectional time because the eternal return guarantees the sequence. This time moves uninterrupted and straight through from past to future. This time denies the will by insisting that what you do next will follow in strict order from what you do now and what is done cannot be undone. Again, the return undermines itself because part of my will exists somewhere else, under the power of a temporal other. I recognize it and with that I deny myself.

Second Affirmation

For the return to work, it must include a second affirmation that breaks it clean away from reference to even the most stubborn reactionary forces. It must break clean away from even itself. Deleuze puts the point in terms of two selections. "But reactive forces which go to the limit . . . resist the first selection. Far from falling outside the eternal return they enter into it and seem to return with it. We must therefore expect a second selection, very different from the first."[21] How different? The central difference involves sequence. The first affirmation was preceded by the imperative to will an act infinitely. When you met the imperative's requirements, you had ascended to the first affirmation and could act. So, attaining the first affirmation meant something like carefully following a set of directions. The way to the second affirmation reverses the order. Before you encounter action meriting the second affirmation, you must have already accomplished the act. That is, in order to realize the eternal return's second affirmation, you need to have already realized the eternal return. No longer a prescription, Nietzsche's idea forges ahead as a confirmation. In sharper terms: if the eternal return makes sense, you have already been spun around inside it.

At this point, Deleuze's Nietzsche veers toward part of Socrates's idealism. Specifically, the notion that a kind of intuitive leap is required. Deleuze: "Truth, as a concept, is entirely undetermined. Everything depends on the value and sense of what we think. We always have the truths we deserve."[22] This claim is not a tiring reiteration of relativism in thought and philosophy. Yes, truth is mainly relative, but Deleuze means something novel. The stress lies on "We always have the truths we deserve." He means there exists an immanent connection between actors and their produced truths. We deserve our truths because we must have already earned them by doing them. This sequence grants Deleuze's notion of truth a pervasiveness any classical philosopher would admire. Like his ontology, Deleuze's theory of truth is restricted; within it, pervasiveness functions, while outside it, capriciousness rules. Socrates's general truth was the Good, Deleuze's particular truth is pure difference which manifests itself in Nietzsche as the eternal return. For both Socrates and Deleuze, persuasion, proofs, imperatives, and discourse fail. They fail for Socrates because his Truth cannot tolerate the impermanence of the written and spoken word. They fail for Deleuze because his second affirmation cannot tolerate the imposition and reaction inherent to public discourse. Thus, Socrates and Deleuze stand in some proximity, momentarily, on the question of intuition.[23] They both need it to reach a point that cannot be imposed with words. From Platonism, Deleuze conserves the idea of a philosophic leap.

Deleuze reverses the leap's direction, however. Socrates's mode of intuition was divine madness. He told us that enduring it was not discovering or learning but realizing something you already knew. In the *Phaedrus*, Socrates insisted upon the soul's immortality and understood it as perpetually cycling between the region of the Gods and material earth. Time in this world, for the philosopher inspired by intellectual madness, meant time spent remembering the otherworldly wisdom of the heavens. In experience, realizing Deleuze's eternal return may seem like Socrates's experience of Providential *deja vu*, but for Socrates, we really had already seen. For Deleuze, any sense of refrain is illusory. It is simply the way you yourself mark your arrival at the produced realization. Recognition no longer refers outside the recognizer to a precedent entity or potential condition. Recognition is the subsequent product of a generated condition; it rises from the eternal return's material, contemporary action as an effect of its own internal distinction. It creates something you knew. Instead of being the goal of Socratic madness, recognition becomes a projection of a new divine madness, a Deleuzean madness.

The telling symptom of this madness is a particular change: ". . . it demands of itself, by the eternal return, to enter into being that which could not enter there without changing its nature."[24] The eternal return does not change your nature. Reverse the order. You must change your nature to get the eternal return.

Nature

What is nature? To answer, Deleuze underlines one of Nietzsche's key insights: the ascendency of slave morality in our culture. Examples: Platonism, Christianity, Nazism, multiculturalism. All these follow from a regrettable split between ourselves and our actions. In the *Genealogy of Morals*, Nietzsche exhausts himself in inflated prose claiming the world originated in a set of hierarchies enforced by sheer power. The nobles were just those able to exercise their wills upon the base. The good were the powerful, the bad were the weak. Whether this state is historical, mythical, metaphorical, allegorical, or simply aesthetic is irrelevant. What matters is that our current condition marks a disintegration from the original. In our time, the nobles have been made to believe that their power is not a virtue, but an embarrassment. Somehow, they have been convinced it is wrong to beat up, oppress, or exploit the small, the weak, and the disadvantaged. If the nobles do oppress and exploit, they are criminals (social condemnation), or sinners (religious condemnation) or louts (political condemnation). And who has convinced them of this, who has convinced them they should renounce their advantage and even pay penance for their superiority? No one but the formerly weak. Those who could not defend themselves from the power of their superiors have convinced the superiors to disarm voluntarily. The tools of persuasion are evident: codes of secular law that demand the imprisonment of violent felons, religious teachings like tithing and social responsibilities like charity that drain the productive class of its resources, the academic edict that mires the day's lecture in diverse viewpoints, the college that implements and aggressively pursues affirmative action policies, the university that creates a new department to honor and cherish the oppressed Central American culture its founder remorselessly exploited a century ago. Thus, the weak, the base, the slow-witted, and the insipid assume lofty positions in society, government, and education, while the powerful and productive resign themselves to penance for their infractions, their sins, and their insensitivity.

The weak have triumphed over the strong. How? By separating the strong from what they can do. The first step toward the nobles' enervation is convincing them that they can, that they must, control their actions. In Nietzsche's original state, no self-consciousness existed. The nobles acted without reflection and then enjoyed the fruits of their crude triumphs. In the modern state nobody acts without first considering. We demand of ourselves: is this legal or illegal? (social evaluation), is this charitable or sinful? (religious evaluation), is this acceptable or incorrect? (political evaluation). The problem with these questions is not the questions themselves, though Nietzsche loathes them too, but before that, the fact that we ask ourselves. This self-consciousness must be smashed. Nietzsche's dictate: act your nature. This is not the same as acting in accord with your nature, which implies you could act in discord with your nature which implies you had a choice. In the eternal return, you have no choice. You have your nature which is your performing. Does this mean the subjects cycling through the eternal return lose their ability to define themselves? No, the idea of a capacity for self-definition in the pallid sense of options no longer exists—nothing to lose. Does this mean those caught in the eternal return are slaves without realizing it? No, they possess an independence that precludes asking the question. The eternal return's liberty lies entirely in an autonomy defined as an absence of dependence on anything outside. It exists precisely because there is no choice. Inside the eternal return, no choice is your liberated nature.

Deleuze takes a long step to ensure that nature stays clear of reaction, he drops down to the ontological level. From *Nietzsche and Philosophy*: ". . . we are able to understand the eternal return as the expression of a principle serving as the sense of . . . difference and its repetition."[25] The return explicitly merges with difference, meaning self-distinguishing processes, as the spawning of experience. Because difference works from the start, the eternal return no longer pertains only to actions, but also to being. Consequently, no abstract, self-conscious, conditioning nature can exist before and rule (and thereby ruin) action because nothing exists before the acts. Deleuze makes the point again: "We misinterpret the expression 'eternal return' if we understand it as 'return of the same.' It is not being that returns but the returning itself that constitutes being. . . ."[26] For Deleuze, the eternal return does not mean some *thing* returns, like a particular, delineable, structured nature. What returns is generating action which issues as a nature. From this production, which Socrates disdained as becoming, every particular being and nature arises. What returns is the process of that arising, not the arisen. When Deleuze writes that your nature must change to enter the eternal return, he does not mean you need to select a different one, more outgoing or more frivolous or something. He means you need to change what a nature is. Nature was a guide for your acts; now, nature is doing, it is the tangible me I feel because I act. It is the me ushering into the world on the heels of performance.

The primary objection to the eternal return—it threatens itself by becoming a prescription for action—has been eliminated. It is no longer a prescription. It is the nature of an ontological state of production. It is also the living embodiment of the productive aspect of difference.

Human Nature

In human terms, what is the nature that returns eternally? Rousseau's noble savage. He acted without respect for others, he stole, he wounded. Through it all, he never doubted because it never occurred to him someone or something alien to the acting will could judge him. Public morality had not yet been imposed. Its appearance at the dawn of civilization and the end of the state of nature amounted to an external will infecting the savage volition with insidious reaction. In the *Discourse on the Origin of Inequality*, Rousseau locates this tragic moment dramatically as the first man to plant four stakes in the ground, claim the blocked-off territory as his, and find others to take him seriously. He had been the savage with inclinations unchecked, unqualified, without doubt, and undeniable. Now, every move he makes also denies itself to the degree he asks: Is this my land? Is this your land? Can I go here?

According to Rousseau's *Discourse*, the crippling, unnerving force behind propertied society is language. Language domesticates the will in two ways: first, by simply giving us words, it necessarily allows abstract characterizations like "courage" or "cowardice." Further, it allows the possibility of asking others, "Was I courageous?" "Was I cowardly?" Peer review has displaced deeds. What Rousseau calls "vanity" follows soon after.

Before language and organized civility, no one judged the savage's actions. Even in the extreme case, when the savage encountered another who was stronger, who arrested the weaker's strength and bent the weaker into conformity with his despotic stick, the weaker could not understand the oppression as an imposition for lacking the linguistically based categories. Importantly, one can be cruelly twisted into the shape of another's whim without suffering denigrating reaction. This benign slavery is very different from the new slavery born of reflection and the degenerate social will. For both Nietzsche and Deleuze, the problem with being a slave is not suffering crude domination at the hands of another. That kind of slavery can still be noble, like suffering pain can be as pleasurable as delivering it. The slavery making Deleuze and Nietzsche cringe follows from the word and the other's saying it.

Rousseau's theory in the *Discourses* poses one overriding question: how do I go back to a prelinguistic condition? Rousseau himself practiced retreats to a nearly deserted island in the middle of a Swiss lake and to remote cabins on country estates.[27] He also speculated on life in savage America. But these gestures fall far short of the deepest problem. As long as common tongues link people, or even each with oneself, the noble can be ruined by formal structures like justice, charity, sensitivity. Language allows these weighty encumbrances as it allows me to recognize myself as a subject in action, not just as a locus of action. In a discursive environment, the disappearance of Rousseau's nobility, along with the eternal return's nature, seems inevitable. For Rousseau, the cure would entail forgetting his own curse. He must learn to undo his language. Normally, of course, we learn through language. Thus, in this particular case, language must be used to forget language. A delicate situation.

The same problem moves forward to Deleuze's Nietzsche. How can the will be reclaimed from reactive volition? How can the will be forced through the grinder of the eternal return? Oppositional dialectics labors in endless resistance. The situation is again delicate. Training the will to repel reaction only lets the culprit in through the back door. Deleuze's alliance with Plato slides back into focus. Both leap. Plato called it divine madness. Deleuze calls it the second affirmation.

The Problem of Time

But there remains the problem of time. After the initial affirmation, the eternal return faced two objections. The second fits within the first's broad parameters, but concentrates on a specific aspect of the apparent imposition: linear temporality. The eternal return read literally from the *Gay Science* demanded life be straight and irreversible. What we have done must return, "all in the same succession and sequence." Here, the return is shepherding its will back into self-denial, denial as refusing to generate time. Deleuze's Nietzsche cannot let time have its way with him, he will have his way with it. Thus, the question blocking the way: can linear, sequential temporality be upset, rearranged, or reversed? Can anybody produce their own time? Someone must, otherwise the eternal return will remain an imposing command.

Titus Andronicus

Shakespeare's Titus Andronicus produces his own time. He reverses linear temporality in conquering a chain of events seemingly beyond him. When he triumphs, he incidentally overcomes the last barrier to the eternal return.

For readers and theater goers, the play runs:

Titus returns to Rome, having led his army in crushing the Goths. The war has taken ten years and five sons. He returns with these prisoners: Tamora, the fallen Goth queen, her three sons, and a Moor Tamora loves. Titus's son Lucius asks Titus for one of the prisoners to make sacrifice. Titus grants him Tamora's eldest. She implores Titus to grant her son mercy. Titus does not.

Next, Rome's emperor takes Tamora as his wife and frees the remaining prisoners to symbolize a new alliance between Rome and her former enemy. But Tamora cannot forgive the loss of her son, and the Moor joins Tamora's family in conspiracy. Tamora commands her remaining sons to ravish Titus's daughter Lavinia before hacking off her hands and slashing out her tongue so she cannot reveal the perpetrators of her infamy. Tamora's offspring also kill the emperor's brother and frame two of Titus's sons for the crime. In the emperor's court, the two innocents are beheaded, but not before Titus can cut away his own hand and send it in a vain plea for his descendants' lives.

Finally, Titus discovers Tamora's treachery and bakes her two remaining sons into pies which he tricks her into feasting upon. Only after her happy chewing does Tamora learn the pies' contents. Now, the play draws to a rapid close in a bloody farce. Lavinia, Tamora, Titus, the Emperor, the Moor all die by sword and amid the audience's awkward chuckles.

As important as the morbid humor laced into this play is the temporality attached to the various kinds of violence. The play sketches three discrete modes of savagery leading in three different directions and to three different players. Their identifying features: distinct relations between action and reaction. Their titles: resentment, blind fury, and revenge. I will approach them in order and then draw out the peculiar temporality beneath revenge. Finally, I will turn to Titus and his own eternal return.

Violence of Resentment

The violence of resentment cannot control itself. I do not only mean emotional control. Certainly this soul rages and escapes the confines of civility. But more than that, it loses control because it cannot escape dependence upon exterior stimulation. Someone or something outside the violent source must bring this savagery into existence and remain codeterminate with it. Thus, resentment can be action, but it must be buttressed by reaction.

Resentful violence can also be understood as a certain production, a wildness made at the scene. But the exterior actor responsible for bringing the resentment into the world immediately monopolizes the force; he absorbs it all. The actress creates the rage, but only to the degree that someone else immediately soaks it up.

The violence of resentment belongs to Tamora. She arrives prisoner in Rome and Titus offers her son as sacrifice. She reacts violently. Because an event beyond her control—Titus sacrificing her son—stimulates her rage, her violence abandons her; forever codeterminate with her newborn savagery is Titus's consigning her son to death. You can say she calculates and schemes expertly and that she manipulates events. But even after her machinations have cost Titus his own hand, his daughter's hands, his daughter's tongue, his daughter's chastity, and the heads of his two sons, Tamora still has not gained control because Titus is still out there. At the rage's origin, he relentlessly waits. And for Tamora, as long as violent resentment burns her, so too will control elude her.

Tamora is caught in a dialectic trap, the same Hegelian moment of dependency and interminable warfare that jeopardizes the eternal return. The proof lies in the fact she does not simply have Titus executed. If Tamora could bring herself to order that, then maybe she could get beyond him. But she cannot order it because she irresistibly needs him, if only to suffer.

Blind Fury

Blind fury is action without any trace of reaction. It is Aaron, the Moor. He allies with Tamora and participates in her schemes, but a world of difference separates their coordinated violences. Unlike Tamora, the Moor does not act in response to anything. He does not act because of anything. He simply acts violently and without discrimination. He sided with Tamora but could as easily have joined Titus. Circumstance determines him. Or, to say the same thing from the other side, his acts obliterate every circumstance without resurrecting them. Thus, though his acts are harmful, they also rapidly spiral into irrelevance. He recalls Nietzsche's ass in *Zarathustra* braying "yes, yes, yes." The ass conflates resignation to the world with power over it. The ass says: because I accept everything, I am above everything. But it is above nothing. Worse yet, it is nothing. "Yes, yes, yes," without "no" no longer means yes and it longer means anything. Like the ass, the Moor is pathetic. Because he acts without any reactive ingredient, he reduces to a senseless machine stammering directionless with as much fury as his years will allow.

As the play ends, Titus's remaining son, Lucius, finally realizes the Moor's vacuity. During the preceding minutes, the Moor has been ranting horrifically and feverishly. Lucius responds: "Sirs, stop his mouth, and let him speak no more."[28] Lucius does not gag the Moor's offensive and violent ideas. The meaninglessness of the Moor's fury has already worked to silence him on that front. Lucius gags him to echo on the physical level what has already happened much deeper. The Moor's physical silence gives us a visual parallel for the poverty of meaning occupying his violent acts. Gagged, the Moor explicitly displays his own blind wrath; it is ferocity without any point, it is silent and irrelevant.

Violent Revenge in Theory

The final violence, revenge, belongs to Titus. It starts at the play's end when he tricks Tamora into eating dinner pies stuffed with her sons' innards. It continues as he executes Lavinia, his own daughter, then fatally stabs Tamora, and finally himself falls under the sword. Titus's spree could be taken as a crazed binge of resentment against Tamora, but Lavinia makes it more.

We have seen Deleuze distinguish active and reactive forces. Reaction is Tamora: he executed her child so she will execute and ruin his children. On the other hand, revenge is active and productive; it relies upon itself, it generates its own motivation. This is Titus. Tamora does not govern what Titus does and she will not be the cause of Titus's revenge. The father will act alone. This does not mean Titus becomes the Moor, a locus of dumb and blind fury. Titus's action includes an element of reaction to the world around him and thus claims for itself some real meaning. But the real meaning does not derive from a given world. Titus projects the world through his action. And that projection manifests itself as both action and reaction. While Titus participates in reaction, he will not depend on a reality he can react to. He will make a reality to react to. So, reaction is subordinate to action, it comes after, it is generated and shaped by the action; it has no being distinct from the action. Meanwhile, it remains true that action has no meaning without reaction, but it can stubbornly cling to being without it. From the ontological level, active force clears space for both action and reaction to erupt as sense with action privileged over reaction. How does this play out? In Shakespeare's drama, it will not be Tamora that harms Titus, but Titus that injures himself through Tamora. In Deleuze's philosophy, there will be a hero who "is said to react precisely because he acts his reactions."[29] This hero models violent revenge. Action generates reaction as a produced medium which carries meaningful action into the world. Reaction is not the cause but the way an active performance manifests and defines itself. Reaction is the trailing edge of a larger swipe of pure deed.

A familiar theoretical problem: how can Deleuze hold a substantial reaction within the bounds of wholly autonomous and productive action? Deleuze answers by describing Titus's brand of subordinate reaction: "It subsists no longer as a power and a quality, but in the mode of being of that which is powerful."[30] The idea of a mode recalls Deleuze's work on Spinoza and the earlier scholastic movement which traced a metaphysically descriptive line from the sole Christian Creator down to the physical world of yours and my bodies. The passage translates in technical terms as infinite substance expressing itself through infinite attributes themselves expressed as spatially extended. These extensions are the modes, like physical subjects. They can be meaningfully distinct from God but still dependent upon Him and in no way a threat to

His supremacy. As a mode, reaction is no longer a quantum of power set against action, like Titus against Tamora as two discrete and forceful wills. Instead, Titus's violent revenge continues as a powered will while Tamora sheds her power but remains tenuously distinct. Scholastic thinkers perceived their own dependance and contingency before God; Titus casts himself in the role of that God and imposes creation on Tamora. She becomes his subject, the product of his demented beneficence.

Revenge in Practice

In literary terms, in concrete terms, it is Lavinia that makes Titus's act pure revenge. She had been mauled and ruined by Tamora's sons, but not killed. At the play's end, immediately after revealing to Tamora the dreadful truth that she has eaten her own young, Titus slides his blade across Lavinia's delicate throat. With that he says to Tamora: the things you have done to my children you have no longer done, I have done them. You, Tamora, you never knew that I produced everything until I told you, just like now you didn't realize you were chewing your own progeny in the half-finished dinner pies until I told you. But I used you for all this. I used you to murder my own sons just as surely as I now leave my own daughter gurgling and dying on the floor. True, my sons' deaths lingered outside me momentarily, they even seemed connected with you, as if they were your responsibility, your deed. But now I kill Lavinia, and with that I take them all upon myself.

The reasoning: because Titus can now execute his daughter, he earlier could have had the ethical and the real power to massacre his sons. More, he did have those powers and he did do those murders. Tamora was an instrument in the killing, nothing more. She was the mode in which Titus acted. When he exercised his own hands and sword upon his own daughter, Titus acted in a different mode, one still including Tamora, but this time only as a spectator and victim. Victim? Victim because as Lavinia dies, Tamora's resenting will—manifested in the infamies she seemingly committed—is being sucked out of her. She shrivels. Now, it is Titus's will, and it was Titus's will all along. Titus orchestrated everything. Tamora stands powerless and empty before the gathering sovereignty.

Obviously, Titus's disturbing autonomy is not normal. His acts and understandings could easily belong to an institutionalized schizophrenic. Both conjure their worlds with only dubious respect for accepted reality. Titus eagerly feeds this comparison with his demented rantings and impulsive killing. But Titus's loose grip on sanity does not bar him from the eternal return. It probably helps him get there. It certainly helps him reach the wild understanding that because he sacrifices Lavinia, he had earlier slaughtered his sons in the mode named Tamora.

At the decisive moment, Titus says this:

> Die, die, Lavinia, and thy shame with thee,
> And with thy shame thy father's sorrow die![31]

The sorrow dragging from Titus until Lavinia's end is clearly not nostalgia for his lost family. Titus has seen the death ten years of war produces. He impulsively and remorselessly runs his battle sword through one of his own sons in the play's first act. Like the Moor, Titus lives well beyond sentimental attachment. The sorrow and festering shame grinding Titus feeds on the thought that his children died at somebody else's empowered hands. He sacrifices Lavinia so that instead of bearing a shameful and nagging sorrow, he can bear his children's demise. The difference between those two burdens is the difference between resentment and revenge.

When Lavinia falls, Tamora becomes simply a relay on suffering's way back to its father. The circle closes a moment later when Titus sets his blade upon Tamora herself. Her physical end reflects the more serious death she underwent seconds before. It reveals— at least in Titus's Deleuzean reality—that Tamora never had been anything more than an image of him.

Two Times

Standard notions of causality determined by sequential and irreversible time must be suspended to make room for Titus's revenge. Revenge orders the play: first, Titus's premier action, he bakes Tamora's sons into pies and watches her eat them. For a tiny moment, depending upon how seriously you take sanity, Titus's action stands identical to the Moor's or Tamora's. If you start by disparaging Titus as a lunatic, then his deed joins the Moor's because it remains shapeless and senseless. On the other hand, by disregarding the mental unbalance, Titus's act can appear initially as a reaction to an earlier wrong, and Titus drops onto Tamora's level of resentment. But in either case, Titus rises up. He gives his action his own kind of meaning by making it a reaction to Tamora while also denying her a powered independence. According to the order revenge proposes for *Titus Andronicus*, Tamora chomping on her own sons and then Titus abusing Lavinia's nubile throat actually inaugurates the play's events; it is the first meaningful action. Only by reference to it does anything else make sense. The other scenes become echos or ripples circling out from that first event. If you push this arrangement back onto a standard temporal plane, the echos actually come before Titus's revenge takes place: when you read the play, you encounter Tamora murdering Titus's sons before Titus executes Lavinia. Tamora's outrage and scheming and all the rest now become forward echos. They are reflections of the crucial, central events bounced ahead in time and thus seen and heard in the play's development before we see their source. The effect comes before the cause. Within this framework, Titus's action has a meaning called revenge because it comes with a fabricated reaction: Tamora killing her enemy's children. But even while stretching away in time, the reaction never escapes Titus. It is Titus. Titus killed his own sons. The only confusing thing is that the fabricated reaction appears before we can see the act, and the hollow actress carries out her mission before we can see the actor that truly instigates everything.

On the audience's level, the reaction (Tamora killing Titus's children) precedes the action (Titus's multiple killing), while, on the ontological and epistemological levels, the action precedes the reaction. Ontology and epistemology clash with perceived reality.

We now have a conflict between two temporalities for the play's plot. On one side, Tamora's scheme against Titus's children becomes only a forward echo of the episode making the entire play: Titus sacrificing Lavinia. Causality is working backward through linear time. On the other side, within the standard temporal framework, the first event remains Titus's allowing Tamora's son to be slaughtered, followed by Tamora's violence and then again to Titus. Causality works forward. The two readings cannot coexist. I am not going to argue which reading should be chosen, but if you choose Titus's revenge as the play's first action, then something needs to be done about the other time flow. On that front, Deleuze provides aid. He claims that the waves rolling out from every side of action have a powerful destructive power. He writes that in the case of reaction subjected to action ". . . the negative [reaction] is aggression, the negation becomes active, destruction becomes joyous."[32] Deleuze claims that—within difference—reaction like Titus's reaches out and rubs out other bothersome readings and irksome, staid conventional times. Preemptive and joyous destruction clears the way for action without dependence on extraneous people like Tamora and irrelevant former events like his sons' decapitation. Titus levels them all and then recasts them as the limiting and defining boundary of his own productive act.

Time in the Eternal Return

Titus's literary accomplishment is reversing time. His power over temporality determines the story Shakespeare chronicles. But Titus's monstrous philosophic accomplishment is producing a time, one we comprehend as normal temporality reversed. From a place no one in the story knew existed, and from a level of rationality no one wanted to recognize, Titus acted coherently within his own time frame to make the story his own tragedy. Not tragic because his children died, Titus does not much care about that. And not tragic in an existentialist sense because the world spirals into disorder and capriciousness; Titus's actions deny disorder, Titus imposes order. This play crescendos in tragedy because of too much control, because even temporality falls under his dominion, because Titus suffers an overabundance of the otherwise enviable power to impose. The play began with a victorious return from a decade of war, a decade of Titus's army impressing its will upon the Goths. The battles were not cathartic. Imposition became the way of Titus's life. In war, he learned the secret of production, a secret shared with Nietzsche and later with Deleuze: destroy the other, then rebirth according to your own creation. This is a curse,[33] the energy of pure production has an intriguing ring in the abstract, but a terrifying and repellent face in reality. This production knows no bounds, neither in space nor in time. When you are infected, there can be no escape because the generation prescribed by difference recognizes nothing beyond itself—nowhere to escape to.

The play's first curtain rises to show Titus leading a procession of conquered enemies fit for sacrifice. They offer palpable evidence of the larger ontological machine now funnelling through

Titus's existence. They are the foreshadowings of a being that envelopes everything around it, flattens its character, and then reproduces it in accordance with a will and a law itself produced by the same functions which destroyed. Titus has no perspective and no objectivity; he has only himself and the manic process that started as war, cycled through schemes, and culminated with a revenge that makes reality his own way by reversing time.

Nietzsche would understand and sympathize with the tragedy: infection by the eternal return. After the petty encumbrances of reaction have been cleared out by the first affirmation, the great obstacle—the eternal return itself—may be faced and overcome. Titus takes a shortcut here, he lived and acted before Nietzsche had spelled out his idea, so the second stage of affirmation presented no challenge.[34] On this point, Titus is most instructive, his secret for entering the eternal return was not knowing it. What Titus did know was a style of action that paid no heed to others, a style that overcame every reaction and every imperative and every time in a frenzy of lurid generation. Three hundred years later, Nietzsche applauded.

One hundred years after that, Deleuze underlined that at the core of the eternal return rolls a tumultuous lesson of production. Titus lived this production, the same production located under the heading difference. Next, limitation.

3

SEE WITH MY OWN EYES: LIMITATION

Deleuze does not grant limitation the same vociferous endorsement and rabid attention he lavishes upon production. In *Bergsonism*, Deleuze sets production at center stage as the movement from virtual to actual. In *Nietzsche and Philosophy*, production manifests itself boldly in two affirmations. In the work on Spinoza, production energizes power and expression. But limitation, how production determines and defines itself, remains ephemeral and understated.[1] Doubtless, this is part of a writing strategy grasping for adequacy to its own content; Deleuze's infatuation with writing the positive aspects of difference mirrors the power arrangement within it where definition always follows generation like Tamora comes after Titus. Nonetheless, delimitation remains vital to Deleuze's idea of difference. Required: a limitation owing itself completely to a generative aspect. Experience must be determined and defined by the same motion that brings the raw force and material of life into being.

Michel Foucault's essay *A Preface to Transgression*[2] elaborates transgression as an operation remindful of Deleuze's difference, but with the accent on the false negative, on the limiting aspects of untainted production. Like Deleuze, Foucault renders Socrates and Hegel obsolete by envisioning generation on a localized and entirely positive field. Foucault stipulates more forcefully than Deleuze, however, that limits are projected, not imposed.

Limitation

Foucault begins climbing into his kind of limitation with a vocabulary shift; he exchanges limitation as a negative quality in the sense of opposition, for limitation as affirmation in the sense of a sovereign production. Limitation is a distinction generated by decree within the singular element. Foucault understands that ". . . the death of God leads to an experience . . . which is *interior* and *sovereign*."[3] The interior's qualification as sovereign stands crucially important because it allows Foucault to separate his notion of the "interior" from its use within idealistic systems like Descartes's. Descartes's interiority constructs a bridge from self to a logical position (I think, I am) and then to a presumably Christian divine. Thus, Descartes's interiority stretches out to a removed God who in turn presses His limiting powers onto Descartes's consciousness as that first realization. Think of Descartes sitting alone in his comfortable chair. He wrote his first irrefutable statement—I think, I am—and immediately turned his consciousness upward. But that gesture to the imposing exterior was unnecessary. Foucault would have him stop and unpack his first claim. 'I am' holds two immediate implications. First, a limited being "I." Second, the affirmation of that "I" as existing. Now, what exactly that "I" is, where exactly its particular limits fall, what other thoughts it holds, what it means, all these are good questions. They may lead to a Christian God, they may lead somewhere else. But no matter what, they all come after the first claim. So, before Descartes turns the power of limitation over to God, he briefly holds it in himself. Solitary, in his isolated cabin, he decrees his own existence. For that moment, limitation functions on the interior, as sovereign, and in the affirmative.

Next, Foucault tentatively suggests a simile for his limitation. "Perhaps it is like a flash of lightning in the night. . . ."[4] Lightning gives the dark a character and presence, not only at its flash, but thereafter and then long after the bright streak withdraws. As a limit, the lightening does not surround the night like a metaphysical fence, nor does it surmount the night like a triumphant master, it delineates the night by charging through the black middle. The lightning becomes an interior limit the darkness quickly transgresses and thus uses to manifest itself. Lightning defines night. Lightning comes from nowhere but within the night, it is the dark's own accomplishment. The lightning is the inside limit the dark shoots out in order to recognize itself.

Going further, Foucault introduces a metaphor. Here, he writes transgression's limit ". . . takes the form of a spiral."[5] Like the swirl of water twisting down your tub's drain, the spiraling point leaves its own limit in its wake. The swirl is not so much the force of oppositional conflict but the produced limit following after a downward movement. Mark the diving tip of the swirl as simultaneously a produced, downward drive and the subsequent limit's edge; the curling water above is the limit's extension. Rather than coming from the outside as an oppositional force, the edges and limitation of the swirl are produced by the motion itself. The swirling cone demands no contrasting limitation beside the self-generated lines it manifests on the way down. The diving spiral makes its own circling ridges as the water drains away.

Foucault's third attempt to enter a mentality of transgression centers on sexuality. Foucault writes that transgression's sexuality ". . . marks the limit within us and designates us as limit."[6] So, Foucault knows a sexuality limited by nothing beyond itself. What does it look like? And how does it differ from sexuality pointing to some thing, and some limit beyond itself? To answer, open Georges Bataille's *Story of the Eye*.

Amputating Institutions

To awaken a sexuality pointing to nothing beyond itself, Bataille first spurns the brands of sex drawing their defining limitation from outside sources. In *Story of the Eye*, Bataille perceives two guilty institutions: the family and the Catholic Church. Both pull sex away from carnality by depositing it in prefabricated epistemological structures. Bataille, writing here as a novelist, is transforming abstract philosophic schools of dialectics and idealism into palpable, human terms. For Bataille, the familial arrangement between parent and child stands near the master/slave relationship, both work through practices of rebellion and domination.[7] Meanwhile, Bataille's characterization of the Church works roughly on Socrates's pattern, both begin from the postulation of infallible law. As Deleuze diverges from idealism and dialectics, Bataille conspicuously amputates both family and Church from his narrative. After he finishes severing, the *Story of the Eye*'s central action comes forward: a sexuality limiting itself. This sex is limited by defining rules, but it itself generates those rules.

First, amputate the family. Bataille's book pictures a daughter whose obscene practices with neighborhood boys ride way past disobedience. The father's rule has already been so ruinously dis-

regarded that Bataille chooses to not even include him in the story.
The deserted mother fights on. She alone tries to inflict discipline.
But this daughter, Simone, doesn't buck mother, she doesn't argue.
She does worse, she ignores. Mom's interdictions fall on deaf ears.
Take this scene:

> . . . very soon, of course, her mother, who might enter the villa
> parlor at any moment, did catch us in our unusual act. . . . She
> was too flabbergasted to speak.
>   "Pretend there's no one there," Simone told me. . . .
>   And indeed, we strolled out as though the woman had
> been reduced to a family portrait.[8]

The mother is a picture, a powerless rendition of familial imposition. She has no luck molding her daughter into a good girl because
she cannot even draw her into an oppositional relationship.

Next, the Catholic Church goes. To eliminate this institution
symbolically, and formal imposition generally, Bataille has his
dubious heroes visit a Spanish Church and promptly batter the
Catholic father to death. But this is not enough. They batter him
with his own holy chalice. And this is not enough. They batter him
while the hero, Simone, energetically rapes him. The priest expires
in his own sin-driven fervor. What Bataille shows quite simply is
that the Church's patterned impositions on action and experience
can be run over by actual practice. The priest cries out sin and sacrilege, but his sanctimonious horror makes no difference. Simone
rides him to death.

Incestuous Perversity

Lines delimiting Bataille's sexuality rise as a natural bound
formed from within, from a completed, frantic expansion of the
desire driving carnal action. Limitation is the climax of carnal production. The process begins: arms and legs and bodies thumping
and pushing, secreting, throbbing, and pressing. Every stretch of
skin, every darkened cranny, everything probed, defiled, and pol-
luted with various implements and unusual materials. The narra-
tor, attired only in a Jacobin cap, splashes like a child in the putrid,
yellow water running down Marcelle's legs. The police surround
the remote cabin and crash through the front door and do not

restore order but destroy it irrevocably. The players rush forward, blindly and capriciously, slapping and churning, until finally, at the climaxing moment, their libidos sink and shrivel. Stop. A natural border of exhaustion has materialized, and materialized from the acts preceding. Before the limiting border, the performance was nebulous functioning appendages and applications and insertions and discharges. Now, after exhaustion has quelled the carnal riot, it is a discrete set of practices we can name, diagram, proscribe, or prescribe. We can even try them again. We can try again because of the fatigue stopping and defining the first time.

We want the definition. This fatigue does not suffocate desire by imposing or opposing; it marks the desire lifting into full extension. Far from contrasting with or stamping out desire, this fatigue is desire's triumph, it is unadulterated victory for the rabid carnality. This is what desiring aims for, its own realization, its own end, its own determination. The desiring libido meshed into bodies and fluids produces this particular end, an end from a specific fatigue that old movies discretely represent with cigarettes for the actress and actor involved.

Bataille's story cuts out two mistaken views of libidinal fatigue. The first characterizes the exhaustion as something sweeping over you from somewhere else, like a flu or the heat on an August day. For Bataille, carnal exhaustion comes from within, it is the residue of carnal action; in Foucault's terms, it is interior. The second mistake associates this fatigue with negative connotations, like depletion of resources. For Bataille, carnal fatigue is not a negative measure marking the continuing reduction of energy like the needle on a gauge drops as gasoline disappears into an engine. In Bataille's book, you work in order to make and accumulate a tiredness. You want it. You decree it. Desire makes fatigue and adds it to the sexual mix. The fatigue is positive, it eventually reaches a critical degree and a defining limit forms. In Foucault's terms, the fatigue has become the interior project of a sovereign.

Looking back inside the limit, a delineated field has been practiced and thus staked out. Name the process of this fatigue perverse sexuality. Like people caught in its throes, perversion disregards all the limits unrelated institutions want to impose. Under perversity's rule, people do not engage in sexual acts, they engage carnally, and their acts produce their own definition as sexual in particular ways. If you have read the book and wonder whether scenes like Simone breaking eggs in the crack of her buttocks are sexual, you should not ask your parents or look for the answer in a Masters and Johnson poll or search through Church law, you should look at Simone's body. She starts out with her rampant libido and defines sexuality at the moment when she can do no more. She defines it as just what she has done. Bataille's characters drive themselves headlong toward their own limits which are not there yet and toward their own definitions which will appear only afterward. Consequently, their entire erotic functioning exists not for the sake of reaching an end, but for producing one. The essential reality is this: the same force generating Simone's adventures on a carnal plane next generates those adventures on an epistemic plane by constructing a defining boundary. Bataille's characters and acts delimit themselves. Carnality limits sexuality. This is perversion.

Perversion and Writing

Perversion's operation easily extends beyond the fold of wanton, erotic vice and the metaphor of orgasm. Take writing for instance, you wake up in the morning fresh and eager to attack your keyboard. As the day wears on, you build up an ironic fatigue finally driving you away from your work. The experience is not of being left empty, like fatigue has drained your resources. If it were that, how could writing ever start again? We would all have one day of authoring in us, and that would be it. But writing does start again. More, writing is excessive, the more you write today, the more you will be able to write tomorrow, the more you will need to write tomorrow; the more ideas you use up today, the more you will find tomorrow, the more you will need to use tomorrow. The opposite question waits here. If writing propels writing and ideas generate ideas, how do you stop, why do you stop? You stop because fatigue has been redefined as a positive accumulation built up from the same source as all the words and ideas. Writing reaches its fullest extension as a resistance to sitting at the keyboard any longer; writing's culmination is not words flying out as fast as they can be typed, but just past that, a point of halting, a point where furious literary exuberance crescendos in stopping. Ernest Hemingway always ended his day's writing in mid-paragraph, in mid-sentence, at a point where he had to go on but could not because he had gone too far. He did not stop because his energy ran low, and he did not stop at a natural pause like a chapter break or after a dialogue. Instead, Hemingway stopped each day in the middle because there, in the heart of writing, he overheated. It follows that when he stopped writing to rest, he was actually dissipating energy, not regaining it.

At the end of the day's work, a field of thought waits (an outline or a rough-draft or a set of paragraphs). It is limited just like perversion limits sexuality. Thus, the act of writing is a type of perversion. And Bataille, author of *Story of the Eye*, could properly be called a pervert, not only because of the lewd acts his heroes practice, but because in writing he repeats their process of generation through produced and entirely positive limitation.

The *Story of the Eye* now splits onto parallel levels. On the most immediate, we find a discussion of perversion in its basest incarnation. This is Simone raping her friends and flogging church leaders. Behind that, the author himself carries out the perversion he envisions his protagonists digging their bodies into. But that does not mean he lures children away from their mothers for depraved adventures, it means he wrote the book.

Sexuality and Perversion

Sexuality and perversion have definitions strictly enforced with respect to each other. Normally, we understand sexuality first, its methods, its allure, its ends; then we understand perversion as some improper variation of sexuality's prescriptions. For Bataille, the sequence reverses: perversion first, sexuality after. Because Bataille's perversion convulses in the absence of sexuality, we can no longer understand it as a rebellion against norms or customs, nor can we understand it as charged with the titillation intrinsic to the forbidden. Perversion expresses pure, libidinous force. It is eroticism generating a defining limit as a product of its operation. The limit is a residual called sexuality, or more specifically, normal sexuality, sadism, fellatio, masochism, masturbation, bestiality, pederasty. All these practices come subsequently. Like a wellspring, perversion leaves a steady flow of memories, formulas, and techniques in its wake.

In the social field of perversion and sex, there is at least one certainty: sometime after Bataille's carnal perversion, and then

after its subsequent stiffening into a particular sexuality, imperializing forces of the family and custom and the Church will flip the
raw physical encounter onto the outside of codified, accepted
behaviors. Perversion now transforms into a space of prohibition
derived from a prior, traditional or metaphysical notion of proper
sexuality. Where carnality had produced its own limit and therefore sexuality, sexuality now acts as an exterior, oppositional limitation imposed on carnality. For desiring carnality, the role of limitation has switched. Before, it was subservient, a product of the
carnal; now it is autonomous and an impediment to carnality, it has
become an enemy frontier. Before, limitation worked for Deleuze's
difference and Foucault's transgression and Bataille's perversion;
now, limitation works for Socrates and Hegel and any philosophy
that wants to drain production of its power to generate everything
up to, and including, its own end. Take as a Bataillian kind of example, the theoretically extreme Catholic doctrine that only reproduc-
tive sexual activities may instantiate any discourse on sex. The
insistence follows from an original, Divine injunction. Within this
framework, any insurgent carnality happening outside the official
practices must be viewed as simply puerile resentment of the
Church's towering force and the metaphysical source of its rule. So,
the limit amenable to procreation comes first. The other limit,
called pleasure, which arises from coitus and variations like
sodomy, arises only after the first procreative act as a gratuitous
and mutant aberration from the accredited practice. Proper sexuality precedes perversion. But don't let this institutionalized and
deceitful sequence efface the authentically former state. The carnal
world did not begin in prescribed and formulated sexualities
before occasionally spilling out of bounds in the hands of
demented libertines. Instead, perversion began. Then it ran up
against its own limit and thus produced the sexual. Finally, institutions entered in to revise history. They put a certain, codified sex
first and then cast the unbridled force of carnal perversion, and its
ability to contrive limitation, outside and into ignominy and, hopefully, into obscurity.

Symbolism

How does Bataille let his readers live produced limitation?
Beside proposing the book as a masturbation tool, the answer goes

to vision, to the eye, and to the symbolism Bataille draws around it. The symbolism requires three stages: eye as granting a limit, eye as disembodied, eye as reembodied in the interior of the very carnality its limit defined. I will take them in order.

First, the eye takes responsibility for delineating and outlining the things around us.[9] Given a choice, I normally see limits rather than smell them or feel for them or run my tongue along them. Where does the bookshelf stop and the floor begin? I look to tell you. Next, confirm the eye's primacy in defining limitation by referring to forms immune from sensory identification. Take an idea, we pass it between ourselves in metaphorical terms, and no metaphor is more chosen than the visual. When I understand, I say, "I see." So, in a physical and then in a metaphorical sense, the eye plays the leading role in bounding and identifying. Bataille's *Story of the Eye* understands and depends on that.

The second stage in Bataille's incorporation of the eye as symbol—its disembodiment—is frighteningly explicit. Simone and her accomplices have just slain the Catholic priest. They stand over the body. Simone: ". . . you must give me his eye at once, tear it out at once, I want it."[10] Why does Simone have the eye torn from the priest's head? Not to render it sightless, the liquid ball still sees, it produces differentiated and limited images reflecting through the cornea and around the globe's back wall. The eye sees even though the visions go nowhere. So, why does she rip the eye out? To distinguish vision from judgment. Judgment works through the priest's mind appropriating and organizing the eye's images. When the eye sat in the priest's socket, it simply fed information for rational division into approbations and prohibitions. True, the eye drew lines around specific entities and limited them through their varying colors, but the eye had little intrinsic importance. It served only as a mechanical conduit for the privileged source of definition; the event's real color and its lasting shape came from elsewhere. Slicing the eye from the priest's head eliminated that elsewhere. Intellectual judgment dies. Along with the priest's discarded mind and body go the other potential sources of defining limitation; the hands and ears and the rest no longer work so the world cannot be defined by the shape and consistency of things touched or by the sounds it makes or the odors it emits. The eye sits alone. Now, only the eye holds importance, only the eye can bound and define. And the information it gleans it keeps. Most important, Bataille's disembodied eye literally and figuratively becomes a source of defining limitation torn away from judgment.

Having established the eye as a force for limitation, and having established the eye as the only source for limitation, the way now stands clear for the eye to symbolize the perverse sexuality Bataille conjures up: defining limitation growing from within the limited element itself. For this to work, the eye must mix into perversion; the eye must generate carnality. Bataille arranges the scene:

> . . . Sir Edmund played with the eye, rolling it, in between the contortions of our bodies. . . . for an instant the eye was trapped between our navels.
>
> "Put it in my ass, Sir Edmund," Simone shouted. . . .
>
> But finally, Simone left me, grabbed the beautiful eyeball from the hands of the tall Englishman, and with a staid and regular pressure from her hands, she slid it into her. . . . Simone was convulsed by the urinary spasm, and the burning urine streamed out from under the eye down the thighs below. . . ."

The aphrodisiacal eye Simone revels in is the same eye she has had torn from the priest's socket. Consequently, this one eye both triggers sensual pleasure and gives a visionary force of limitation we could clumsily name as an abnormal sexual practice involving urine. As quickly as that, an affirmative, positive limitation has emerged from Bataille's book. The eye limits itself, the carnal eye sees and therefore bounds itself as a provocative, productive sexual tool. Foucault and Deleuze benefit, their philosophies have found an important literary ally. But a problem remains, the triumph of perversion's limitation lies exclusively in the book, it lies in flimsy text and ephemeral symbolism. The example seems merely technical. Deleuze, Foucault, and Bataille all claim to be more than literary aesthetes. To be more, the idea of produced limitation Bataille conjures up for his readers needs to escape the book. It must get into us as we read, it must involve our eyes. To be more than literary showmanship, Bataille's distance and difference between reader and book must disappear into a single eyeball invested with the strange and explicit power of producing and then limiting a carnal/sexual episode.

Our Own Eyes

Our own eyes play the central role in limiting Bataille's carnality and giving it meaning. How? Read the passage again. It is
highly visual. When reading the scene we do one thing before anything else, we picture it. Granted, we get a sense of volume when
Simone shouts and there is the heat Simone feels on her legs, but
beside that, only images. We have the contortions of their bodies
and the round globe caught in their navels and the eye that is beautiful and the Englishman who is tall. Simone pressed the eye with
a staid and regular pressure. She does not say she uses a staid and
regular pressure, and Bataille does not put us inside her consciousness to understand her thoughts. How do we know what she does?
We see her pressing. Then we see her convulsing. We hear nothing.
We see the stream. We smell nothing. The character's thoughts, and
what they hear, what they taste, what their hands feel, what they
smell have all been banished. The eye remains. But the eye that
remains is our reading eye, an eye outside and watching the actual
perversion of the episode. The earlier problem—the symbolic eye
as ineradicably textual—has a complement in the reading eye
which simply watches the scene without joining in the carnality.
For limitation to work in accordance with perversion, our reading
eye must also be caught up inside the limited episode's action. Our
eye must join the eye we see pictured before us.

Pushing our reading eye into the text requires first stepping
back and looking at Bataille's story in a broad sociological context.
Clearly, the bizarre sequence reaching from Simone's demand for
the priest's eye to its discomforting employment does not depict
actors playing to society's expectations. Just as important, but not
so evidently, what happens does not constitute a rebellion against
formalized rules; the scenes are too original for that domestication.
Bataille understood Hegel, he knew writing against the grain
would eventually be turned around and incorporated into the prosaic. To escape incorporation, Bataille pictures Simone beyond the
space of tension between morality and defiance. Simone does not
break society's rules. She doesn't acknowledge them, she doesn't
even know them. As a result, a palpable distance opens up between
Simone's act as we experience it on our immediate reading, and the
act as we make sense of it over time and through social mediation.
The gap opens as follows. The actions pass. Because the text is so

highly visual, only our eyes watch. We hear nothing, we smell
nothing, we touch nothing, we think nothing. Our eyes delineate.
Later, when the time comes to account for what happened, when
somebody asks what the book is about or how it fits into the social
and political trends of the moment, the vision gets subordinated to
reactions defined by forces beyond the immediate, sensed reality.
Normal rational responses like disgust with the sordidness,
amusement with the zaniness, scandalization, indignation because
of the objectification of bodies, and anger about the treatment of
everybody involved, all these have the (negative) power to serve in
a nonvisual defining capacity. These judgments owe their origin to
a meddlesome society or a stagnant custom, and they blind the
eye's experience.

A palpable distance has spread out between the immediate,
visionary reading and the subsequent judgment provided us by
society's accredited reactions. Reading the book evokes this distance. Examine your immediate reaction to the text. As a reader in
the book's private world, how do you respond to Bataille's sentences? Are they funny? disgusting? aggravating? intriguing? All
the limiting judgments supplied by the social canon and literary
tradition fail miserably. With respect to normal genres, Bataille's
narrative seems incoherent. We don't know how to react. Nonetheless, we read and we do react. So, there must be something we react
to. And that something is the text and the scene we see before we
judge it. We read the text, we see the scene, we react. Only in the
last stages do canonized categories enter in to restore literary order
and turn our reactions over to universally recognized labels.

Now, what gives the immediate reading a defining limit and
what allows its existence before society's canon enters? In this
highly visual passage, it is the watching eye. We, the readers,
watch. Before us pass colors and shapes entwined. At least on first
read, we cannot make the move to a second level of judgmental
delineation based on mores or social dictates or custom or personal
experience. This allows us to be literally drawn into the story. We
become the priest. And don't think the priest comes out to us, we
go to him. The events we see pull our eyes out of our heads. Bataille
draws us into his text by momentarily holding off our socialized
judgments. He forbids our judgment, but he keeps our eyes.

Thus, the eye watching the event is our eye, is our eye torn
from our head, is the priest's eye, is that same eye we see rolling

between the bodies, stimulating them, and finally being engorged with urine. It is your eye. The same eye sees and causes the convulsion and the urine and the entire event. The eye sees from the inside. Perversion's limit comes from inside.

Deleuze has found partners in Foucault and Bataille. Difference as production needs these partners and this limitation. But only insofar as it had already, implicitly, made them.

The secret to Deleuze's difference is a production responsible for its own limitation. Difference spins production for the subject perceiving no original split between self and act. It adds a limitation extending back from production and mediated by production and meaning nothing more than a climax: the end of desire as determined by desire cresting.

Nietzsche, Titus, Foucault, Bataille, Deleuze, each one finds a way in. For Nietzsche, it was the possibility of living the same moment forever, not forever because time stops or the world literally repeats, but forever because the only thing that ever happens is a production generating all time right up to eternity. For Titus, it was the realization that there is a world where insanity no longer marks a distance from reality, insanity makes reality. For Foucault, it was the sovereign interior. For Bataille, it must have been a lover, she drew him out and then he found a repose to realize what he had done and what every man has done. For Deleuze, it is a difference which differentiates internally, which differs from nothing beyond itself.

On a number of points, Platonism has already been reversed. Socrates bridles because less can be more, because ontologies can be restricted, because the whole is generated, not given, because experience comes before theory, because production on earth comes before reference to heaven, because Nietzsche's idea of the same returns eternally from what we have done instead of determining what we will do, because Rousseau's nature follows from what we have done instead of determining what we will do, because for Titus the present comes before the past, because Foucault's transgression manufactures its own limits, because Bataille was perverse before he was sexual, because Deleuze insists metaphysical identity is second.

In the next two sections, difference reverses Platonism on two further experiences, both more complicated and more compelling:

the meaning of possession and the depth of alienation. Crucially, these two locations restrict themselves. They are not cornerstones in an effort to build an overarching ontology that challenges the tradition of identity because such projects make difference into just another identity, just another, newer tradition in the history of being. Difference works aggressively within its territory; it explains some things better than Platonism, then it stops—outposts on the plain of Socrates's one.

PART II

POSSESSION

No one has schizophrenia, like having a cold. The patient has not "got" schizophrenia. He is schizophrenic.[1]

—R. D. Laing, *The Divided Self*

If possession is the activity of another, of a virus, a psychosis, or a demon wrestling for control of my bones and my muscles, then I should respond defensively, respond with exorcisms, medical, psychological, or mystical, in an attempt to reclaim my territory. But difference denies territories exist before its own production commences. So, for Deleuze, a possession conditioned by difference cannot mean viri or demons installing themselves within an already existing body like a parasite attaches to its host. Instead, possession makes the bodies it inhabits.

Possession works with the rules of production and limitation difference pioneered to conjure an existence that owes no debt but to itself. Possession uses bodies without respecting them. It slices off the limbs and parts it wants and then regenerates in accord with its own reason. Possession takes and remakes the hands of a man, Scott Fitzgerald, curls them over a typewriter, sets them in feverish motion. Possession grabs the body of a woman and transforms it into a surface for screeching fingernails and blunt fists. Possession pulls tongues from mouths and slips them through other bodies to form unions that never should have happened. Possession resurrects author's intention in literary criticism. Possession does all this not by invading hands, skins and tongues, but by recreating them. Possession is a refined case of difference, it is the motion of difference as it hovers around and then assembles identities.

The Platonist Augustine carries forward in his *Confessions* an identity impermeable to Deleuzean possession. By writing a continuous autobiography, Augustine claims: I am now, have been, and will be roughly the same skin-contained body and self that years ago stole pears from a neighbor's tree and later sank into the vices of Rome before finally discovering Christianity. At times, Augustine may well have considered himself possessed—by thievery, by lust, by greed, by religion—but he never fully identified himself with those things. Neither thievery nor lust nor Christianity made Augustine. They happened to him, they got under his skin, they invaded that base notion of self that subsisted through everything.

Possibilities: put body and self before possession, put possession before body and self. Deleuze takes the second. True, Deleuze does not use the word 'possession,' at least not significantly. Neither does Augustine nor Socrates before him. But it has always been there, waiting, a pivot for Platonism's reversal.

Chapter 4 concentrates on possession as conveyed by language. In Chapter 5, the study becomes concrete, a body is possessed. In Chapter 6, possession breaks bodies apart. Importantly, this chapter is not dedicated to reiterating the story of the fragmenting subject. That labor is negative and reactive insofar as its main impetus is a challenge to traditional notions of selfhood. I will repeat those challenges, but only as a by-product of the positive and central articulation: possession manifested as constructing multiple bodies, foreign languages, and innovative identities. In Chapter 7, I investigate how possession can be elicited into our world.

4

Verbs and Nouns

To repeat the phrase that became anathema in my ears during the
last months of our trying to make a go of it "expressing oneself" I can
only say there isn't any such thing. It simply doesn't exist. What one
expresses in a work of art is the . . . destiny of being an instrument
of something . . .[1]

—F. Scott Fitzgerald

In *Logic of Sense*, Deleuze lays out two series, one in language,
one in experience. In language, start with the verb, nouns come
next and then propositions. In experience, start with a pure event,
connect it with things and connect that to states of affairs. In language: verb → nouns → propositions. In experience: pure event →
things → states of affairs.

The two series correspond. This is not an early Wittgenstein-
ian claim about referentiality, it is not like each particular word
firmly connects to a defined part of experience; instead, language
and experience fall into parallel orders. Both express difference's
reign over identity.[2]

Along the series of experience, Deleuze begins with events he
qualifies as pure.[3] The fastest way to overlook events in their purity
is to start from an arrangement that leaves the event out, like a
before/after scenario. For example, the sentence "Myrtle Wilson's
now prone body had left an uneven dent in Gatsby's fender" completely misses the event even while communicating it. Implicitly,
we know the fender was smooth and straight, and now, after the
car knocked the life out of her, it is dented. We understand the
event—Gatsby's car slamming into Myrtle Wilson—after understanding the surrounding things and states of affairs. But Deleuze
wants the event first. He wants things and their states to follow

from the crash. Even stronger, he wants to wipe things and states of affairs out of the world and recondense them only after an event. So, before there were any cars or any fenders or any people, Deleuze's revered events, events like crashes, subsist in a vacuum. These are the pure events. Pure events generate things and states of affairs. But, can there be crashes without presupposing cars and people? Can there be events without things? These questions require allusion to the linguistic series: verbs, nouns, and propositions.

Distill the Verb

Deleuze cites a text by Emile Brehier to begin explaining the verb:

> . . . when the scalpel cuts through the flesh, the first body produces on the second not a new property but a new attribute, that of being cut. The attribute does not designate any real quality . . . it is, to the contrary, always expressed by the verb, which means that it is not a being but a way of being. . . . This way of being finds itself somehow at the limit, at the surface of being. . . .[4]

What is the cut? An attribute, not a property. Attributes belong to verbs. Verbs cause attributes while escaping. Verbs are elusive, they leave their marks without leaving themselves. Properties, like adjectives, belong to nouns. Nouns are captured by properties. Nouns are ponderous, so when you have the property you get the noun too. Because the cut is an attribute, it is the effect of a verb. And because a verb is evanescent and fugitive, the empiricist is drawn to ask whether it has being, whether it connects to anything, or, most directly, where the verb which caused the cut has gone.

Conventionally, we have nouns, and by having them, we have their properties. For example, we can have a noun, a forearm, and we can have a noun with properties, a forearm that is strong and worn. The strength, the tough, wrinkled skin belong to the limb, they pass their entire existence locked on it. This same forearm can be cut. The cut attributes, but it does not belong to the limb. True, the cut's *effects* can be understood as belonging uniquely to this sliced roll of skin, but then this specific cut has already devolved into an adjective, a property. And the cutting, which should be grasped with the verb's logic, has calcified into a noun. Deleuze posits that before the particular cut slashed through to this particular muscle, there existed the general cut belonging to no arms and no skin. It only appears occasionally as an experienced slicing. We see the verb as an attribute given over to a strip of skin, but we don't see the verb, we don't see the event. Yes, we see me and my knife swinging wildly and slicing a forearm, but these are only the people and things surrounding. If we do see the cutting itself, than we see it at the very edge of things and within the shortest burst of time: we see the skin splitting. But even in this case, the noun, the skin, has mediated. At best, the cut and its attribution of cutting get through only at the extreme Brehier called "the limit of being."

You can set your hands solidly on me, my knife, my victim, the wound, even the wound immediately after it opens, but not the cutting, you can't grip that. Attributes aggressively mark the failure of any particular, static entity to capture their cause. Attributes are like properties that elude domestication. Thus, the forearm displays both properties and attributes, the properties stubbornly cling to the arm. The attributes subsist in the same place, but they function differently, they push attention toward a conspicuously elusive source.

Deleuze versus Socrates

Deleuze's reading of properties and attributes conserves, in a perverted fashion, an ancient conception. Socrates postulated that any thing in this world holding a property received it from the larger and absent idea—in the *Parmenides*, he went so far as to wonder whether this held true even for things like hair and dirt. Socrates's speculation privileges stasis because he favored nouns. Deleuze moves this construct over to events. Now it is actions that dispense attributes to particular cases while themselves proving elusive and absent. Verbs become the metaphysical stimulants.

But metaphysical in a different sense. None of the homages Socrates paid to apotheosized nouns bestow any honor upon Deleuze's verb-driven pure events. Socrates cherished eternity. Events, however, do not want stability, they want to come and go: in history, some verbs simply stop happening, feudal courtship practices for example. Socrates also aimed at universal applicability for his highest nouns, but the event—like difference generally—restricts itself: not everybody has cuts across their forearms. A longer string of distinctions could be formulated, but the important point is, Deleuze is not just substituting events for the objects of Socrates's philosophy. He is transforming the character of the philosophy. Nonetheless, a short parallel remains: where Socrates started from things and then postulated and privileged external, metaphysical Things, Deleuze starts from events and then discovers pure events. Socrates valued Forms which manifested themselves as properties derived from previously apotheosized nouns. Deleuze values pure events which manifest themselves as attributes derived from happenings, from verbs.

Properties and Attributes

The separation between properties and attributes is not so much a division: some qualities are properties, others are attributes. The separation is more like a sequencing: properties are attributes that have lost their misty connection with the elusive cause lodged in a pure event. Qualities start as attributes. But when time or phenomenological carelessness severs the connection between attributes and verbs, nouns insinuate themselves. Next, the attribute slips into being a simple property while the noun involved assumes the role formerly occupied and then abandoned by the original verb. A forearm with the property "wrinkled" was once a weathered arm. As weathered, it displayed attributes escaping the limb's dimension; a weathered arm implies hot, burning sun, ripping wind, hours of their tireless punishment. These things have vanished, leaving the static appendage to claim the features as its own. Once attributes, now properties. Once, the weathered arm indicated verbs, it indicated burning, ripping, and punishment, now, it is simply an arm with wrinkles.[5]

Nouns versus Verbs

Nouns versus verbs is a debate about privilege. Normally, nouns control, then verbs come in terms of the nouns directing them. Deleuze calls this common sense. Common sense insists on univocity.[6] Nouns understand and order themselves first, then the verb enters and exits through the doors and in the direction nouns determine. Cars and people determine the character of happenings. Reverse the privilege. Verbs rule nouns. On the level of the sentence, the verb must be read first. Nouns function at their service. What is this like? Deleuze turns to Lewis Carroll's *Alice in Wonderland* and notes ". . . the innumerable examples dotting Carroll's work, where one finds that *cats eat bats* and *bats eat cats*, . . . have one and the same sense."[7] The sense Deleuze finds in Carroll's book is very different from the common variety staking its authority on there being an exclusive disjunction between "cats eat bats" and "bats eat cats." Uncommon sense works where one arrangement of objects and nouns becomes as sensible as another; we have to be assured only that the verbs regulate. The assurance amounts to the verb successfully expressing itself. Thus, since "cats eat bats" and "bats eat cats" equally well express "eats," both sentences work equally well. Both sentences have the same sense in an unusual way. True, nouns need to be there and function, but which one is where slips into a secondary consideration—nouns reduce to foils, they play bit parts, one easily stands in for another.

Deleuze crystalizes the lesson in verb priority around his preferred infinitive: to become. The specific example involves Alice's age, and the nouns do not even need to be rearranged for the verb to assert itself while the subjects and objects whirl into confusion. Deleuze insists that when you say "Alice becomes older" you mean she constantly becomes older than she was, but by the same verb, and in the same sentence, she becomes younger than she will be. Again, the substantive Alice that stands before me and ages becomes older than she is now, but she is now becoming younger than she will be. At the same moment and in the same sentence she is becoming in both directions, older and younger. For the verb, all that matters is that she becomes. In which direction that becoming points fails to register on Deleuze's screen of uncommon sense even while a shrill alarm goes up in noun-ruled language. Deleuze:

> It is neither at the same time, nor in relation to the same thing, that I am younger and older, but it is at the same time and by the same relation that I become so.[8]

In the first part of this sentence ("nor in relation to the same thing"), Deleuze maintains we should not read by relation to things. That strategy would cede the words' meaning to the substantive nouns surrounding the event. In the sentence's second part ("by the same relation"), Deleuze stresses the relation which extends out of the verb "to age" and determines what is relating. "To age" makes an older Alice becoming younger or a younger Alice becoming older, either one, but both in the name of declaring itself, in the name of declaring becoming. The active relationship has replaced the relation determined by the things that relate. When reading by emphasized things, we have univocity: I say "Alice ages" and we all know what I mean and we all know exactly how she relates to herself. We all know how she changes. But if the relating steps into relief by using Alice's relation to her changing self as a channel through which the becoming specific to aging exercises its action, then whether the aging goes forward or backward matters zero. Consequently, what the noun 'Alice' is in herself matters zero, even she has no being in herself, she could be a subject getting older or she could be the subject getting younger. It doesn't matter. Take your choice. What does matter and what is not a choice is the motion, the aging, the becoming, the verb. One way or the other, the verb brings Alice into a specific becoming. And because Deleuze reverses Platonism, becoming leads in turn to a more specific Being.

Dimension of the Verb

Deleuze gives his readers a list of negative qualities tailored for the infinitive: "It is pre-individual, non-personal, and a-conceptual. It is indifferent to the individual and the collective, the personal and the impersonal, the particular and the general—and to their oppositions."[9] The individual, personal, particular, collective, and general all play central roles in thought guided by the noun's original stability. Deleuze wants to begin from intractable instability, however. He wants to find liquid forces that produce the stable unities we know in our language as meaningful sentences and in our experience as things that hold their definitions stubbornly while time passes. For Deleuze, the individual, the personal, and the rest do not imperfectly imitate original being, they do not imitate it at all. The path of resembling substantives, of noun-resemblance Socrates followed out of his cave and up to Being, actually and necessarily misrepresents genesis. Original being is a differentiating machine inaccessible to thinking led by the hope of stasis as destiny. Beginning to think about being requires starting from instability only, and this is the verb's field. On the way there, we cross the decidedly non-nouns, the pre-individual, the non-personal, the a-conceptual.

We reach the start of being, namely becoming, in language with the infinitive, with the verb retracting every specific declension. Take the verb "to drink," the infinitive is before the individual, conceptual, general. It holds not even a trace of the personal or the particular. Obviously, the verb cannot be thought directly or exclusively. Thinking it requires plugging it in: I drink, they drink. But the infinitive form of the verb nonetheless insists the action exists on its own, it exists before the first person singular, the third person plural, and the rest. This is what Deleuze calls the extra-being[10] intrinsic to the verb, it is the being going past the immediate experience of people and things in action. When the infinitive does hook up—I drink, you drink, she drinks—it becomes vulnerable. Now we can think it in terms of substantive bodies, and we can even push further and say it is the substantive that makes the drinking, the noun makes the verb; it is because of the "I" that I drink. But the true sequence works the other way. No categories of individuals or collectives or one or many enter the original scene. Start with "to drink." Next, the drinking makes a subject, and I am drinking. Only now do the qualifications Deleuze began by renouncing enter: conceptual, individual, collective, personal, particular, general.

The infinitive leaps from I to she to you to they. And these language stations are powerless to stop it because before I, you, he, it, she, we, they, and the alcohol, there was simply to drink.

Writing Bodies

After *to write*, me. *To write* generates me as a subject to express itself. The *to write* possesses. Over the horizon of all the bodies that have been subjected to invasions—emotional, mystical, and physical—there agitates a more extreme version.

For Scott Fitzgerald, writing was the possessing verb; he literally owed his life to it. This means more than romantic and hackneyed propositions like "writing was the most important thing in his life" or "he lived to write." Those sentences do not go nearly far enough because they imply Fitzgerald existed independent of the figure bent over the typewriter. They imply that writing was something Fitzgerald invested himself in, something he attacked with gusto and devoted himself to. The real story is less glorious. It starts like this: Fitzgerald, as a writer, lived entirely within the structure of being the infinitive "to write" projects into substantial existence. When he was working, Fitzgerald's material surroundings constricted drastically. On the other side of the choked-off reality the fictional reality of his book expanded. It is that reality which surges back into the world of things to make typing fingers and eyes following along after the new sentences. What is the experience of this writing Fitzgerald? In any creative writing class, the first thing every student learns is to imagine a scene as strongly and completely as possible before beginning. The strength of this imagination can be gauged by the remove it sets you from your immediate physical surroundings, the furniture nearby, your posture in it, the weather outside, whether you are hungry or thirsty. As these things fall away, the corresponding imagination is gaining intensity and a fictional reality gains texture and color. Then, as displayed by the physical book being written, the ephemeral writing energy comes back across to the material world and resurrects the body that had been abandoned to the imagination. My own characteristics, which had been effaced so that my conjured characters could have believable but different qualities, my own hands which had been amputated so that my characters may occupy themselves differently, my face which drooped expressionlessly so my characters could smile and frown and color, my body which slumped so my characters could stand and sit and hurry, now they all return to me. They come back into being, through the expanding book, as my fingers moving and typing, my face leering at the screen, my body poised over the keypad. It is because of the book—because of my absorption by writing—that my own hands move and my own face tightens and my own body contracts and my own writing identity rises. The imaginative world causes and vivifies the material world. The writing vivifies the writer. Most important, I am not writing; the writing storms through, bringing fingers to life in its wake. On Deleuze's ontological plane titled difference, where philosophy has lost its global force while preserving the right to discuss the origins of experience, a limited account claims legitimacy: during those minutes of pouring words, my physical existence is because I write.

Meanwhile, another Fitzgerald, one who went to the market and courted Zelda and lived from day to day, was historical and substantive. His material body preceded any action he undertook like his stable identity preceded the projects he invested himself in. In language, he was structured by nouns. He was born in St. Paul, Minnesota, in 1896. He lived on the city's most prestigious avenue, in a house one tenth the size of his neighbor's. He went to high school at Saint Paul Academy, enrolled in Princeton, joined the army, and sometime thereafter doubled. The multiplying was not one Fitzgerald giving birth to another, like both could be traced back to a common root; the new, writing Fitzgerald existed irreconcilably with the historical version.[11] While the substantial identity biographers trace went about living the exotic life of a wildly successful, young author in Paris and an expatriate on the Riviera, another Fitzgerald in another dimension lived under writing's sway. This latter Fitzgerald did not write to finish the story, to prove his talent, to redeem his relatively underprivileged youth, to make money, to attract women, to create immortality. If those things happened, they happened back on the dimension of the man who put his substance before his action and his unified identity before his productive changes.

So, two distinct Fitzgeralds: one was born every time writing began and evaporated when the day's last sheet turned out of the typewriter. The other was born in St. Paul, married Zelda, had his name on the cover of famous books.

The writing Fitzgerald existed on a plane without space and time. Again, what is this like? As a writer, Fitzgerald may have seemed to have been at the typewriter for twenty minutes while the watch on his wrist might have registered seventy-five minutes. Seventy-five minutes is vital to the material man who lives inside schedules. But it holds no consequence for the author. This experienced dichotomy symbolizes the entire disjunction between nouns and verbs. Like substantives and infinitives, Fitzgerald's two times split. The scene does not call for a Heideggerian analysis of temporality, this is not an authentic kind of time reified by ontic, irresolute society into clock time. Abandon conciliatory projects. On one dimension there is twenty minutes, on another, seventy-five. Because of the separate temporalities, it makes no sense to try reconciling our common world with this writing Fitzgerald appearing and disappearing. True, you can say time is still essentially the same for the writer, just a stretched or contracted version of the hands turning on the historical figure's wristwatch, but that misses the point. The point is, for the writer, it doesn't matter whether you were working thirty minutes or three hours. You can't tell the difference. And even if you could, even if you agreed the writer's time was the real time or the substantive time was the real time, where does the novel's time fit in? If Fitzgerald wrote for seventy-five minutes—which seemed like twenty minutes—and covered four days of Gatsby's life, how long did he write? Twenty minutes? Seventy-five minutes? Four days? Enough to say writing used the hands and the machine it could work.

The same on the subject of place; it makes no sense to ask where Fitzgerald did the writing. Enough to say writing used the hands and the machine it could work. Of course, we can look at the various static locations: St. Paul, Princeton, Paris, Antibes, but they mean nothing. Fitzgerald could have been at Princeton, Princeton could have been at Fitzgerald. Commonsense subjects and predicates are only accidental qualities the writing inhabits and claims for itself and makes as an extension of itself. Trim the biography of every author to one word: writing.

The problem with the Fitzgerald born from the infinitive and only subsequently embodied in nouns is that the infinitive is itself evanescent, transient, and viewable principally through its effects. And because the writing never appears without the substantive body, there ensues a temptation to confuse the effect for the cause, a temptation to privilege nouns over verbs, to privilege the historical Fitzgerald over the writer, to privilege the physical body over the infinitive force, a temptation to say Fitzgerald writes instead of writing is Fitzgerald. Still, the infinitive does manifest itself. And not only as a negative theology, not only as determined through a string of nots: not substantial, not individual, etc. Listen to Ernest Hemingway, he has seen and positively chronicled the writer:

> [Fitzgerald] had told me at the Closerie des Lilas how he wrote what he thought were good, and which really were good stories for the [*Saturday Evening*] *Post*, and then changed them for submission, knowing exactly how he must make the twists that made them into salable magazine stories. I had been shocked at this and I said I thought it was whoring. He said it was whoring but that he had to do it as he made his

money from the magazines to have money ahead to write decent books. I said I did not believe anyone could write any way but the best he could write without destroying his talent. Since he wrote the real story first, he said, the destruction and changing of it that he did at the end did him no harm.[12]

Hemingway clearly sees the two Fitzgeralds. One is writing, a man coming into existence so that the words of really good stories can make it from the verb's dimension onto a blank piece of paper. The other Fitzgerald wakes up as from a dream, finds the stories already substantially written and hacks them into form for the magazine, for the money, for the notoriety. Publicity is the destination. But the writing Fitzgerald shuns publicity, he is reclusive. He is also those things Deleuze has already listed pertaining to the infinitive's dimension: pre-individual, non-personal, and a-conceptual. He belongs to extra-being, he exists as an effect.[13]

A specific effect is *The Great Gatsby*. This book is both palpable, material object and infinitive expression. The writing Fitzgerald produced *The Great Gatsby*, the substantive, material Fitzgerald needed the book to sell. That makes two Fitzgeralds and two different books, but between them exists only one, the *Gatsby* published by Charles Scribner's Sons in 1925. Thus, with *Gatsby*, the material Fitzgerald meets his own extra-being; the two Fitzgeralds relate across one text. Implicit in their meeting is the monumentally significant convergence of things and events, of substantives and infinitives. Hemingway remembers:

> Scott was puzzled and hurt that the book was not selling well but, as I said, he was not at all bitter then, and he was both shy and happy about the book's quality.[14]

This man who was not bitter, who was shy and who was happy was a verb. In a flash, the writing shows through the features and words of the historical Fitzgerald who suffered puzzlement and hurt that sales, and thus income, were not meeting expectations. Hemingway's report recounts the fleeting moment when the writer allows itself to be seen and even speaks through the mouth and expression of a historical man always tied to material things and usually dominated by them.

Years later the infinitive deserted, leaving the historical

Fitzgerald destitute; he struggled forward. In this later time, after writing left, Fitzgerald found himself in Hollywood. His wife was insane. His stories and books failed to excite publishers and simply writing them for their own sake was no longer possible. He tried writing movie scripts. But the substantive man simply could not write. He had no talent. What does this mean, to be talentless? Under the verb's regime, talent does not register a capability, like something a body can do. It indicates susceptibility, susceptibility to possession by the infinitive. Talent for writing is not something you have and something you can express, it is something that has you and expresses you. Talent for writing is being a conduit for *to write*.

The substantial Fitzgerald could chop first-rate prose into pulp fiction, but when writing disappeared, and he had to write from nothing, nothing good came. Hemingway watched from a distance. He recalled it melodramatically, but also clearly:

> [Fitzgerald's] talent was as natural as the pattern that was made by the dust on a butterfly's wings. At one time he understood it no more than the butterfly did and he did not know when it was brushed or marred. Later he became conscious of his damaged wings and of their construction and he learned to think and could not fly anymore because the love of flight was gone and he could only remember when it had been effortless.[15]

The transition Hemingway records goes from writing possessing a man to a man who tries to write. It goes from the verb generating the subject to the subject making the verb. In human terms, the transformation moves from the Fitzgerald writing *Gatsby* to the Fitzgerald pecking away at an enemy typewriter for some Hollywood studio. Of course, the hack Fitzgerald had been there all along, but he is no longer occasionally displaced by writing itself. He is no longer displaced by a writing that produces words and books and him in the absence of substantive reasons or motivations.

Hemingway's lesson is simple, writing possesses. Writing requires surrendering identity, and not just the shallow surrender requisite to writing about others, not just the surrender to a different dialect or a different background or a different race or another

sex. To write the way Fitzgerald wrote means surrendering yourself to something entirely inhuman, something as foreign to substantive humanity as the infinitive verb.

Possession by the Infinitive

Possession by the infinitive occurs everywhere. Take a walk or
a hike. Walks begin with a defining set of nouns: the people going,
where they will go, when they will return. After stabilizing all those
static and preliminary items, we allow the verb to enter and legs
begin moving. But sometimes, on long walks over uneven terrain on
hot days, the moving itself leaps through and takes over. Remember
a hike taken along a dirt path occasionally blocked by a fallen tree
and constantly diverted by rocks and the earth's own jutting shape.
This hike starts out as a walk, with you and your goal and your mind
regulating each step on the way to the end. Eventually you get
thirsty. But your water is gone. The sun gets hotter. Your hat soaks
through. You wipe your forehead with your sleeve, but the sleeve is
already dripping. Your shirt pastes across your chest. Your destination slips out of focus. Each step requires complete concentration.
The temporal horizon shrinks. You started out with the whole day in
mind, then narrowed that to the next hour, and now you can only
think of the next step. The horizon contracts to zero. A reversal of
polarities takes place and you are no longer planning each step; the
step is directing you. You are no longer there to walk, but the walk is
going on and you are following along for the ride. You no longer
map progress. No more destination. Legs move automatically. You
are the pure event of hiking; the hiking, the movement is controlling.
You are locomotion—your self, your identity arises from the fact legs
are moving, avoiding boulders, stretching over fallen tree limbs.
    When we rationalize an experience like this, we attribute it to
lightheadedness caused by fatigue and the sun. But, instead of denigrating these moments as times when the body and consciousness
failed or stuttered in the face of harsh conditions, think of them as
times when motion came alive, driven by the force of pure event,
the infinitive *to hike* possessed you in the name of the sun and the
heat. During these fleeting moments the body thrives while dis-
missing cumbersome burdens of identity, destinations, and pro-
grams. Eventually, there comes a point when the body stops for
rest. This is not a rational decision, you don't think, "Now I'll stop."

You find yourself plopped on a rock. The motion stopped itself. A temporary endpoint or destination has been produced from the hiking. Rather than saying we hike to reach the endpoint, say the destination arises because we are hiking. The fatigue produced from the hiking fashions the destination. The substantial place and pause has followed from the motion. And only now, in the pause the motion has made, do you regain a sense of your body as finite and yourself as its captain.

Lecture

The same on the philosophy circuit, giving papers at a conference or in a colloquium series. At least when you're young and just starting out and nervous, you read and then find yourself answering questions, and under the pressure and in the excitement and as your mind rapidly fatigues, you stop thinking through your responses. They ask and you answer. You amount to nothing more than the ideas spilling out; instead of you constructing answers, the answers construct you. You stop defining yourself as a controlling locus exercising decisions; you start defining yourself by what you have said because you are watching and critiquing yourself just like they are. It is only now, in the wake of responding, that you can be defined because it is only now, subsequently, that you exist. True, your body was out there even before you started, but that body is gone now, wiped out of being. Responding gives you a new one: look at your hands gesturing awkwardly, shaking, feel your lips tighten, your mouth getting drier and drier, a sheen of nervous perspiration. Where is the water glass? Why is it so hot? The experience is not your having a body that responds, that gestures, that shakes, that sweats; responding, gesturing, shaking, sweating makes your body and you. They define you. The proof? You hear yourself answering a question and you feel yourself cringing inside, saying to yourself, knowing, "Oh, oh, there's something wrong with this position being staked out, there's something wrong with this position I'm staking out . . ."

Infinitive Moves

In *Logic of Sense*, Deleuze repeatedly associates his pure events with phantasms.[16] Socrates used 'phantasm' to disdainfully name things coming into being independent their ideal inspiration; he banished them from his city. Deleuze argues for bringing the phantasm's category back into active philosophy.

Begin by tying the phantasm to the infinitive. On the level of our common experience, which is run by substantives and organized by categories amenable to stasis, the infinitive appears with a conspicuous trademark: evanescence. Deleuze pushes this mood to the limit by injecting suggestive words like 'quasi-causality' into his writing: "Events are never causes of one another, but rather enter the relations of quasi-causality, an unreal and ghostly causality. . . ."[17] We are verging on the occult. Infinitives connect with events connect with phantasms connect with ghosts. Ghosts, even though they are here and now, cannot be. Their mystical existence in the present juxtaposed with their real, physical existence in the past spins vertigo. We lose the bearing of time. Simply as a logical matter, ghosts should set two epochs at odds by eliciting our demanding questions: which is your real time, in what year do you actually live, were you real then, as a physical woman on earth, or are you real presently, as a roaming spirit? But what does the ephemeral ghost care about these things? These are noun, substantial questions. A crack that has always been there widens out, not one between the material human of the past and the spirit you see now, but between the philosopher who asks questions on this subject and the philosopher that doesn't, between the philosophy that sees a temporal contradiction in the ghost and the philosophy that just sees a ghost. What a ghost does is not so much threaten the there and then with the here and now by appearing in both, it rattles the certainty of any time and place; it throws into question the value of time and place.

Experience splits onto two dimensions, one with fundamentally important times and places, one without. One that starts from time and place, and one that enters times and places accidently. One ruled by stable things you can really touch, by questions about what is real, the other ruled by ghostly causes and the unreal. One ruled by nouns, one ruled by verbs. One with possession invading bodies already living at certain locations in certain years, one with possession making bodies and spreading locations and years about itself. One with solid people, one with spirits. Occasionally, these dimensions curve together and experience reverses; consciousness governed by substantive control over action gives in to a usually fleeting moment of infinitive control over things. On the hike, that moment was tagged as lightheadedness or extreme fatigue. These derogatory names and their phenomena fit into the same box as phantasms, the box marked as slag extraneous to the real and important aspects of life. Only on narrow bands of the world, among strenuous hikers and possessed writers can these phenomena gain positive definition. For the writer Fitzgerald, the moment the verb curves into the plane of nouns the fingers spring to life and paragraphs appear. Time and hunger and location and responsibilities and the other concerns of normally ticking subjects vanish.

Two Daisies

Two dimensions. And two choices: one, we can deconstruct them, tie them together, make them into masters and slaves. This can go on forever. Or, we can use them. We can work one of the privileges, penetrate it and see where it functions positively to read and transform the world. The second, practical choice is always Deleuze's. I follow him.

American literature permits us a grand figure of infinitive possession, Gatsby. His verb: to desire. It surfaces through Daisy. He met her before the war, he was sent to Europe, the allies won, he tried to return, but was diverted to England by military capriciousness. He passed his days at Oxford relentlessly beseeching the bureaucracy for release to come back stateside. While his petitions for leave were threading through levels of command, Daisy met and married Tom Buchanan. By the time Gatsby arrived in America, Tom and Daisy and their infinite money had vanished into the nascent world of American beautiful people. Years later, Gatsby tracked her down. He bought a grand mansion directly across from hers, on Long Island Sound. Eventually, he schemes a way to meet and they begin again. Tom finds out. The argument ensues:

"Your wife doesn't love you," said Gatsby. "She's never loved you. She loves me."

"You must be crazy," exclaimed Tom automatically. . . . "Daisy loved me when she married me and she loves me now."

"No," said Gatsby, shaking his head. . . . "Daisy, that's all over now," he said earnestly. "It doesn't matter anymore. Just tell [Tom] the truth—that you never loved him—and its all wiped out forever."

She looked at [Gatsby] blindly. "Why—how could I love him—possibly?"

"You never loved him."

She hesitated.[18]

Her hesitation gives us time to see two independent Daisies. The first is substantive. To this one, when Gatsby pleads, "Just tell him the truth—that you never loved him," the sentence outlines a field of competition between discrete and precedent men—Gatsby and Tom—for Daisy's affection. What they tell each other is strictly within their control and a product of their substantial selves. This reading starts with the material present as particular woman and men, and we understand their acts as cast from their static beings and continuous identities. Thus, we see characters manically trying to mold their current situations to the fixed dreams they hold.

The second Daisy comes from fluid desire. Not Daisy desires Tom, or Daisy desires Gatsby; desire, and therefore Gatsby and Tom and Daisy. This story could as easily manifest itself as Daisy desiring Gatsby or Gatsby desiring Tom. But though the specific arrangements are accidental, they are not irrelevant. Here, Fitzgerald diverges slightly from Carroll. Each desire-fueled version of each person retains a difference from the others, but nonetheless, through them all, Gatsby desires Daisy, Daisy desires Tom, desire comes first and arranges the players as a locus for itself and as a by-product of its fervid expression.

On this second, Deleuzean dimension, the players, Daisy for example, no longer have a character or anything independent of the roving desire momentarily surfacing to make them. I can no longer write "Daisy is aloof" or "Daisy is indecisive" or "Daisy is careless," because herself, Daisy is nothing. Start with desire, desire manifested as Daisy and then expanding again into her identifying characteristics. So, I can again write "Daisy is aloof," but only with the understanding that desire makes her to be so. Instead of Daisy controlling her public image, she is the localized project of an impersonal force. If desire leaves, she leaves too. On this reading, Gatsby's insistence, "Just tell [Tom] the truth—that you love me," no longer reveals a competition between two men for one woman, Gatsby is not verifying his hope with some frozen, substantial reality. The desire working here makes a Daisy that never loved Tom. The Daisy made by desire could do nothing but repeat to Tom the thrust of Gatsby's words because Gatsby's very insistence is the force making her. Importantly, the insistence does not belong to Gatsby either, the insistence makes him too. Daisy and Gatsby are little more than the imperative sentence. In this version of desire's story, we attribute the sentence to Gatsby, and place Daisy on the receiving end. But that could be reversed. And this reversal is not of the deconstructive or dialectic variety because it carries no opposition and almost no philosophic relevance (though it does carry literary relevance). Reversibility is only a symptom of a certain ontological stage Deleuze calls difference, difference manifested here as desire.

According to the rules of desire, the characters have no volition because they are nothing but infinitive volition. It is not that the characters have been sapped of the ability to act, no privative negative inhabits difference; the verb has overwhelmed the characters and left them with no option but to act, and act in accordance with the single wave of desire forming the entire episode.

At the story's crucial moment, Daisy hesitates. The words Gatsby insists she say do not come. But desire insists they must. Everything hangs in the balance. Which Daisy will continue? If she repeats Gatsby's sentence, she has already been abandoned to the desire that drove him all these years. If she refuses to say the words, she claims herself as a material woman who controls her actions. The choice is between two dimensions: the infinitive and the substantive.

Gatsby

Gatsby is unique because, for him, there is no choice. He lives exclusively in the infinitive, as a product of desire. The objects constructed for Gatsby to desire changed through time; first it was a desire for the privilege and hauteur only old money can provide, later it was desire for Daisy. Either way, Gatsby was nothing in himself. This is not pejorative. Gatsby was one of the many locations desire finds for itself on earth. Desire made him to change his name from Jimmy Gatz to Jay Gatsby, it made him to claim he was an Oxford man when he had only spent several months there waiting for the army to send him home, it made him to claim Daisy never loved Tom but loved only him. According to the desire channeling through Gatsby, all these things were true, they had to be, it is tautological because desire made all the things. On the other dimension, little of it was true.

Reading

When reading Fitzgerald's book, you could as easily read that Gatsby makes his famous parties or the famous parties make him. In a literal sense, it is Gatsby that provides the place and the prohibition-era alcohol. But it is the grand mansion and the notable guests that make Gatsby a mythical and intriguing figure. This is a quibbling distinction, however, in view of the massive divide between noun and verb privilege. The verb insists desire makes both Gatsby and the parties. In this Deleuzean dimension, the pleasure of reading lies in drawing close to the fleeting and mysterious verb. The work of reading follows after in determining what the philosophic conditions for this force are, what kind of experience it makes, and how it can be invited into the normally substantial world. On the other dimension, which belongs to the substantive, the pleasure of reading lies in drawing up close to the characters, in relating to them and seeing what fibers they are made from. The work of reading lies in explaining why it is that certain characters act as they do since all their actions must be traceable to a static and almost material object we call their personal identity.

Infinitive Inhumanity

The infinitive's dimension excludes humanity. By humanity, I mean the humanistic and existential version of the subject. For the humanistic subject, experience begins from the integrity of a certain embodied self that aspires, suffers, hopes, accomplishes. Even in the extremely flat case, think of Camus's stranger, his actions are bizarre but still distinctly his. In the end he suffers in his own way for them. On the inhuman, infinitive dimension, a coherent story focused on elaborating the acts and consequences belonging to Camus's protagonist would be tenuous because of the verb's intrinsic anonymity. The anonymity begins with the infinitive's promiscuity, it skips from first person to third and then to animals and things. Polymorphous applicability betrays faith in the regular subject. Like the infinitive itself, the verb-driven storyline can skip from character to character, one individual may act, another may continue that action, still a third may end it. This kind of book would have no central protagonists, only lines of personified action grinding through the machine created by the book's central verb. Protagonism will be like fame: everybody will have it for fifteen minutes. The characters fade, the operating mechanism of being famous endures. Not a character, and not fame itself, but being famous, this is the protagonist. Substantial individuals enter solely to give the action a place. Then they cycle through.

Humanity is reducing to a very different absurdity than Camus wrote. For Camus, the trademark of absurdity was its recognition. We, as readers, recognize the impossibility of the human condition because God died and rationality failed. On the infinitive dimension, we are denied even Camus's recognition because no subject exists at the story's center to crystalize the lessons in futility. Something as anonymous and alien as an infinitive verb has monopolized the plotline and claimed any lessons for itself.

The inhuman character of the verb reaches an even starker manifestation with time. In *Logic of Sense*, Deleuze breaks temporality into *chronos* and *aion*. *Chronos* is the time Socrates lived in and tried to control. It fills with substantives. In theory, it is the shortest of times, it is the infinitely fast and always passing moment we call now. In practice, *chronos* projects into the future and drags along the past. To gain hold of the many nows to come, it employs plans, aspirations, predictions. To drag behind, it relies on memories, lessons, customs. Thus, *chronos*, the time that should be razer quick, stretches itself out. Still, it is the present moment.

Aion belongs to the infinitive verb. It is the vast composition of future and past as it reaches out to eternity. The *aion* does not include the present, it does not stretch from the past to the future through all the moments in history. The *aion* presents a differentiating block occupying a temporal level separate from now. What purpose does it serve? First, it is a conceptual necessity; it is only because we have the *aion* that *chronos* can understand itself as moving. It is only because there is a past as past that the present can carry the movement necessary to implying a past that every now falls into. And it is only because there is a future as future that the now can imply a movement forward. Because we have the *aion*, the present can come to be and pass away. But even though *aion* provides space for past and future, it is not itself exactly past and future; it is a plane constantly expanding outward but limited in the middle. So, paradoxically, while *aion* enjoys unrestrained access to everything that has been or will be, it never enters the present. Its motion is a constant peeling away from that one temporal state that disassociates from it. Still, the unconquerable sliver of time is not *aion*'s lack, it is not a break down the center of a great block; the present marks the passage to a foreign dimension. *Chronos* and *aion* are irreducible. One dashes from now to now, the other rests comfortably in the swing through eternity—though a very different eternity than the one Socrates promised to his philosophic soul. Socrates's eternity held nouns and static conditions. Deleuze's *aion* flows with infinitives, it fills eternity with impersonal verb action, with cutting and writing and desiring.

Like *chronos*, *aion* presses its own limits. Where *chronos* stretches the maximum from its present, *aion* is pinching impossibly close on both sides. Remember the cut. To cut belongs to *aion*, to that vast space of quasi-time[19] outside now. We never see the cut, it is never happening. But we see the forearm immediately before and after, we see the knife, we see the blood, we even see the skin splitting clean on either side of the sharp edge. Still, nowhere in all this is the cut itself. So too with desire: we see Gatsby, we hear about his grand mansion and opulent parties, we know he does all this after being possessed by the verb, but we never see the actual verb. Fitzgerald understood this and communicated it opaquely when he wrote the book; he cloaked Daisy and Gatsby's original falling in love in the ill-defined past, before the principal storyline began. Fitzgerald also had Gatsby understand the love as always something in the future, as a state he never reached—this is the green light at the end of the dock, it glows from the *aion*. Daisy, like Daisy and Gatsby together, existed all along, but only in the past and in the future that could never arrive in the present. Fitzgerald's famous lines:

He did not know that [Daisy] was already behind him, somewhere back in that vast obscurity beyond the city, where the dark fields of the republic rolled on under the night.

Gatsby believed in the green light, the orgiastic future that year by year recedes before us.[20]

Desire made this scene, and did so in accordance with its own time that never touches now, even while always squeezing close, squeezing as close as Daisy's moment of hesitation and Gatsby's sturdy aspiration.

Listen to Gatsby reminisce, he reflects on a reality that could be sensible only in the infinitive's dimension and on the plane of time unhinged from the present:

> "What was the use of doing great things if I could have a better time telling her what I was going to do?"[21]

We could simply shift a few words in this sentence to come up with another one just as true: what was the use of doing great things if I could have a better time telling her what I had done?

Gatsby: the man perpetually floating in the past and future. He is a man, but because of his strange time, not human. Everything that defines him, old money, mad love, an Oxford education, they belong to extra being, to the never quite here.

Possession

The infinitive's time zone is Gatsby's deepest secret and the secret to the possession preceding him. At some point before the book began, Gatsby was a man who acted in the present and lived where people controlled their deeds. Fitzgerald tells us he was Jimmy Gatz then, a Midwestern boy in a dirt poor family. Three transformations swept across this subject, all at approximately the same historical moment: his name changed to Jay Gatsby, he entered the military, he met Daisy. These events fit together, they offer perspectives on the cataclysmic occurrence shoving Gatsby into infinitive reality: his possession by the verb *to desire*. Everything changes.

The most obvious biographical sign of possession is the name switch. A given name claims to have the power of stockpiling. Over the years, continued gathering allows Jimmy Gatz to assume an increasingly palpable and definable material being. Like he accrues memories, Jimmy Gatz assumes a personality. As a result, he becomes predictable: he is quick to anger, charitable, calculating, determined. The various patterns making up his identity push into increasingly sharp clarity as the passing years allow each characteristic to carve its signature deeper. At a theoretical extreme, the process will be complete, and if nouns control verbs, every action will reach perfect predictability. His name change mocks that predictability, it loudly renounces everything a real name values, especially the accumulated identity that names explicitly warehouse. Because Gatsby has renounced accumulated, material being, there is no longer anything about him you could pick up and say, "Ah, here is the man." True, he surrounded himself with artifacts seeming to play defining roles: a vast mansion, a library stocked with sophisticated books, upper-crust friends. But all these things were counterfeits. The mansion was old, but Gatsby's money was not. The books were the kind an Oxford man would read, but Gatsby was only in Oxford for several months. The legion friends were always at the parties, but when Gatsby died, only one appeared to mourn. Gatsby as a stable identity had, and was, nothing. He had no books that meant anything, no friends that endured, no past he could admit, no character that was his own, no true present moment, and, like a summation of it all, no real name.

To imply Gatsby's slip into the infinitive, Fitzgerald also uses the military into which Gatsby was so disastrously inducted. What happens when you are drafted? Your hair comes off, then your clothes. You are bathed, issued shoes, socks, underwear, pants, shirts, hats, and guns indistinguishable from those given to the recruit in front and the one coming after. You get a number and now this is all you have. Board a bus with everybody else who all might as well be you. Like the army strips away your physical appearance, the infinitive destroys everything personal, everything you have and everything allowing you control. Still, this military version of anonymity is inadequate to the experience of possession. When the military levels you, it starts with the assumption that people have unique and incorruptible characters. Elaborate psychological means are then utilized to minimize the uniqueness. The infinitive dimension bypasses such procedures, it simply refuses to acknowledge any formative individual character. Entering the infinitive means thoroughgoing anonymity. It means you are nothing and have never been anything and never will be anything but what the verb makes you. Possession.

When Gatsby fell for Daisy, he slipped out of the material present and into the verb's *aion*. He slipped from a man who had a character to a desire that had a man. He shifted from the land of humanity to the time zone of the inhuman, a time with a past and a future that repels the reality of now. For readers of Fitzgerald's book, the first temptation is to report that the Daisy Gatsby loved was his own creation, she became his version of the ideal woman so many men have seen flickers of in their various lovers but never successfully arrived at. According to this story, they met, fell in love, the war pulled them apart, and in her absence his memory inflated. From then on, their love was ruined because she had become more than any woman could be. I deny this plot. A verb conjured both Gatsby and Daisy and their love from a dimension no material man or woman will ever touch. Rather than starting out as an attractive woman, Daisy started with Gatsby in the evanescent and inhuman realm of desire. This doomed them. They never happened together because even when their material bodies and static identities met, they could not get together because they were never in the present; they were always being tugged apart by an origin disallowing the present. This is the philosophic complement to the social reality Fitzgerald won fame for writing. This is like the ambitious Midwestern boy trying to match the old-money, establishment woman. There is always something back there, something they can't entirely overcome, some internal difference at the core of their love. In society, the difference pulls through disparities in clothing and lineage and refinement and manner. In philosophy, the internal difference is an unconquerable disparity isolating material bodies from the evanescent verb. According to this philosophic story, even when Gatsby and Daisy whispered and touched, they were still not together because they both also traced back to origins without the tangible substance requisite to physically being together. Their delineable, corporeal identities were born from pre-singular, impersonal desire. This mismatch is the true cause of their futility. And this is the true meaning of possession: material bodies and a desperate love and a bestselling book all owing their existence to a force manifested in language as the infinitive.

In the next chapter I move from a linguistic to a phenomenal account of possession by applying it within the confines of a specific human body that possession creates. I take up the psychological case study of a patient possessed by a murderous alter-identity.

5

EMILY, THE PATIENT, BLISS, DELEUZE

For years, the patient has been arriving disoriented in doctors' offices or hospital emergency rooms, bruises and cuts across her face, blood dried under her fingernails. She has no explanation; the wounds miraculously appear on the other side of prolonged naps or inexplicable skips in time. Her doctor's skeptical eyes and suspicious questions finally elicit mumbled, stock excuses: "I fell," she claims. Or, "I had a bad dream and knocked into the bedboard." "No, I'm not married," she insists, "I don't have a boyfriend either." A breakthrough solves the mystery. In *Archives of General Psychiatry*, Eugene Bliss, her psychiatrist, reports this experience:

> . . . in my presence the patient transforms herself into [Emily] and begins to hit herself with her fist . . .[1]

So,

> . . . now the cause is evident. Emily, her suicidal personality, is responsible. Under hypnosis, Emily affirms, "She (the patient) is weak and I am going to kill her."[2]

Emily is possession, she is the verb manifested in Bliss's unnamed patient.

Normally, when doctors like Bliss take up cases like this, cases where a body seems to be invaded by another identity, they begin with skepticism. Even if the new identity proves to be authentically other,[3] they insist the invader must have her roots in the suffering patient. Thus, they begin their diagnostic procedure by searching for latencies; they dig into the patient's secret places, they look for things that happened to the body, suppressed things, forgotten, or simply overlooked things. This is always Bliss's assumption, that something happened long ago, usually something traumatically sexual, and it forced his patient to break off part of herself in order to bear the weight of the gruesome reality. Incest, for example, can be managed by a young girl who splits off part of herself to hold the memories of father's appearance every Friday night. This one part passes her entire existence enduring Daddy. The main personality has no knowledge of the goings-on until years later when the split surges into the mainstream of consciousness, perhaps as a source of suicidal fits.

I reject Bliss's conventional reading of multiple personality. Deleuze's thought can be used to see multiple personality as the verb curving into the noun's dimension. Emily injects extra-being into the patient's existence; she is an infinitive that births an identity not previously possible. This has nothing to do with the past. Emily comes from somewhere the patient has never been. True, the scene of Emily's appearance is the patient's body, but she does not take the body as the patient knew it, she does not inhabit it, she destroys it and recreates it as an expression of her own law. Thus, contrary to what Bliss would insist, no battle exists between Emily and the patient for the one body. It belongs to Emily from its genesis.

When Gilles Deleuze read Bergson in the 1950s and early 60s, he fastened onto one overriding distinction, the distinction between the movement from possible to real as against the movement from virtual to actual. The movement from possible to real is developmental and always accompanied by a loss of what Descartes called reality, because a possibility becoming real renders other possibilities impossible. According to the rule of development, change dilutes being. The quickest example is your life; when you decide to marry, you have developed by closing off myriad futures and thus an entire horizon of possible being. So, development means change tainted by contraction. But not all alteration implies contraction. Deleuze follows Bergson in considering sentient life generally. Could the human race have developed over billions of years of narrowing? Could it really be that the process of you and me growing out from the primal swamp meant the withering of potential being and reality at each step? If I was a possibility waiting in that swamp eons ago, along with legion other possibilities for different species of intelligent life that were precluded by the emergence of humanity on earth, then according to the possible/real model, we must concede that human beings have less potential, less possibility, and less significant matter than a lifeless bog. Deleuze understands Bergson to comprehend better the appearance of humanity on earth by moving from a developmental model to an evolutionary one. This is tantamount to moving from a possible versus real division to one separating virtual from actual. The virtual evolving into the actual comes with an upsurge of being. When the virtual becomes actualized, when humanity finally appears at the end of an evolutionary trail leading back to a muddy riverbank in Mesopotamia, being has gained, and it has gained at each step along the way. Capacities and abilities are acquired, and each leads further upward, as learning one foreign language makes the next one easier and learning Kant makes Hegel more comprehensible. Writing a book leads to another, even if the first was philosophy and the second popular fiction. Possibilities multiply with change. The movement from virtual to actual means innovation, it means transformation picks up reality.

In the *Inferno*, Dante stationed Cerberus at the gates to Hell. The more the horrid dog ate, the hungrier it got. Hunger bred hunger. Actualization participates in Dante's nightmare: created reality spurs more created reality.

Emily's appearance is the actualization of a virtual possibility. She did not accompany the patient at birth, she did not accompany her through adolescence. Only when Emily suddenly evolved did she arrive. So, for the doctors investigating Emily and her patient, it will do no good to bring in hypnotists and therapists to search through childhood mishaps for suppressed traumatic episodes. Those things may exist, but they fail to explain. Emily outstrips the patient, she adds something. In fact, she adds everything.

Dr. Bliss realizes none of this. His ignorance will preclude both a successful diagnosis of his patient's malady and an understanding of Emily. Nonetheless, his diagnostic failures will be instructive. They will demonstrate the flailing vanity of developmental thought when confronted with a differential production, and they will allow us to look at the face of pure difference in the mode of possession. The face belongs to Emily.

The Nexus: Sex/Family/Body/Self

Because Bliss functions entirely in the substantive dimension, he relies on a static conditioning structure or nexus of ideas to diag-

nose and treat his patients. He forms his nexus, implicitly, by binding the patient's family and sexuality to her body and her selfhood.

Begin with the nexus' sexual component. For Bliss, the traumatic incidents founding multiple personalities occur in dark, corner rooms, center on the genitalia, should not have happened.
Upon consummation, the men and women, boys and girls dress
and hurry away. But prohibitions continue weighing on their acts.
In their minds, the shame expands.

The prohibitions and subsequent shame come from the family. Bliss thinks of mother's open blouse, father's castration threat,
the changed diapers, the baths, tickling the stomach, rubbing the
thigh but avoiding the chest, avoiding the genitals. These rituals of
parenthood slice the child's body into distinct territories and color
them alternately with frivolous pleasure and black censure. Certain
places may be laughed over, displayed, others must be hidden
beneath two layers of clothing. Perversion occurs here, in the family. Long after the child has grown into adulthood and taken a room
in some anonymous city, the sexual acts with virtual strangers will
titillate by violating original familial encodings of condemnation.
The places you want strangers to touch are the places your parents
forbade.

The surrounding components of Bliss's static nexus of understanding are the body and its particular selfhood. Bliss reports saying this to one of his patients: ". . . she is the real person since, after
all, there is only one body and one head. . . ."[4] Linking the body and
the "real person" enables Bliss to station his idea of selfhood
between sexuality and the mother/father operation of familial, sexual territorialization. In order for the family to apply its particular
brand of sexuality, the child onto which they express their discipline must be tangibly malleable and reflect their shaping hands.[5]
The child as concrete, specific, sexually active, and skin-contained
fulfills these requirements.[6] Now, the child's identity—the real person—can emerge from the sexual encodings parents lace onto the
body.

Bliss's clinical terms, diagnosis, and treatments will all
(latently) carry the sex/family/body/self structure of presump-
tion. It regulates his evidence, his procedures, his conclusions. The
nexus will form identity and multiple personality disorder on its
terms. And these are the terms of development, of possibilities
diverted and deferred and reappearing. There is no room here for

anything coming from outside the closed theater of the patient's past and the material, corporeal possibilities she was born into or had applied to her skin during the early, formative years.

Body and Self

Bliss's central diagnostic shortfall: his concept of selfhood never leaves the physical body. Like the physical body, the treated self rising from familial sexuality is singular, self-identical, and rigidly determined. Like the physically healthy body, the healthy psychological self matures and changes, but only gradually. The body is predictable: tickling her feet means laughter, a frigid day without a hat means a fever. The nexus-self is predictable: being jilted by one's lover means short-term depression, lethargy, frustration. Normal vividness eventually returns. The body delimits and claims the individual's field of physical responsibility: you swung your arm, you knocked the vase from the table. The legitimated self delimits and claims the individual's field of moral responsibility: your ideas, your words, your guilt. Bliss's treatment idolizes this responsible, almost corporeal self abstracted from the physical.

But the suicidal personality, Emily, will not fit into the body-centered model. Bliss observes that ". . . acts of self mutilation . . . are perpetrated by [Emily], with the added grace for the subject of no pain."[7] Emily's immunity is pivotal to understanding her story. Because Emily can beat on the patient without suffering pain, Emily's identity cannot be combined with the bodily centered identity of the subject she strikes. In the midst of punishment this severe, the only way Emily can escape pain is by escaping the beaten body. Emily disembodies. For her, this is easy because she erupts from the immaterial dimension. She can act without suffering because, at first, Emily is nothing more than action; she herself has no material sensible to pain. She comes into the material world by using a body to express her action, but she does not exactly take this body from the patient because if she did, she would have to take its essential functioning, like pain following from a thrashing. Instead, she razes the corpse in generating a new kind of body, one immune to hurt. This is the crucial moment in possession.

This is the moment when Emily reveals herself through material (the body she tears) while also revealing herself as immaterial infinitive (the body sensing no pain). The old patient's body is

gone. The new possessed body exists only to receive self-mutila-
tion. It exists because it is mutilated. As a palpable substance, its
actuality is not already given but follows from intense savagery. On
the level of personal identity, the body exists solely for the purpose
of Emily recognizing herself. Where it had lived in the patient's
domain, a place where punches hurt and scratches sting, the body
now lives on Emily's dimension where scratches and punches tell
the terrifying but painless story of another self birthed into the
world. The body was a formal condition of identity for the patient,
now the body is simply an accessory Emily uses to expose herself.
The body was a delineation imposed on a woman, a quasi-Socratic
Form imposed on the world, now a madness generates its own limiting body as a way of producing itself.

No Understanding

Emily confronts us with a case of multiple personality more
extreme than Bliss is equipped to deal with. It should come as no
surprise, then, that the family- and body-centered discourse Bliss's
treatment employs strikes Emily as babel. Bliss remembers that
". . . when I ask her why she is doing it, the patient denies the [self-
mutilating] act, but Emily admits, "Yes, I'm doing it but it isn't any
of your damn business."[8] Of course, Bliss responds by trying to
make it his business. But he is misinterpreting her. "None of your
damn business" does not mean "Leave me alone," it means "You
couldn't understand if I told you."

Bliss as Idealist

Deleuze's *Anti-Oedipus*, coauthored with Felix Guattari,[9]
throws critical light on the psychological approach Bliss represents.[10] Most important, Deleuze would understand the Blissian
approach as Oedipal. For Deleuze, Oedipal does not only mean the
Freudian Oedipus complex bending the intelligibility of guilts and
anxieties into an inclination for killing the father to possess the
mother. More generally, Deleuze uses Oedipus as the rallying call
in a smear campaign against any technique of understanding that
reduces psychological phenomena to a single confining structure,
the kind of structure we have grown used to hearing from Socrates
and the kind I have just developed as Bliss's nexus. Deleuze writes

summarily: "Oedipus is the idealist turning point."[11]

In Bliss, because selfhood goes through the familial, sexual body, it aspires to the material body's characteristics, to something approaching absolute singularity, regularity, predictability, and normalcy. Bliss wants to combine his patient's personalities into a self at least as immune from character shifts as the normal, healthy body is from day to day physical changes. But how realistic is this Blissian ideal? Who has not resorted occasionally to the explanation "I was not myself earlier?" Who has not done things still making them cringe five years later, "How could I have said that?" "What could I have been thinking?" At the extreme, we have seen pillars of society slipping out of porn shops and heard of parents abusing their own children. But even more prosaically, no one goes from day to day without major, even inexplicable deviations from the line of behavior their self-defined or socially defined or doctor-defined character dictates.

A gap opens between reality and Bliss's ideal individuality. Because the ideal is precisely that, it cannot be criticized or problematized. So, treatment failures, failures in the integrity of identity, must be located on the immediate level of an actual patient and doctor, not with the standards the patients are being held to. A failure is the patient awakening one morning with bruises and cuts across her body. When Bliss reflects on the problem, he stays with the physical body that had started the original process of forming an identity susceptible to apotheosis. Bliss explains to himself that perhaps he failed to notice all the patient's hidden personalities. Perhaps the prescription was too weak. Whatever the relapse's cause, the malfunction exists in the mechanism attaching the treatment to the patient, and never in the assumptions or categories of the nexus-ideal itself. So, the doctor never asks whether we should stop holding people to body-modelled identity, he only asks what went wrong with this particular treatment. The doctor continues blindly pouring himself into his work and accomplishing nothing. Bliss suffers: "In my experience the treatment of these patients is both difficult and frustrating, with success counterbalanced by distressing failures."[12]

Idealistic theory's impunity from empirical refutations creates the potential for obsession in the clinic. The ideal persists through every patient's distressing failure, absorbing every labor. Wrongheaded assumptions deflect blame from themselves and focus it on the doomed practice. Bad treatment reproduces. The downward spiral of defeat tightens and speeds. Every patient's regression demands more devotion, stricter care to unanimity, additional sessions, and increased study. Unifying the multiple personality never ends. Except possibly in grinding compulsion.

Theater of Healing

I will give one brief, specific example of Bliss's Oedipal practice—a practice sending treatment spinning into hopeless, decaying failure by relying upon assumptions which deflect evaluation and treatment from the assumption's own inadequacy. The nexus-bound Bliss understands that ". . . the patient disappears when the alter ego assumes the body."[13] Because Bliss ties identity to the body, in order for him to have any hope of pulling a multiple personality back together, he must assume a continuity between the various personalities' bodies. Thus, they all "assume" the same body. But what would it mean for Emily to assume the patient's body? Bliss wants to integrate all of the multiple personalities to form one normal person. But what could it mean to integrate the uniquely corporeal Emily with the body-centered patient? The questions slip past Bliss while he administers his futile program of hypnotism and abreaction toward the proper self born from familial sexuality and a past that holds all the keys to today's developments. This is the disaster that waits in Oedipus: even though his program cannot possibly succeed, Bliss presses on.

Next, because Bliss blindly refuses to relinquish his corporeal idealism, the helpless patient has no recourse but to take the entire case upon herself. The doctor continually insists a cure is possible, even inevitable. He says, "Remember, there is only one body and one head so only one you." But there is not only one body and not only one her. Therefore, to satisfy his cloying demands, the tired and frustrated patient finally has no choice: she must devote herself to momentarily impersonating the deranged personality as well as she can, then she can absorb her dramatic mask.[14] This way, at least the doctor is satisfied. Unfortunately, the treatment process is no longer about melding the multiple identities, it is about refining the skills of pretending to meld. Instead of practicing psychiatry, Bliss is unwittingly directing a theatrical performance. Bliss himself encourages this particular futility, these are his own remedying words to the suffering patient: ". . . visualize these experiences as if happening on a stage."[15] Taking the doctor's cue, the patient goes up on stage and performs the ritual of multiplication and then integration. When the play is finished, she may come down. But the emergent, cured patient is only an act. Emily is still out there.

Where is the lunatic? Surely Emily, the disembodied spirit clawing violently at the arms and legs around her, qualifies. And the treated patient, she dips into insanity by suffering multiple personality disorder. That leaves the question on Bliss. True, he doesn't see things that aren't there, and he doesn't hear voices no one else does. He doesn't seem violent. But his patient's recoveries can only be artificial. To the degree he accepts these counterfeit episodes as progress, Bliss disassociates from reality. That mental infirmity is comparatively minor, however. The real problem Bliss faces, but can't see, lies in the particular nature of his practical failure. Somehow, Bliss got into a professional position where the energies extended to solve a certain problem turn against themselves. Bliss's specific debilitation: the energy used to comprehend multiple personality asserts itself only by negating itself more fundamentally.[16]

Bliss's practice manifests psychologically the plague of reaction permeating Western culture, the plague that Nietzsche first identified and Deleuze underlined. Everything about reaction is stifling contradiction. Reactive forces express themselves only by repressing themselves. They choose values only by ceding to others the higher power of creating values. With every step, the reactive consciousness drives itself deeper into its own suffocation. Bliss suffers reaction on at least three fronts. First, he seeks to control multiple personality disorder, but only by unwittingly relinquishing control—Bliss takes on multiple personality by excluding the recalcitrant personality from the process, thus gaining command of the patient by forsaking any influence over Emily's behavior. Consequently, multiple personality disorder dominates Bliss because he imagines himself to be treating the disorder, but Emily, the multiple personality, is actually orchestrating the doctor's futility. Second scene of Bliss's reaction: Bliss's treatment practice defines itself only by sacrificing its guiding assumptions to something outside itself. Bliss relies on represented metaphysical ideals to construct the regulations for a human identity which is actually tangible and physical. Third, Bliss himself becomes an active practitioner only by responding to the world's norms. The denigration of multiple personality disorder as a scourge requiring correction only follows as a reaction to socially determined unpalatable effects of the malady, waking up without memory of the last thirty-six hours, for instance. It goes without saying that such an affliction is not necessarily unsavory. Of course, for this particular patient waking up with welts across her body, it seems sensible to define the disease as problematic. But the Oedipal character of Bliss's practice takes him further. Even if he will not admit it explicitly, as a condition of the idealistic precepts he uses to even begin, Bliss drifts toward psychological fascism: any flux in the regularity of a certain identity must be stamped out.

Where is Emily now? In Bliss. His own practice labors against him, it attacks his efficacity, it silently drains him. Against it, Bliss stands powerless because he cannot locate the source of his illness. As the patient loses consciousness whenever Emily appears, so too Bliss remains blind to the insidious onslaught of his other, namely, his practice's stridently reactive essence. In both the patient's and Bliss's cases, only the other's effects exist: lacerations, anxiety, ulcer, failure. Like his patient, Bliss wakes up in the morning and his scars are there and growing (". . . the treatment of these patients is both difficult and frustrating, with success counterbalanced by distressing failures."). Notice that the Emily inside Bliss and ruining him is Bliss's Emily. That is, Emily as Bliss understands her and imposes her on his patient. This Emily rebels against the patient like Bliss's method rebels against his practice.

Self-Creation

Deleuze's entire oeuvre focuses against the Emily Bliss has stumbled into. Deleuze wants a differential force working without constant recourse to reaction and rebellion. He wants a subject without idealistic impositions on sexuality and on identity. He wants Emily, but not Bliss's Emily. He wants the infinitive's version, the one ushering from an immaterial dimension to create a subject and only subsequently a material body. For Deleuze, this infinitive Emily is the only sane person here. She calmly eludes the ruinous, self-destructive codes and ideals Bliss forces sexually energized families to impose on their children and Bliss himself imposes through the conventional body. Emily makes up her own kind of body. More generally, she composes herself without reference to the detritus surrounding her. See it in her denying Bliss's demands for attention. "None of your business," she tells him.

Recently, Richard Rorty has used Nietzsche in taking up an investigation into creative forces like Emily's.[17] Daniel Conway puts Rorty's attempt to conceptualize an identity free from derivative reaction this way: "To create oneself anew, [Rorty] explains, is simply to fashion for oneself an enabling narrative; a liberal pluralism would not only encourage such self creation, but also foster a tolerance for the self creation of others."[18] Emily begins to fit Rorty's definition because she creates herself. She writes a perversely enabling narrative in her own language free from Bliss's sexuality, family, and identity. Emily's words come though as bruises and cuts across an inhuman body. But tolerance? What kind of tolerance does Emily have? None. Listen to her. "[The patient] is weak and I am going to kill her." Emily would not fit into Rorty's liberal community.

Nor should she. Demanding that Emily be tolerant reduces her force to a docile body. Her identity would gain definition mainly by reacting to airy, utopian dictates. Emily refuses reaction and she refuses imposed tolerance. This does not set her at war against tolerance; she simply has nothing to do with it. The same goes for the patient. Despite all appearances, Emily never reacts against her. The patient only mediates Emily's existence, she is the way Emily presents herself. Emily does not say: "She is weak and therefore I am going to kill her." Emily says: "She is weak." And: "I am going to kill her." No causal relation, no reaction exists between the sentence's two parts. True, Emily generates her own being and identity by inflicting wounds onto the patient's body, but this body suffers no pain, so it no longer belongs to the patient. Therefore, no rebellion because nothing to rebel against. And Emily could just as easily produce herself through other channels. She could choose a different expression, she could be something as mundane as the habit of chewing on finger nails. Or, Emily may bring herself into existence altogether outside of body's language; she might be a mental compulsion, like the inability to forget a certain screeching sound. Emily may be what the ancient Greeks called a muse, an inhuman moment of inspiration like Plato endured in realizing his conception of *eros*. The result was his *Symposium*. Or, Emily could be related to the Fitzgerald who wrote *The Great Gatsby*. The important point is, Emily does not depend on the patient's body. She possesses it.

Emily draws a self-defining line to generate definition where none of the other lines and rules functioning in Bliss's idealistic world work. Her process of encoding strikes us as cruel. But that does not make Emily cruel. It is not that Emily is fundamentally cruel and then she draws her violent line of self-definition. Emily is not anything, so adjectives cannot describe her. She belongs to movement and force. She draws the lines generating her own being, and the experience we take from that is her cruelty. The cruelty is subsequent phenomenon; it comes through the process of self-definition. In making the same point in general terms, Deleuze remembers Artaud's teaching that ". . . cruelty is entirely determination. . . ."[19] Emily erupts as Artaud's determination. Emily is indeterminate force determining herself by tearing at a body she generated to painlessly receive violence. She is possession manifested as viciousness. For that, she makes no apology.

Like Titus Andronicus, Emily is a symbol and a remainder that violence frequently accompanies difference in ontology and possession in our human world. This violence is not bloodthirsty; it is oblivious to the needs and values of others.

Bliss understood identity as stability and singularity and above all as a thing, a noun. Emily forces us to think of identity as sudden change and multiplicity and above all as a verb. Bliss starts from bodies, identities develop from there. Emily starts from action, bodies are the means she employs to move and evolve. When Bliss looks at the world he sees substantives. Emily enters the world as infinitive: to tear, to scream, to split. Verbs drive language, Emily drives experience. Her force gives bodies lives and identities, just as verbs possess the nouns in sentences and give them vivid meaning and a reason for being.

Finally, even though Emily has broken the equivalence Bliss postulated between the physical body and the self, she has done nothing to break her self-expression away from the traditional concept of the coherent and continuous body. When Emily possesses a scene, the territory she recreates as her own corresponds perfectly to the territory the patient would call her physical self: Emily remains caught inside two legs, a torso, two arms, and a head. She denies that identity follows the bodily lead in maintaining singularity, and she insists that the nexus body is not a precondition of existence, but the effects of Emily—the flailing arms and ravaged flesh—stay in the standard nexus body. What Emily leaves undone is the final effect of possession: the full liberation of possession-identities from traditional corporeality. The next question is, how can possession go on to create an identity by creating its own outline of a body unrelated to the one the patient would recognize as her own?

6

DESIRE, NOT WANT

Just as for Dr. Bliss and his patient, for early-modern empiri-
cists, the skin formed an impermeable shell that made the body one
and unified through all its diverse movements. A specific and
familiar notion of identity followed: as my body was unified, I was
unified. Identity and the body subscribed to the same rule of pervasive singularity. John Locke keenly sensed this. He wrote in 1690
that his person ". . . has reason and reflection, and can consider
itself as itself the same thinking thing in different times and
places. . . ."[1] Locke proposes that unity governs the subject, and
does so in two dimensions: place and time. In terms of place, my
body determines and guarantees my unleaking singularity because
I cannot break apart from myself. Where one part of my body goes,
the rest must follow. In terms of time, conventions like responsibility and the promise clamp me together. If I promise not to steal a
pear, the responsibility for the vow does not disappear as though a
number of hours could pass it through my system. I remain bound
to the promise days and years later just as I remain trapped in my
body. For Locke, these two planes—place and time—hold unified
identities.

But Locke was not sensitive to every experience. Take this
report on identity published in the *American Journal of Psychiatry* in
1960: "During moments of actual violence, they often felt separated
or isolated from themselves, as if they were watching someone
else. . . ."[2] The subjects here are criminals, individuals both historically and temperamentally far removed from Locke's model. By the
criminals' own accounts, their dirty hands and violence came from
elsewhere, from somewhere outside neat, singular bodies. To this
experience Locke cannot reply. The reality is, in certain recalcitrant
cases at least, unifying principles for conceiving identity fail. And
they fail in a different and more severe way than they did for Bliss's

patient when Emily arrived. At least that patient never had to watch Emily destroy a life.

Multiple identities acting through one body is not necessarily destructive. Deleuze, along with his sometime collaborator Felix Guattari, look for the positive. Listen to them reflecting on their condition while writing their first coauthored volume: "The two of us wrote *Anti-Oedipus* together. Since each of us was several, there was already quite a crowd."[3] In their claim of multiplicity, I find two things. First, a statement of solidarity linking Deleuze to the phenomenon of people exceeding singular containers. Second, the questions guiding this section: how exactly does Deleuze understand his identity as multiple by getting beyond body containers, and thus beyond Emily? What philosophic concepts underlie Deleuze's position? How does this experience bring possession to full extension?

Undermining Singularity

Deleuze's conviction of multiplicity produces two possible but radically divergent positions. I will recognize both, but Deleuze would subscribe only to the second.

The first stance takes multiplicity to mean that each unified, enclosed personality spawns several unified, enclosed personalities. We had Gilles Deleuze, we have Gilles $Deleuze_1$, Gilles $Deleuze_2$, Gilles $Deleuze_3$ . . . Gilles $Deleuze_N$. Each Deleuze represents the homogeneity of singularized identity. The same orthodox categories and epistemological values applicable to Deleuze the solo laborer easily cover each of his multiple instantiations. Here, nothing fundamental about identity changes, the number of stubbornly singular examples merely increases.

This mundane conclusion condenses on the psychological front. Increased acknowledgment and investigation of multiple personality disorder has failed to cause paradigmatic shifts in diagnosis and treatment.[4] The psychiatrist summons each of the multiple's persons individually to the surface (frequently through hypnosis), tramps through normal topics of childhood trauma and burdensome, repressed episodes of guilt, and then moves on to the next personality just as though calling the next patient into the office. This clinical situation is as maladjusted as the illness it administers. Treatment is generating multiplied, ideal, singular individuals, and each one is reinforcing assumptions and procedures deflecting the practice from its true subject, a person without singularity.

The second position extending from Deleuze's claim of multiplicity pulls the individual out of the atomistic straitjacket. The unity that psychologically ties the individual through responsibility and promises, and the unity that physically ties the individual through a conventional and integral body, both cease their regulatory functioning. Identity diverges from singularity. But a problem lies in the separation; how can the subject come free from singularizing assumptions? If it is true that concepts of individuality were bequeathed to our era wrapped in unity, then to even take up the question of the individual tacitly endorses unity's categories. Denying those categories falls short of Deleuze's mark because the denial is reactive—the claim of multiplicity depends on the singularity it spurns. Under these conditions, a true multiplied identity can never emerge. And what we should expect to find in practice is just what we do find: psychologists treating multiple personalities not as multiplicity but as multiplied unity.

Further, this roadblock does not wait exclusively in doctors' offices and other stations far removed from contemporary theory. Even the most recent philosophical books refuse to relent on the hegemony granted unity over identity. Their weapons for refusal are usually the same, an appeal to the unified subject shaping the discussion in the first place. Take the following from Renaut and Ferry's recent book translated as *French Philosophy of the Sixties*. Here, Lyotard stands in for Deleuze. Renaut and Ferry write: "When, within this tradition, Lyotard describes the task of 'making philosophy inhuman' and, . . . that 'there no more exists a subject . . .' to *whom* is he addressing the definition of the task and the call to assume it?"[5] Written another way, Renaut and Ferry's objection comes to this: how can a subject claiming multiplicity not, in the end, reduce to proclaiming the position from the spot already occupied by a singular human? Renaut and Ferry have a point. Arguing directly against singularity works like pulling against a choke-chain; the harder the theory rails against unified subjects, the more obtrusive the particular, unified theorist/objector becomes.

Deleuze anticipated the problem. Work must be done before raising the question of identity so as to clear an independent space for a new subject removed from singularity. Deleuze manufactures concepts initially unrelated to the issue of identity, concepts that can later come up from under normal categories to produce a separate, multiple subject without reference to the former and its inescapable unity. Thus, when Deleuze says he has multiplied, he does not mean he has broken his single self into bits. He means his philosophic work has manifested itself obliquely as a new way of reading and understanding identity right from the start. So, singular, body-centered identity has not been overthrown or even engaged, it has been circumvented and rendered obsolete. Two of the concepts central to that rendering are desire and partiality. I will address them in order. Unlimited possession waits on the other side.

Desire

Desire for Deleuze does not imply prior lack. Lack still exists, but it follows after desire as an effect or a symptom.

Deleuze's relation between desire and lack reverses Platonism. To reach Deleuze's desire, track through its ironic forerunner, *eros*. Socrates is the thinker driven to suicide by the sheer bleakness of his own philosophic vision. His first word about any earthbound person or thing: inadequate. From police action to individuals, everything is first imperfect. The police, for example, may act in the name of Justice, and some crude justice may even be done. But their action remains incomplete. Perhaps too much force was used or one of the suspects escaped. If not, if the act seems beyond reproach, remember it occupied only a brief time and limited parcel of space. A bad neighborhood recently cleansed of thieves and drug dealers unequivocally foreshadows another sector's infestation. In one way or another, any justice done here on earth equally stakes out its own shortcomings. The problem is inescapable. Because metaphysical justice always remains exterior to its own incarnations, the physical example never encompasses the original. Earthly justice exists essentially and systematically as privation. It is not only more justice needed now, in the new bad neighborhood, but more justice is always needed, even before the first just act. Socrates's desire always comes after this staggering inadequacy. Desire expresses Socrates's inescapable original need.

The Socratic subject also falls short. Our lives take shape first and always against what we are not. Aristophanes, the *Symposium*'s comic mouthpiece of truth, made the case that each person once attached along the back's line to another. When Zeus halved us all, each individual life became the erotic, desiring process of searching out that missing half. We are all lovesick, our identities doomed to frustration and want for the whole lost somewhere back there.

Augustine works on the same model. Original sin smacks our birth with lost perfection. We work to regain it. We pray because we never can.

Mainstream psychology follows along. Multiple personality disorder can be forced to imply an absence, an ideal whole caught in the misty past and rent into pieces by some terrifying affair. Then, each of the multiple personalities becomes an individual intrinsically struck by loss. The other selves become recalcitrant, but immanently connected, Aristophanic brothers and sisters. Doctor Bliss recalls treating the multiple Andrea. He forces her to recollect and adopt a certain episode belonging to a different personality:

> "Lets go back," I suggested to her, and haltingly, she began.
> "I don't know how."
> "Go back . . . to your father raping you. You have the ice pick."
> "I can't, I'm so tired—"
> "You must!"[6]

Socrates echos the imperative. She must go back, even she must want to go back. All our wants and desires flow out of earlier defects, they flow from missing parts of ourselves, from missing times in our lives. Before we want anything, we want that missing thing.

But what if Andrea does not want to go back, what if she does not miss or care about her recalcitrant sisters? Deleuze enters here. He agrees with Plato and the tradition in making desire crucial. But for Deleuze, desire produces lacks. This is Dr. Bliss screaming, "You must!" Bliss's fervid desire for his assumptions, for his method, for his psychology, generates the inadequacy in his patient. Before Bliss's appearance, she sensed no lack, no reason to go back, nothing to go back to. But Bliss fabricates an insufficiency and teaches her it has been there all along. The desire comes first, then the lack.

Deleuzean desire begins as Platonism reversed. It continues as an autonomous productive force, a nonreactive force. Desire steers away from two extremes. First, it operates free from the herding manipulations of hereditary privation. Second, at the other end, at the furthest remove from pandering reaction to an original perfection, desire stops short of confusion with pure spontaneity. Deleuze writes that desire is "constructivist, not at all spontaneist" (*spontaneiste*),[7] because at root spontaneity for Deleuze remains a response to the ideal but missing state. Granted, spontaneity is sightless and leaderless. But spontaneity is only the backside of Socratic lack because it obtrusively insists an original unity never existed and that it itself follows nothing: every act must prove arbitrariness, and spontaneity becomes slavery to the ideal's absence. For desire to work, present or absent ideals need to be irrelevant. Thus, Deleuze's desire does not find its place *between* need and spontaneity, but distant from their continuum. Kant adopts similarly painstaking reasoning to align his ethical freedom. For Kant, freedom must avoid both determinism and random action. Kant's solution: freedom legislates its own law. Likewise, Deleuzean desire articulates its own expression by regulating itself. The employed regulation provides a kind of lack, but a new, derivative lack. Lack now exists insofar as we need regulation for desire's coherent (not arbitrary) operation, but the regulation only follows from the operation's churning activity. Lack—in the form of regulation—is generated, like the limitation following difference's production.

Deleuze finds an idea parallel to his desire in Umberto Eco's writing on literature: ". . . the work as a whole proposes new linguistic conventions to which it submits, and itself becomes the key to its own code."[8] Codes are like regulations are like lacks. Code means the existence of the text's stating and defining itself. The code did not antedate the work, it was not the writer's or the reader's first thought. The code came after the book was read. The narrative came after the book was written. And the narratives keep coming after. With each new book or reading, a series of codes develop and continue by eluding localization, by generating the next conception of a text and then the next. Instead of saying each writing brings us closer to the ideal but presently absent book,[9] closer to the ideal code of writing and to the reason we began writing in the first place, say each writing makes a new literature and gives reasons for having written afterward, if at all. Hemingway cited the writing Fitzgerald to understand that this comes closer to experience. You do not write for reasons. You write.

Reasons come after action. Lack comes after desire. Ask anyone who has ever been in love.

As animated by his notion of desire, Deleuze's conception of justice tied to police action cuts back across Socrates's. For Deleuze, justice reappears after each episode, from each episode. Thus, the police
constantly produce not only justice's several heads, but the entire
legal code. Then, following from the code's production, a corresponding need for an ideal justice as a justification for the constructed
code, and following from that the need for police to enforce the legal
code. It follows further that a police state can generate itself by generating the need for itself (Nazi Germany). When the police are
through and today's criminal sits dejected in the cell, a new justice has
appeared. Each time it will be a new justice, as each day produces
new criminals where yesterday there were only innocents (prohibition, 55 mile-per-hour speed limits, new laws against kiddy-porn).

Advances in medical science constantly provide specific
examples of this Deleuzean kind of generated justice. When a new
apparatus enables a prematurely born baby to live, though in
severely debilitated condition, parents and doctors face a decision:
disconnect the machines or not. Sometimes related cases offer guidance. But as the speed of technological advance increases, the number of precedents dwindle. Dilemmas arise in ethical vacuums; no
applicable regulations or imperatives exist before the concrete
choice. The exact nature and effect of the infant's incapacity
remains unknown. Nonetheless, the decision must be made. It is.
Any attached conviction of moral rectitude comes subsequently,
like the lawyer thumbing through precedents trying to justify and
connect this newest instantiation of morality with the preceding,
codified versions.[10] Socrates would have it that Justice guided the
act, but here the specific act has generated the general rule of justice. Only afterward do we know what we need to do in similar situations in the future. Only after the practiced instantiation of justice can we define when justice is lacking.

A qualification needs to be added. Deleuze's desire is not itself
a stable, foundational element seeping through experience like
classical Being reaches through ontology and then into the world.
Instead, for desire to maintain its privilege of production over formal elements, it must tirelessly repel Socrates and his static utopia.
The quality stirring this innate repulsion is partiality. I elaborate
that next.

Partial Objects: Excess

The term 'partial' traditionally denotes imperfection and remoteness from foundational, idealistic unity. Deleuze accepts this meaning. But Deleuze's partial objects are not fallen entities. They are not less than they could be, not pale versions of what they should be; partial objects distance themselves from the perfect whole through overperfection. They are more than perfect, too perfect, too self-sufficient.

In literary terms, the tragic flaw exemplifies. The difference between tragedy and a sad story is the source of demise. The authentically tragic figure suffers an overabundance of an otherwise enviable quality. The sad figure never has enough. Socrates is Plato's saddest persona. He never had enough justice, enough vision, enough political keenness to establish his ideals. Socrates tried to love exclusively at the highest level. He ignored or staved off blatant come-ons from Athens' irresistible men, he quaffed volumes of wine but refused the alcohol's effect, he disdained accolades from fellow citizens. He wanted only the mental ideals. He discussed them and related stories about them and reflected on them. But the morning after the *Symposium*, he left with Aristodemus, not the Ideas. At bottom, Socrates's eros was insufficient. If he loved more, enough to die perhaps, he could have what he needed.

Othello suffered the other partial and imperfect desiring love: Deleuze's. Enraged by wild, overloaded eros, Othello suffocated his wife beneath her pillow. Why? His terribly mistaken belief that her devotion had wavered and she had loved another man. The authentic tragedy follows from Othello's prolific desire. Had his love flowed from an incomplete soul, he could not have shoved her as far away as death, he could not have shoved her away at all. His response would have been forgiveness and cloying attempts to win her anew. Incomplete souls can only repeatedly lunge after the source of their lack, never overwhelm it. Othello overreacts. His excess multiplies itself; if she left once for another man then she must leave irrevocably. Love accelerates from romance and adoration to rage and murder. Later, after they carry her away in her wedding night sheets, solitary Othello is left to reflect on his own kind of eros. It arouses itself, without external need, without preordained lack. It prodigiously yielded a loving wife, then a sexual traitor, then an innocent victim.

Deleuze sometimes designates partiality's manic process with the word 'machine' (*machine*). He wants machine to carry the connotation of perpetual motion, of self-sufficiency. Even more: overproduction. Machines perpetuate themselves while churning out. True, engine machines need something: they need gasoline, maintenance, and oil. But Deleuze's machine is not exactly an engine. Deleuze's machine is a weight lifter arriving at the gym each day at noon, doing ten reps five times on the primary muscle group equipment, then running three miles. It does that and tomorrow will manage ten reps six times and run three and one-eighth miles. Or, a machine is the historical novelist researching a past decade to write one book. Through the study, other connections and leads perk up. Finally, the original manuscript lies finished, but three new ones have already started: a writing machine.

In Deleuze's terminology, partial objects are beyond perfect. And their gains drive them away further still.

Partial Objects: Combining

Partial objects rarely subsist on their own. They function and endure through combination with other partials. Combination means blending elements irreducible to each other into a third wholly distinct from the previous two. Partial objects combine in the fashion of heterogeneities.

Deleuze's own, somewhat strained example is the wasp and orchid.[11] Each summer, the orchid contorts itself into a beguiling double of the female wasp. The attracted male wasp enters the flower then pollinates it in his tormented confusion. Deleuze interprets the event as follows. The wasp and the orchid are two heterogeneous elements. They combine, forming a third element heterogeneous with the previous two; the resultant object cuts away from the preceding. This predication forbids understanding the wasp-orchid combination as a form of interaction, because interaction demands the participating entities preserve some of themselves while simultaneously mixing into another. Deleuzean combination sacrifices the original entities. Wasp and orchid form a single, isolated block of becoming generated autonomously: wasp-orchid. Wasp-orchid juxtaposed temporally with wasp and orchid. Juxtaposed but not connecting with them.

How does that work? What happens to the individual wasp

and orchid as they combine into this third, unrelated entity? The question cannot be answered in positive terms because the response then encircles and destroys the irreducible difference it means to justify. The argument for heterogeneous juxtaposition must work indirectly.

Wasp, orchid, wasp-orchid. Were they not heterogeneous, were the wasp not wholly alien to orchid and wasp-orchid not wholly alien to both, the way opens for a singularizing regimentation from the outside. Such regulation can work through dialectic channels by outlining contrasts and then slipping in a larger singularity. For instance, the wasp has a different color from the orchid, but both participate in the more fundamental category of color. Idealism enters when the particular color becomes irrelevant. Here, Deleuze's project to conceive multiplicity is collapsing. But Deleuze's interpretation can resist idealizing unification with arguments like the following. The participation in color supposedly shared by wasp and orchid does not come intrinsic to the wasp and orchid; it is produced separately and subsequent to the wasp-orchid block. And it forms still another wasp and still another orchid: the wasp-color, the orchid-color. Yes, this wasp and this orchid join into dialectic or idealistic interaction under the patronage of color, but that is a different production on a different level. On a separate plane of explication, the heterogeneous elements retain their divergence and combination guards its Deleuzean accent. Extending this argument allows loads of combining partial objects to file through the single encounter of wasp and orchid: wasp's confusion, orchid's pollination, wasp, orchid, wasp-color, orchid-color, wasp-orchid, wasp and orchid, the biology machine naming the episode a fertilization, the Socratic machine finding in the flower raw versions of metaphysical forms like Beauty, the Kantian machine finding the idealism of nature's purposiveness, the dialectic machine finding codependence between orchid and wasp. All these combinations are not separate viewpoints, as a single physical event invites many perspectives. Each combination makes its own event. And each series becomes a separate reading in Eco's sense: not just different construals of a natural text, but different generations of the rules by which the experience gains meaning.

Returning to the physical example, the wasp finally escapes. The wasp-orchid encounter breaks down, leaving a new wasp and a new orchid, both discontinuous with the previous wasp and orchid. And the new wasp and orchid, what are those but new heterogeneous combinations: wing-body, petal-stalk, each producing their own codes and definitions. True, the emergent wasp can be associated with the previous, we can say both have wings, both occupy the same amount of space and behave in similar ways. But that systematic classification comes after the new wasp's existence. The unified idea of any particular wasp continuing through time and enduring various encounters with the world comes after the particular element as an artificial construction, not before as an immanent quality or essence.

Take another example, a book. It can be read. Alternatively, it can be stacked next to others on rows of shelves to form a literary wall covering. In both cases, the book combines with other elements in forming a production. But these productions cannot be circumscribed by what a book-in-itself would be. In the former case, the book combines with a reader generating a reading or an enjoyment. In the latter case, the rows of volumes claim a cultivation or level of education for their owner. Fitzgerald's Gatsby had walls full of books combining in this second operation. He arranged for his more educated guests to find their way into his library where they naturally fell under the spell of monograph after monograph. Here, reading plays no role. Gatsby certainly never opened his books. He hadn't even bothered to cut the pages,[12] so they could not possibly be read. The point was the books' existence and their cultural message. In this library, books combine with other volumes and with the evening's guests to produce forces of respect or envy or, in certain cases, love. All those forces aim at Gatsby. The peculiarity of Gatsby's books lies in their orientation. They incorporate not their reader but their owner. They don't become a reading, they generate a patrician. The books reach out for Gatsby, even though he may be in a different room, or out on the lawn, or away from the house for the evening.

The differences separating Gatsby's volumes from books for reading are unconquerable. For one of Gatsby's guests to begin actually going through a volume sentence by sentence would be at best a faux pas, more likely an offense or even a type of sacrilege. So it is not that these books have various facets or uses all eventually referring to a single, regulating ideal; it is that Gatsby's books exist in a different mechanism of becoming than read books. Partiality manifests its presence here by making the books combine and by channeling them into unrelated projects and elements.

Conclusions on Partiality

Partiality is the condition of terminal becoming: no impenetrable unities, instead, leaking imperfections: no perfection, instead, overperfection: no singularity, instead, heterogeneity. Because nothing is perfect in itself, the formation of episodes, people and objects must be combinatory, and continuously so. The notion of a single person or a single event or any idealized, impermeable entity comes after the entity has produced itself and in the midst of its production toward different combinations.

Conclusions on Desire with Partiality

Partiality invests desire. First, desire exclusively generates; motivations, needs, and static identities are products, not intrinsic conditions. Second, desire has no destiny except breakdown and incorporation in other mechanisms. Third, desire functions in combinatory blocks of heterogeneous elements. Fourth, desire's remove from perfection stands on the other side of the whole: not less than perfect, more.

Desire and Identity

Deleuze's linked concepts of desire and partiality will clear space for a multiplying subject that escapes the constricting singularity the tradition imposes on its heirs. As a result, a way will open for possession to completely create reality on the level of the subject. Possession can not only create the subject as it did Emily, but also the definition of what constitutes a subject. To see this happening, we need simply follow through Deleuze's conception of multiplicity, keeping in mind that possession is working through the verb 'desire.' I will develop Deleuze's multiplicity in two ways: first, by noting a historical precedent for multiplying identity startlingly similar to the one Deleuze's desire produces. Second, by using desire as a tool for reading Steve Erickson's novel *Days Between Stations*.

The archaic, pre-Socratic Greeks anticipated the Deleuzean concept of partial identity. They understood themselves as bundles of limbs, as arms and legs constantly in the process of mechanically combining. Kathleen Wilkes puts their view this way: "From vase paintings of the eighth century BC we can see that the human form was thought of as an articulated collection of limbs—the arms, legs, torso, and head are pictured as prominent and rounded, while the joints are unstressed and wasp-like. . . ."[13] The body is not a static whole; it is a tenuous collection of elements. Wilkes continues: "When Homer needed to talk of the living human body, he used one of two plural forms both meaning "limbs.". . . So man was a physical aggregate."[14] That aggregate only gained vitality as a functioning, unified entity after the limbs had combined into it. For the archaic Greeks, as Wilkes envisions them, the body does not condition and regulate its limbs; the limbs leave a notion of embodied unity behind their cooperative action. The limbs are partial objects combining into a physical aggregate in turn responsible for the now canonized epistemological notion of unified corporeality. But for the archaic Greeks, because the modernist orthodoxy had not yet entered into the limb's process, we had no intrinsic, body-centered unity.[15]

The Greek experience reappears today every time somebody receives a back rub. As a masseur's hands ripple down our back, our legs and arms relax, then fade away. Desire animates the entire operation by cutting our back and the masseur's hands off from the other limbs and other body parts before recombining them in a single, transient block of kneading muscle and skin. The hands are no longer separate from the back. Part of my body and part of his body form one temporary body while my other parts and his other parts diffuse. Desire produces an identity here. It is transient and malleable, the borders constantly extend and retreat. More importantly, the borders are not understood in contrast to an idealistic whole. They move in relation to themselves. Identity slips over or retreats from the very limits it has just defined through its own motions.

The pre-Socratic Greeks' aggregate body subordinates a skin-enclosed individuality to malleable, partial combinations. Possession enters as the weaving of these partial objects into self-centered identities, into Homer's heroes, and into puddles of rippling muscle.

Days Between Stations

Reading via Deleuze comes with this imperative: do not interpret in terms of skin-bound identities, understand in terms of desire. Steve Erickson's first book, *Days Between Stations*, exemplifies. A protagonist, Michel, invites his upstairs neighbors, Jason and wife Lauren, to the night club he manages. That evening they arrive and are shown to a table. Michel takes a break from work to join them.

> Michel and Jason talked. Michel signaled the waitress and ordered a drink. . . . "A landmark?" the waitress asked Lauren. Michel looked at Lauren for the first time. "No, thank you," said Lauren. . . . Michel shrugged. The waitress left.[16]

We could describe this brief scene by starting from Michel and Jason as integral characters. Then we would say they talked. Two static identities come first, then the action joining them. We would also note that nothing happened between Michel and Lauren.

Alternatively, we can deny privilege to the physical bodies and start with the most obtrusive manifestation of desire in the episode, the conversation. Name it Michel-Jason. The conversing works to form two people talking. Say: because of the conversing, two conversants. As identities, they come subsequent to desire's action. Simultaneously, and less distinctly, a disconnected level of action runs in silence generating the juxtaposition of Michel and Lauren. This level continues in silence, even becomes a mechanism producing silence. The silence operates within desire's rules, not as a wall between two self-identical individuals Michel and Lauren, instead it makes those two individuals in accordance with its own wordless code. So that silence can exist, they exist. They exist after silence as two people not talking. Now, after they are two people, we can string a muteness from one to the other separate from their formative condition. It is that second silence we refer to in saying that not a word passes between them. Desire's first silence is not the broad soundlessness forming the backside of another's conversation. And it is not the patterned silence that speech needs to delineate its words. And it is not the anxiety strung between two people's stilted conversation, the nervousness as each asks, "What should I say next?" Desire-produced silence works as a positive force, not an absence born from lack. As autonomous, it perpetuates itself independent of conversation. So, later, when Jason and the conversation leave the table, the tangible, productive, fecund silence continues. Michel and Lauren sit quietly. No pleasantries are forthcoming, no apprehensive questions initiate a talk. Erickson writes it very simply:

Jason went to the toilet. Michel and Lauren sat at the table, neither saying anything.[17]

Literary interpretation starting with the idea of characters casts Lauren and Michel as foils or contrasts for the talk between Michel and Jason. As for themselves, they are only individuals barely aware of each other and failing to connect. But seeing them failing to connect already implies they exist as selves in need of connection. Desire refuses that premise. Reading energized by Deleuze's desire understands silence actively constructing Lauren-Michel, a single becoming. Nothing more is needed, or, if something is needed, the need comes after they have become. In terms of the story, it no longer makes sense to divide these two. The real body in action springs from a silence delineated by four arms, four legs, two torsos, two heads. Again, this one body emerges from a powerful and demure silence, one just as fruitful as conversation. Later, it can be broken in two, as Lauren and Michel can be broken into two people.

With Michel and Lauren, one silently driven identity complicates or comprehends two bodies. Only full-blown possession can accomplish this. In the last chapter, in Emily's case, possession recreated the patient's body; Emily claimed it totally, but she could not break away from the confines imposed by the convention of physical bodies understood in the post-archaic Greek sense of corporeal wholes. Now that last barrier has been flattened. Silence creates an embodied subject not by deferring to traditional presuppositions but by creating a body in the course of making an identity. This new body has no relation to the one Dr. Bliss knew. This new body can have more than two arms and two legs. Every conventional quality has become variable; corporeality changes with possession's action.

Before going on to see how this possession and this reading works out for Lauren-Michel, consider the story's ramifications for Michel alone. In him, desire works the other way, as breaking down; one conventional body will simultaneously house multiple subjects. One Michel works with Jason splicing sounds and their quiet absence into words. Another Michel uses intriguing silence in combining with Lauren. Deleuze names this doubled state schizophrenic. He means something like what psychologists call multiple personality disorder, but not exactly. Psychology views multiplicity along time's horizontal line. One person maintains a single identity in a single body, then transforms into a different but still single personality in that same body. With Michel we are going vertical, his body becomes at once two, with each subject alien to the other. This is not the limp idea that one side of Michel works with Lauren while another side functions with Jason, and on some higher plane both sides reconcile. Reading by desire makes the singular Michel overproduce himself; leave the identity locked in a sealed body aside—it cannot contain Michel's desire. Construe this part of the story as two flows of possession halting and igniting: Michel-Jason, Michel-Lauren. One drives from conversation, one drives from silence. Michel works disjointedly in two places simultaneously. In this scheme, bodily delineated identity hinders our approach toward the real subjects in action, subjects with two heads each, subjects from talking and subjects from silence.

This scheme, and this reading, and these Deleuzean subjects are entirely dependent upon the silence. For Lauren-Michel to form one subject from two conventional bodies, and for Michel to see his one conventional body break into two subjects, silence must be something; it must be every bit as tangible as conversation. Silence must act. Like conversation, it must produce effects in the world. We see that next.

The book continues. Jason and Lauren spend their evening in the club and go home. They park on the street, walk, and pause below their building's exterior stairway. Jason notices the power is out. He returns to the car for a flashlight. Lauren starts up alone, through the dark. The wooden stairs climb past Michel's door on the third floor before making hers on the fourth. Lauren stops on the third floor landing. She waits.

> . . . listening, and in a blackness that would not have allowed her the sight of her own hand inches from her eyes, she saw [Michel] move.
> She said nothing.[18]

The Michel-Lauren working silence reestablishes itself here, on the third-floor landing. A single, momentary, partial object alien to Lauren and Michel replaces Lauren and Michel. Neither one acts in what follows. Neither one makes decisions. True, decisions are made, but no one is there to make them. Erickson writes:

. . . he could not have predicted the decisions she'd made, since she hadn't yet made them.[19]

Like the characters, the decisions (the manifestation of lack in desire), will only come after the event they ostensibly condition. This is the event:

> . . . if she thought to mutter anything at all he caught the sound of it in his mouth. . . . he would not break the kiss and his face wouldn't leave hers. . . .[20]

No words passed between them, but that doesn't matter. Silence has manifested itself as efficacious.

What makes this liaison? Not interaction between the characters, neither would have dared this, even if it was only a simple kiss. At the club, they hadn't exchanged a word, their eyes never locked, they hardly noticed each other. Further, so much dissuades them: plain fear, the morality, the husband. Michel would have thought again and retreated. She would have hurried upstairs. But desire's rules for combination insist neither he nor she are there, at least not before desire. This sequence—desire and combination before he and she—makes the possibility. Instead of thinking of rational characters balancing their choices and acting in ways unified with their past and future, unified like their impermeable body, think of desire making action and from there the choices, and then the possessed bodies following along the already marked way. This reading allows an explanation that drives beyond their individual fears and hesitations, and beyond the prudish objections that they have nothing in common, nothing to share, no conceivable future. The event transpires. The causes, the arguments for and against follow later. The conventionally embodied characters and their particular rationales for action come last as admissions of guilt and receptacles for secrets and forgiveness.

Reading starting with the characters forces standard questions: what circumstances brought them together? What do they find attractive in each other? Why this night at this time? Reading through desire devalues the characters and their questions. Now, we need to start by asking: what breed of desiring-possession composes the identity? Where does it start? Where does it end? What bodies, what parts of bodies live here? The answers are always changing. Sometimes subjects follow from possession as conversation, sometimes from possession as silence. Some subjects materialize in restaurants, others on third floor landings. Some end when the bars close, some keep going. Some desiring possessions use mouths and gestures, some use eyes, some use embracing arms.

The book continues and Lauren-Michel have their affair but conspicuously refuse marriage. The refusal is important, it again distinguishes the desire Michel-Lauren embody from need-based desire. Lurking around marriage are many of the idealisms exercised by characters invested with singularity born of lack. Marriage can name the striving upward to finality, toward some unrealized perfection, toward the whole as blissful pairing. Or, marriage can lean over backward to some perfection lost; it incessantly gropes for the first date or the first time. Marriage has counselors to serve its frequently lost ideal.

The other desire yields characters and events without privative want. That frees a way for understanding identity without responsibility to the cleanly delineated and impermeable bodies that have come to represent idealism here on earth. Deleuze's desire yields narration like this:

Do you feel my tongue there? he said. She nodded speechlessly. Can you feel it in the chambers of your heart? . . . no sound came from her when she saw the tip of his tongue wind up through the aorta, along her throat and dart before her eyes.[21]

It starts with a stretching tongue and ends with wide eyes. In between, a subject forms from sensations in the chambers of a heart and up through the aorta and along the throat. Possession as desire materializes this as a speechless identity. Nothing else and no one else peoples the scene, no comforting, traditional bodies, no safe, impermeable singularities. And why should we want these things or anything or anyone else? Desire for Deleuze means we already have more than we need.

Desire, Partial Bodies, Possession

Every correspondence between the conventional human body and identity breaks. The archaic Greeks started out with a whole body that was one only after its composition from parts. Deleuze's theory mixed into Steve Erickson's book has produced an identity composed of two conventional bodies (Michel-Lauren in silence), it has produced multiple identities simultaneously from one body (Michel's vertical multiple personalities), and it has produced the single identity attributable to a tongue curling all the way through a lover. That body pierced symbolizes the lesson Deleuze's work liberates from *Days Between Stations*: impermeable identity enjoys no privilege.[22] A tongue generates its own subject on its own terms. Underline the production; the main point is not the negative one about bodies coming apart. At this stage in philosophy's history, discourses about fragmented selves can only sound redundant. The positive point: the subject rises from possession. And going beyond Emily, possessed identity may be two bodies or it may be a tongue darting before her eyes.

Or, the subject of possession could be just the conventional body. That's fine. It normally is, almost every moment of every day passes under the assumption of consistently singular and body-centered selves. Deleuze is sober enough to recognize this, and prudent enough to accept it. He is not a reactionary. He is not bitterly against the present age as Rousseau was. Deleuze writes only in order to reach "the point where it is no longer of any importance whether one says I."[23] What is important is that when someone does say I, we recognize that 'I' as an after-effect. I am an after-effect of an inhuman force that has spent two thousand five hundred years producing most Western subjects in terms of conventional bodies and singularity, but which could just as easily have generated a culture of lives and understandings like Erickson proposes in *Days Between Stations*: a culture of torsos and tongues and legs and piercings and happenings without initial reasons. A culture of possession.

Having blown possession all the way out, the next chapter will ask what can bring possession on.

7

INVITATION TO POSSESSION

It is unusual, but occasionally it happens to almost every writer that the writing of some particular story seems outer-willed and effortless; it is as though one were a secretary transcribing the words of a voice from a cloud. The difficulty is maintaining contact with this spectral dictator. Eventually it developed that communication ran highest at night, as fevers are known to do after dusk. So I took to working all night and sleeping all day. . . .[1]

—Truman Capote, *Other Voices, Other Rooms*

Possession is transient. It cracks out part of my biography for its own momentary projects. Sometimes, as for Emily, the crack runs along time's line: first one personality, then another. Sometimes, as Michel displays in *Days Between Stations*, the crack breaks a single identity into simultaneous multiples. Either way, difference passes through. Deleuze teaches an underworld, a subterranean agitation of possessions forging upwards into human lives, taking them, using them, all the while maintaining such overriding privilege that the partial bodies in question gain no claim on the forces. When Emily seized the patient, she indulged guiltlessly the time that would otherwise have belonged to some other. She dug long, red furrows into the skin without remorse. Then she left, utterly. So, when the patient awoke, the time was completely blotted out, and were it not for the welts across her flesh, she may never have suspected anything but that she was prone to awesomely deep slumbers. Emily is transient. Like all possessed beings, like all beings forming their existence from generating difference, she does not submit to description in terms tailored for static states. She accommodates writing that promotes the entrances and exits of possession. Consequently, the least intrusive interrogation does not sift experience for a steady condition, it is not a form of: what is it like to live original difference? The least intrusive question asks: how does possession enter?

How has possession entered? For Michel and Lauren in Erickson's novel, as for Emily in Bliss's case study, possession was something the characters and patients found themselves in. They never saw it coming. They can hardly be blamed. Palpable bodies in experience and substantial nouns in language almost always provide the guideposts and coherence guiding lives. Possession challenges this hegemony with a blitzkrieg of difference. Remember Michel and Lauren on the third floor landing, them together had not entered either consciousness, no foreshadowing, no anticipation. But that does not mean possession cannot be anticipated. It can be. It can even be solicited. This is crucial. The fact of solicitation underlines that possession is not necessarily fearsome, it does more than ravage the security seated in our bodies, it does more than ruin traditional identities. It makes identities. It opens possibilities. It invests its targets with capacities. It made Michel-Lauren, it opened a space for them together where no possibility otherwise existed. It graced Fitzgerald with the capacity to be his generation's best writer. Possession vitalizes and explains the exceptional parts of us. It should be invited. So, in this chapter, possession enters experience following an invitation.

Writing Can Be Possession

As Fitzgerald taught, writing can be possession. In introducing one of his collections of scatological ramblings, Charles Bukowski agrees: ". . . the writing got done by itself. There was not the tenseness or the careful carving with a bit of a dull blade, that was needed to write something for *The Atlantic Monthly*."[2] If the writing got done by itself, writing does not belong to its author. It takes its author. Then, the energizing writing ironically hides itself within as an artistic skill, as something Bukowski could be responsible for. We say, "Bukowski is an obnoxious writer," or, "Bukowski's energetic prose . . ." We understand writing like the shirts he wears, like he has a choice, like the white one or the striped one. Beneath this convention, Bukowski is appearing text with a human body and its decisions attached subsequently to give the book an intelligible locality in our material world. Writing precedes Bukowski means writing precedes both his body and his thought. A very serious question waits here. If writing precedes even thought, how can any comprehension get underway? It is no longer a question of whether or not another's words can be well understood, but whether they can even begin to be understood. Can the hermeneutic circle even get started? I follow this worry in the next section. For now, the text creates the author.

And there is no reason to suppose that the identification is strictly one to one, no reason to think that this particular writing existed only once and generated solely one body; there is no reason to believe it erupted for the first time with Bukowski and then disappeared forever. True, the writing did arrive and leave, but it may just as well have arrived elsewhere before and come again following, again elsewhere. A likely candidate for a past manifestation of Bukowski's possession: Ferdinand Louis Celine. And in the future, where might it strike? Impossible to say. But, we can ask, what might catalyze a reappearance here on earth of the particular writing now attached to Bukowski. What can facilitate its presence? The general question—how can possession be solicited—has narrowed to this: how can a distinct form of possession's writing be tempted back into existence?

This is the central question Jorge Borges takes up in his celebrated literary tract *Pierre Menard, Author of Don Quixote*. Intellectually, the question becomes increasingly tantalizing as the distance between a certain writing's manifestations stretches out. In Borges's enigmatic narrative, the specific writing we are looking for has not surfaced for three centuries. When it finally emerges again, it comes into the world as alien, as unsuited to contemporary language and cultural practices. But along the narrow strip of its generation, possession leaves all those static things in its wake, so these apparent hurdles obstructing the reappearance are rapidly set aside, again leaving the central question: how do we invite a force that can remake the world in accord with a writing?

Pierre Menard, Author of Don Quixote

Borges presents his answer in an ambiguous mix of fiction and reality. The ostensible subject of possession, Pierre Menard, is, the *Dictionary of Borges*[3] informs us, a fictional character. But Borges portrays Menard amid references to nonfictional persons like Paul

Valery, at factual places like Nimes in France, and in the midst of real social debates. Daniel Balderston, a contemporary critic, pushes the confusion beyond irony; he cites a published book by Menard, *Writing and the Subconscious: Psychoanalysis and Graphology*,[4] and devotes an entire chapter of his own book *Out of Context* to describing Menard's cultural milieu and works. He concludes that Pierre Menard must have been born in the 1860s or 1870s in Nimes. Menard devoted himself to letters and became a modestly consequential speaker in French critical discussions. Most importantly, and here Balderston's biography joins Borges's fiction, Menard struck upon the following project: write *Don Quixote*. There are two things this project is not: first, not an attempt to write a contemporary, updated version of the old, stalwart novel. Menard did not envision his toil as analogous to theater writers adapting canonized plays—Shakespeare's *Lear*, for instance—to the current world, with Lear presented as a broken politician or senile businessman. Menard's intention was to remain much closer to the original text. So near that the result of his labors could be identified in advance of their completion. Menard was to write *Quixote* as Miguel de Cervantes had earlier written it, verbatim, word for word, line for line, with identical paragraphs and the same number of chapters all in the same order. This sounds manageable enough. But Menard's task was more complicated than it sounds. He did not see himself as a human Xerox machine; his task would have nothing to do with dumb copying. Borges stresses that "[Menard's] aim was never to produce a mechanical transcription of the original."[5] So, the book will be neither a contemporaneous adaptation nor a mechanical secretarial service. The book cannot be different from the original and it cannot be the same. Suddenly, the task is dumbfounding. Menard admits as much in a letter discussing his work:

> My intent is merely astonishing. . . . The ultimate goal of a theological or metaphysical demonstration—the external world, God, chance, universal forms—[these things are] no less anterior or common than this novel which I am now developing.[6]

Philosophers have found nothing but trouble in trying to understand the meaning and reality of the external world, in trying to prove God, in trying to justify causation, in trying to harness universal forms for ethical and political purposes. Now, Menard wants to tie another knot into the tangle. The name for this tying is possession by the writing of *Quixote*.[7]

Inviting Possession

The invitation to possession according to Borges's report on Menard: sink yourself deeply into the circumstances which first manifested the writing. For Menard, a Frenchman of the early twentieth century, the initial steps were daunting but at least readily discernable. He needed to forget history between 1602 and his present. He needed to embrace the Catholic faith, learn Spanish, and not Spanish generally, but a specific, antique idiom. He needed to visit the place, see the landscape, sleep above the same street, know the people, know the people as they were then. Do everything. Read all the history books, all the biographies, then cut through all the contradictions to assemble the flawless comprehension of the time and the faultless picture of Cervantes himself. Even read *Quixote*, but don't memorize the words. Push deeper into the pages, uncover the author's intention, his reasons, his motivations, his demons. Then Menard needed to begin writing the book, and even when he knows he is going wrong and that what he has is just bad draft, he must keep adding words and sentences and then, when it becomes hopelessly wrong, he starts over again. And over and over again. All this is like housecleaning, an eradication of Menard's twentieth century sentiments, it is all preparation for the old writing to revisit earth.

One very unexpected problem undercuts all these efforts, however. According to Menard, his method threatened to make the project "too easy."[8] Menard does not mean he was facile with foreign languages and cultural anthropology generally, though he very likely was. The project risked becoming too easy because he, Pierre Menard, could do it, or at least take total responsibility for it. Granted, the task would be burdensome, it would exhaust his concentration, tax his constitution, leave him haggard physically and psychologically. But this is the point, this is why the route is finally too easy, because all these things and everything that will happen, happens to *him*. Menard does not want something to happen to him. And on the other extreme, he does not want simply to become Miguel de Cervantes, who is just another him. He wants to be nobody and become the insubstantial writing of *Don Quixote*. Provoking this overwhelming breed of writing is much more difficult and much less certain than you simply putting your head down and driving mercilessly into the past, into another language, another time, another culture.

In grammatical terms, the problem: Menard's single-minded devotion to his project, to the fact that it is his, will block possession because it forces the infinitive 'to write' to accommodate itself to a precedent subject. 'To write' gets frozen into 'Menard writes.' Possession demands, however, that subjects follow and be drafted by the verb. Menard, the substantive, should accommodate the infinitive.

In theoretical terms, possession lies beyond the grasp of any individual's conscious efforts because possession comes from a different order of being than individuals. We cannot enter possession's dimension and bring it back across, because entering is tantamount to sacrificing all the standard presuppositions about ourselves and how we operate; it means sacrificing the privilege of discrete, singular identity and linear, irreversible time and lack's priority over desire and everything that a philosophy or practitioner of difference, like Titus Andronicus, overturns and disregards. Possession, on the other hand, can maintain itself while crossing over. It recklessly breaches our world and claims our bodies and identities to remake them in accord with its own exploits. It can even remake them in counterfeit accord with the privilege of substantive over infinitive. This scheme clearly illustrates the nondialectical nature of the relation between writing and authors, between possession and corporeal bodies, and more generally between active and reactive forces, and even more generally, between difference and identity. Writing, possession, activity, and difference share a dominion over their respective others. They are different but not opposed, not dependent. For this reason, everything from possession's writing to pure difference can break onto the other plane and make authors and identities without sacrificing themselves. Meanwhile, authors, their bodies, reaction, and identity claw at their respective others: authors enter interminable warfare with their writing, bodies constantly struggle to control their acts, reaction claims to be action, identity purports to shepherd difference. Dialectical dependence chafes in the midst of all these conflicts, but only from the side of authors and identity. From the other side, writing, possession, activity, and difference rely on nothing outside themselves, they define their own limits. Writing defines itself by fabricating an author. Subsequently, and only subsequently, the writing contrasts with, and therefore relies upon its author. So, several steps down the line from the ontological genesis, a certain reliance emerges, but only as created and artificial. This derivative reliance plays a role in the dialectical history of misrepresenting being, of understanding that generation only comes with an equally original and comparably powered negative limitation. But, in accordance with the limitedly true, nondialectical structure of being, possession fabricates and subsequently and ironically relies upon a material body, active forces fabricate and then ironically rely upon reactive forces, difference fabricates and then ironically relies upon identity. Any reader of Nietzsche and Deleuze has been pelted with the insistence that active is nobler than reactive and that difference precedes identity. Several privileges have been added: possession precedes corporeal bodies and writing is nobler than the writer.

The personal experience of the nobility intrinsic to the philosophy of difference is possession. Menard shoots for it. When he moves to Spain and sleeps in the same bed and learns the dialect and speaks it even though no one living there speaks quite that way anymore, he is trying to entice a force out of three hundred years of hiding. When he begins writing for the seventh time after six catastrophic failures, he is trying to create conditions that will attract possession to him. But he is never working toward it because that labor is logically impossible, because possession means the end of all projects with impositions called goals, and because possession means the end of him. Consequently, when possession arrives, all the preceding work he did, all the books he read and every preparatory draft he wrote will be reduced to irrelevance. They have served their purpose. Next, possession will level everything in generating its own world and its own book, its own *Don Quixote*. *Don Quixote* again.

Borges reports that Menard took extraordinary care to burn beyond recognition every shred of the early drafts for those chapters he was finally blessed to write. He burned them scrupulously to avoid a confusion. Normally, when we look at an author's early drafts, we see nascent ideas and articulations, ideas developing and focusing and growing out and being shorn back and coming into focus again, tighter focus. Possession works differently. Its books are not planned and developed, because people plan and develop with nouns. If books are planned and developed, then we should be able to write the introduction and conclusion before even starting on the interior chapters. We should write to get to the end, a certain static point out there. Books should come from outlines. But anyone who has ever written anything of any length knows the outline comes after the book. It is only when a book is finally finished that an introductory overview comes into focus and a conclusion becomes possible because it is only when a book is finally finished that it at last dawns on you what writing has been doing. Only at the end do you clearly realize what, exactly, you have been writing about. And the reason for your delayed realization is simple. It is not that you hadn't thought the ideas all the way through. And it is not that they were caught in your subconscious waiting to work their way out. Your realization is delayed because you have not been writing. Writing has been going through you. Only when writing finishes are you—as author—finished. And only when you are finished can you see what the constructing energy was all about, how the chapters fit together, where everything was headed. On the subject of the book, synthesizing authors first appear when they sign the title page or attach gratuitous redundancies to the main text, when they write introductions, conclusions, tables of contents, indexes.

Menard wants to write a book without knowing what it will be until written, but he also wants to control the experiment totally, so he defines that book he will not know, *Don Quixote*. With the definition intact, Menard is no longer free to write by accident, to produce random words and then call that a book. Possession's writing is not chaos, it is internally structured and rigorously controlled. It is just that the structure and control no longer precede the writing and condition it, they follow out of the writing and delimit it. Returning to the question of Menard burning the early drafts, it makes no sense to look at his early efforts because they have nothing whatever to do with his *Don Quixote*. In fact, Menard's early drafts are even antithetical to it and misleading. Studying them, even seeing them, gives the wrong impression of what precedes writing's possession. It is not a planning author accumulating and refining ideas, it is invitation. Granted, invitation looks like planning, but it isn't.

Question: if the burning symbolizes the stark break between the writer with projects on the one side and the infinitive project possessing a body on the other, why does a conspiracy seem to exist between invitation and possession? That is, if it is true that possession razes the author before resurrecting, shouldn't it be as likely that I begin writing *Quixote* again as Menard? As likely me, even though Menard has done all the footwork, learned the language, studied the man, visited the place? Given what possession does, how can invitation have any effect at all? Unfortunately, answering the question ruins the positive force of possession, it deposits possession's writing in the world of projects and teleological privilege and final answers and everything Socrates wants. The exigencies of possession determine that the question cannot be answered satisfactorily. But the problem can be eluded. At the same time that the question of how invitation works is rising and finding no response, the idea of invited possession is working as a hermeneutic tool to explain Borges's plot. And in the previous chapter, possession alone explained Michel and Lauren together. And in the chapter before, it explained Emily's unique, mysterious violence. And in the chapter before, it explained Fitzgerald's passion. Cling to these successes. Deleuze privileges explaining power over self-reflexive handwringing. Philosophy needs to be evaluated in practice before in theory. Evaluate what has happened instead of what should happen. So, there exists a lacuna in possession as theory: how can invitation work? Why does possession follow invitation? No answer. But in exchange for our surrender and the lingering annoyance buzzing from this particular failure, we gain twice: first, we have faced the divide separating authors who write from writing that makes authors, because accepting philosophy with a bottomless hole is tantamount to accepting an unmeasurable distance between writers and their writing—a distance crossed only by writing, not by us. Second, and more importantly, we have acquired powerful tools. Invitation and possession give us a way to explain Menard's ersatz-plan and understand Borges's story, and they will give us a way to read the history of philosophy and a way to interpret texts by a refurbished author's intention. In return, we only need to bite our Socratic tongues.

New Center

In the end, Menard's method of total immersion in the Spain of Cervantes proved too easy because instead of dipping into the murky task of entering a different order of being, Menard himself insisted upon acting. What he must do is resign to an ontology that can never explicitly enter human-centered history.

Polarities reverse when possession comes through Menard. Before possession arrived, Menard read Cervantes's texts so that he could approach the book's originator. Now, with possession, Menard becomes the originator and his body manically produces the very text he had studied. Memory plays no role, the explanation is much simpler. The book being written again is the same thing happening again (the eternal return). The only confusing thing is that the substantial character and the time in history have altered drastically. But because possession privileges verbs over nouns, the transformations in players and times matters hardly at all. To push the point further, Menard could go on to write other books that could equally well be attributed to Cervantes even though the historical figure called Cervantes never wrote them. So, instead of reading novels and biographies to understand what Cervantes thought and believed and feared and communicated with his pen, Menard now produces those things. He is no longer trudging through famous literature and language barriers to get to the center, to get to Cervantes, he is writing Cervantes by sending pages of text rippling out from the new source of *Don Quixote*.

The Same Book Again

In philosophy too, the same book has been written again, though not with the precision of Menard and his *Quixote*. The repeaters? Rousseau and Nietzsche. Start with Rousseau's *Discourses on the Arts and Sciences* and *On the Birth of Inequality in Society*. Then stack the *Social Contract* on the end. Rousseau's thought in the *Discourses*: We ushered from a blessed, noble, savage condition of nature. We crossed out with the triple and nearly identical discoveries of language, thought, and property. As a result, we find ourselves in the worst possible state, our freedom lost twice. First, we no longer recognize our own desires, they atrophy under the weight of social custom. Second, even if we could recognize our desires, vanity, the acquired habit of evaluating ourselves through the eyes of others, disallows the expression of those desires. No recognition of desires plus no expression of desires equals no freedom. The particular character of this freedom lost is anonymity. We are not enslaved because someone is forcing us to do something, we are enslaved because we have lost ourselves to the headless monster of society. What to do? We can't go back. So push forward. The exigencies of our current affliction have the redeeming value of making us pregnant with a future. By driving anonymity—the loss of freedom—all the way, we can recover a new kind of freedom unattainable and obviously unthinkable for the noble savage. This freedom is the freedom of sovereignty, the freedom embodied in the political state following the citizens' complete alienation to the general will. In the *Social Contract* Rousseau envisions a human organization outstripping us all, and because of that, allowing us to become it. This new state appears as a democracy, but it is not. When prospective laws are put to a vote by the people, as every law is, the question is not, "Do you want this enacted?" But, "Is it the general will that this be enacted?" When your vote finds itself in the minority and the law is enacted, you have not been overruled, you have simply misjudged the general will you began by alienating yourself to. Thus, given the conditions of the sovereignty's formation, the resulting state can never be anything but an expression of your freedom, even when you disagree. This obviously is not your personal freedom that has disappeared, but little matter because society had ruined that anyway. The new, political freedom promises a future heretofore unseen. It promises an authentic, communal freedom. And it reminds us that sometimes people need to be forced to be free.

The same in Nietzsche's *Genealogy of Morals*. Not exactly the same, but not close either. No room for degrees of success in this discussion. Either Nietzsche (at least part of Nietzsche) was Rousseau (or part of Rousseau) again, or he was not. He was. Nietzsche posits a beginning in a state of nobility pointedly savage in nature: the good were just those able to acquire what they wanted. More directly, what is good is what I want. As in Rousseau, Nietzsche cuts out social mediation. Nietzsche's noble does not ask first. And again as in Rousseau, Nietzsche's savage morality has now vanished. For (Deleuze's) Nietzsche, because of consciousness' dawn over the brutal utopia, the reactive forces discussed in Chapter 2 have been able to separate the nobles from what they can do; they have separated nobility from intrinsic, thoughtless action. The reprehensible hierarchies of Platonism flow over the West. Instead of the good reigning over the bad, the strong over the weak, we have the reverse, the weak over the strong presented publicly under the euphemistic title of Good over the Evil. Social and religious regulation, coupled with trite maxims like "what goes around comes around" have given pause to noble morality. The pause is fatal because it gives us time to think about what others would think. Can we get back to thoughtless nobility? No, consciousness, our "weakest and most fallible organ"[9] according to Nietzsche, is ineffaceable. Like language for Rousseau, once we have depressing self-consciousness, we have it. Before acting, we cannot help but defer to something stultifying, something like protocol or Kant's law. But again, as in Rousseau, we have also become pregnant with a future. Our new conscious capacity forbids savage morality, but it allows the overcoming of civilized man. As with anonymity for Rousseau, we find salvation by driving our flaw to the maximum. It is in being fully conscious of our deplorable state, in being repelled by it with all of our senses and our mind, that we are driven to a novel, different kind of savage morality. Instead of imposing pitilessly with the brute power of muscle, we can now hope to impose pitilessly with the conscious power of philosophy. Nietzsche's bitter dream: bring the world to its knees under the force of his books. Regain nobility by imposing values. He may be succeeding. Whether he is or not, redemption waits on the other side of our fallen nature, just as for Rousseau. And for both, it is something in the fallen state that promises the redemption.

Are there differences between Rousseau and Nietzsche? Yes, but not every occurrence of possession needs to be as tightly controlled as Menard's. We are searching for something more elusive than straight isomorphism, at least more elusive than isomorphism on the substantive level, on the level of things. True the books are not indistinguishable, but they are something more than similar, more than two authors stumbling into structural congruence. Wittgenstein might say they are like twins, but which sort, fraternal or identical? An open question. Did the *Discourses* and the *Social Contract* happen again as the *Genealogy*? Irresolvable, but look at the *Genealogy*, whole sections could be peeled out and seamlessly pasted into Rousseau's *Discourses*. Take the sixteenth section of the second essay, for example. But again, evidence on the one side or the other can go on forever.

The Deleuzean claim: the writing that happened as Rousseau happened again as Nietzsche. The verb, a specific version of a specific verb, repeated. What does it mean for verbs to repeat? For nouns, the answer is simple. The same thing happens again, and the thing that is the same regulates what is happening. But we have seen that for Deleuze, repetition is not governed by things but production. What appears as the same thing happening again appears after the repeating (the generating) as an effect. The idea of a book's repeating follows the book's completion. Neither the *Discourses* nor the *Genealogy of Morals* plays a governing role in any historical return of the same. Things do not return. Difference makes things cognizable as having returned. Any material book only marks difference's encore appearance as a reappearance. On the other side, the noun's repetition is busily elaborating itself by determining what came first, second, third. But in the infinitive realm, that aspect of repeating, the ordering, vanishes. The infinitive makes everything original. But original in a vertiginous sense, original without contrasting with copy or with a second coming or with a repetition of the same thing. Later, along with noun privilege, a second meaning for 'original' enters the scene; copies accompany this original, copies and questions about before and after. But back on the infinitive plane, whether Rousseau or Nietzsche wrote first hardly matters. What matters is writing, a particular writing which is new every time, even when repeating. From this verb-powered side, even the invitations Rousseau and Nietzsche mailed out, the study, the learned languages, the hours of discussion, lonely reflection, all that slides away. Nietzsche and Rousseau were just there, both writing the same thing originally. Just like Menard and Cervantes.

Even if you refuse to go all the way with Deleuze, even if you refuse to believe that verbs run the world and the same verb can appear again, we can still use this strategy as a hermeneutic device. While holding in abeyance doubts about the reality of infinitive-driven experience, we can dedicate ourselves to discovering how many times, in how many languages and places, a certain book, say Menard's book, has appeared on earth.

Hermeneutical Ramifications

Don Quixote's resurfacing in Menard equally resurrects—in a drastically transformed state—the old hermeneutic method of reading for author's intention.

Since Nietzsche told us everything is interpretation, and since Freud opened a new vista of psychology snagging current actions in childhood trauma's, the technique of reading literature for the author's intention has lost its constituency, mainly because it has become impossible to discern satisfactorily what the author wanted to communicate. In the *Genealogy of Morals*, Nietzsche demonstrated that passing time shifts the meanings of words, rearranges the importance of ideas, and transforms the categories determining our knowledge. Foucault followed up in books like *Madness and Civilization*. What is good, what is bad, what is reasonable, what is insane, all these and most everything else is constantly open to major reconstruction. Reading an author's intention back over history's inevitable epistemic divides becomes a forbidding task. Further, even if the general culture from which a book appeared could be mastered, could someone like Menard equally well grip the individual Cervantes? To approach the author's intention as traditionally conceived, it is not enough to know the public elements of a discourse, everything private must come to light as well. The list of requirements begins with Cervantes's youth. According to Freud, we need to know about his mother and his father, what did they teach him, especially about sex? What were the rules of his childhood, where was his rebellion, and for what reason? We need to know all about the first years. This is too great a burden.

A second problem with justifying literary interpretation by appeal to what the author wanted to communicate rises from our era's paranoia of fascism. In the 1990s, no one wants to impose, and certainly not impose readings. Literary theorists familiar with Emmanuel Levinas have acquired a potent weapon for defending against imposition, the word 'violence.' For Levinas, to imagine you can comprehend another person is not only false and vain, but also a brutal and repressive encroachment upon the other's infinite and unique depth. The same idea can be moved over to a literary work, now referred to as a text.[10] Since we cannot know exactly what an author intended, to report on an author's book as though we could is a violence. And in philosophy's world, where the highest standards must be upheld, this imposing violence summons up dramatic remembrances of Hitler's Germany. When we read and then write that "Cervantes meant so and so . . ." we are regimenting Cervantes, lining him up, marching him off in a literary process of asphyxiation. No one wants to do that. So, the two problems with justifying a reading by appeal to author's intention: it is impossible, it is fascistic.

On the other side, the objectors to author's intention have their own objectors. Their backlashing claim: to interpret without the author at the center, and to be so intimidated by the paranoia of fascism that you can never say one reading betters another, leads to a base community of readers. Dignity disappears because rank order has been shuttled into the basement, and because the idea of an *agon*, a battle between readings that brings out the best in both but ultimately crowns one as better than another, has been stigmatized as too ruinous to the self-esteem of all but an obnoxious few. The objectors to the objectors perceive unbridled relativism stomping interpretation into the ground. While inoculating the practice of reading against interpretive insensitivity, fears of violence and fascism reduce reading to senseless babble.

Possession defuses these problems and satisfies both sets of critics by instantiating its own version of author's intention. No longer is the exact intention impossible to attain, it can happen, even though it cannot be worked for so much as only invited and then hoped for. Within possession, we come perilously close to the author, so close that we do not discover the intention, we become it by first writing. Consequently, possession is delivering a very different meaning for author's intention. The author no longer originates the intention, but is produced from intention. And intention no longer guides the writing, it follows from the writing. Because the writing makes the intention makes the author, it no longer makes sense to object that the author cannot be comprehended, because the author's intention has become a product of us, of our writing, of the writing you and I do.

The next objection: interpreting by author's intention is fascistic, it violates the author's infinite uniqueness. Possession defies this objection. It claims Menard is the original author even though it is Cervantes's book. Or, better, it claims both Menard and Cervantes are the original authors of a book that belongs to the infinitive. No possible fascism.

In general terms, the objections to interpreting via author's intention can all be traced back to a (phallogocentric) privileging: the author over the intention. When the true ontological order is restored, when the writing itself instantiates the intention and the author follows, the author can again take the center of interpretation.

So, the objections to reading by authors' intentions have been overcome. And on the other side, the objectors to the objections should be satisfied. Fascism has evaporated even while a way of objectively rank ordering readings has stepped smartly into view. If only we can separate true possession from the pretenders, then we can immediately set up objective standards for the quality of interpretations. Two important points about these standards: first, they will emerge from within the writing itself, they will not be the result of dogmatic regulation. And, as an extension, this hierarchy will operate like a restricted ontology. That means a traditional metaphysician could still object that reading has been swallowed up by relativism because from some safe and distant vantage point, one beyond all the material particulars of writing, it appears that one rank order could arise just as well as another. True. But possession starts from the claim that no such restful, exterior point exists. Everything ushers from the force of writing itself, and within that maelstrom, right and wrong, better and worse exist just as surely as Menard had to burn draft after draft of failed, not quite possessed writings.

Inviting Possession

Invite possession by sinking yourself deep into another life—one lived before or one constructed from fictional material. The sinking cleanses, it loosens accretions and calcifications piled up during years of living the same way in the same place among the same people. Adopting another life is trading in defining nouns: your name, your language, your parents, your children, your home, your values, what you desire, what repels you. All these and everything shifts. Importantly, these shifts happen and remain on the noun's level; authors and readers establish new locations even while the jurisdiction of writers over writing and identity over difference continues. But at the same time, the rumblings wake possession and invite it. What follows is not a premeditated shifting of substantial identities but an anonymous fabrication of infinitive identity.

Why have writing and literature volunteered themselves as privileged examples of possession? Because as part of its day-to-day work, authoring, especially authoring fiction, entails exchanging defining nouns. If it is a good author, like Fitzgerald, who imagined himself as strongly as possible as each unique character when writing their words for them, then writing dialogues becomes an invitation. When Gatsby spoke with Daisy, for example, Fitzgerald himself first became Gatsby, then Daisy, then Gatsby again. Even better, when Fitzgerald wrote exchanges between three, four, five people, his work became rapid-fire invitations, rapid fire noun shiftings. Hence, writing naturally leads to possession.

Still, there are no directions all the way in. Possession can be solicited but not caused. At the closest approach, the invitation is crumpled and discarded just as possession enters.

Structurally, possession resembles the eternal return. Adopting another life is like the first affirmation, it awakens the issue. The second affirmation is possession, it is Titus rewriting time, or rewriting the entire play even though four of the five acts have already passed.

In 1940, after he had lost his talent, Scott Fitzgerald famously wrote: "There are no second acts in American lives."[11] Wrong.

Of true possession it is impossible to be afraid. Who would be afraid? Which body? What person? Since possession builds the subject, no one exists before possession so no one is there to be afraid. This is not always true; people exist and carry on in accord with other rules for identity. These others cross paths with the possessed; they may not know it, they may know it and be captivated, they may not care, they may be scared. Dr. Bliss's patient was terrified of Emily. She should have been. Still, even while manic horror stirs around, no subject consummate to Emily could feel fear of anything coming from beyond themselves because there is nothing beyond.

Fear is a trap, a way of staying with Socrates, a way of living in reaction. To sink in it, I need only dwell on weary structuralist and then poststructuralist claims about identity. Yes, the much abused Modern subject is decentered and fragmented and broken down. First, thanks to Emily, absolute singularity falls away. Pushed to a higher degree, Michel's degree, one body simultaneously holds multiple identities. Higher still, combinations produce malleable bodies and indiscriminate identities; a tongue combines with a lover's innards and a subject is made. The weight falls here. The subject is not broken, the negative has not overwhelmed the positive; production has overwhelmed tradition: identity generates. The moral is entirely affirmative, it is about the liberal construction of subjects and what they can do now, what they can write now, how they can love now.

Possession's crudest lesson is disenfranchisement of the substantial body in the name of infinitives. The subject freed from its skin container breaks out everywhere verbs congregate: in bars, in silence, in writing, in conversation, in kissing. Identity still breathes through skin and organs, but its verb-center frees it to take only those sections it wants while neglecting the rest. When Michel and Lauren joined, the possessed subject invested the tongue and the insides. The rest disappeared, not just rendered momentarily obsolete or extraneous but gone, not there. Under possession, no material is there except that being actively driven by a specific verb. In the chapter on difference, I wrote about restricted ontology—the parameters of being compose themselves without regard for global viewpoints—the same holds for possession. Under one substantial and physically based ontological framework, Michel and Lauren still have their bodies attached as they fall together. But when possession takes them, those integral bodies no longer place a legitimate claim on existence because they are not part of the infinitive's core fabrication.

Why possession? Because it explains some of the best things we do. Fitzgerald as author was the finest thing he did. He owed that to possession. Emily's violence was the most noteworthy thing the otherwise anonymous patient ever did, she has possession to blame and to thank. And where would Michel and Lauren be without possession? And how could we truly understand the writings of another without possession? Possession hurls us past every constriction. On the physical level, the body no longer stops you. On more rarified planes, obstacles like reasons and needs fall away. It is no longer a panic, like can the body maintain its integrity? And it is not a trepidation, like why are we doing this? It is invigorating possibilities: what identity will rise? What can be understood? What will be written? What can get made? These are the questions that cling tightest to possession and to Deleuze.

These are not questions that came easily to Socrates. He wanted to know how we could get to the true identity (*eros*), and how we could understand the Forms (*Parmenides*, *Republic*), and whether or not writing itself betrayed idealism (*Phaedrus*). Finally, he wanted to know how everything refers back up to the timeless metaphysical zone. Deleuze finds the voice to ask his different questions because his reversal has gained momentum. In language, nouns and verbs reverse. In physical experience, things and events reverse. In emotional experience, desire and lack reverse. In literature, we no longer read to understand authors, we write to become them. Then we write and become something else entirely, something Socrates does not believe in.

PART III

ALIENATION

Possession, like difference, runs on reflexive production; it relentlessly sucks everything back in. So, unforgiving, unrepentant, and remorseless, it is solitude that characterizes these bodies. And even though it might be true that from some global perspective the structural mix of production and limitation retains the same form everywhere difference rears its head, still, possessed subjects hold no uniting power because difference's subjects cannot get beyond themselves because they each take full responsibility for limiting themselves. Difference's dominion over identity is culminating. Identity has been so trodden, so defeated, that even when identity exists, it no longer has the strength to reach out to its fellows, much less bond with them.

On scattered occasions, philosophy has come close to realizing alienation: the anonymous ascetic wandering through ancient wildernesses, Rousseau's reveries of a solitary walker and his aphasic state of nature, Camus. Not Marx, the alienation in this section's title has little to do with Marxian reflections on labor. Alienation in this book denotes extreme foreignness. Maurice Blanchot approached a bedrock version in his compact book *The Unavowable Community*. Blanchot read Marguerite Duras's *The Malady of Death* and shortly afterward wrote this of love and Duras's enigmatic lovers:

> . . . during the nights they spend together she belongs to the community, she is born from the community, while making felt, through her fragility, her inaccessibility and magnificence, that the strangeness of what could not be common is what founds that community, eternally temporary and always deserted.[1]

Here, Blanchot seems right on top of alienation. He lingers on ideas of inaccessibility and strangeness and what is not in common. He reads Duras's thousand-word book with care and with admiration, and he stands ready to accept what he finds there, but, finally, Blanchot falls short. Not short in the qualitative sense, like his text's minimal grace could be improved with a little editing or a few extra paragraphs. He falls short only of the extreme alienation Deleuze's philosophy prepares his readers to envision. True, Blanchot's pages hold an alienation, one inspired by Duras's elegiac story, but they never accomplish purity. In trying, Blanchot invokes Levinas's ethics: "An ethics is possible only when—with ontology (which always reduces the Other to the Same) taking the backseat—an anterior relation can affirm itself, a relation . . . [that] feels that the other always puts it into question to the point of being able to respond to it only through a responsibility that cannot limit itself."[2] Blanchot falls short. He seems to succeed in disavowing any collapse into an original union by refusing to let ontology melt the other into an always implicit same. But then he lets a foundational community in through the back door by accepting a strong notion of responsibility to others, even by setting up a position around that responsibility. But what do the possessed have to do with responsibilities to others? What did Titus Andronicus care about others?

This is the problem: Blanchot edges up to alienation by implicitly conceding an original and ruinous deference to social unity. See it in his title, the book is not called *Alienation* or *Solitude* but *The Unavowable Community*. Blanchot reaches isolation after community; he starts from community and then feels his way out toward its absence. Blanchot understands alienation with the terms, categories, and presuppositions of unity. Granted, those terms and categories have been drained of their association with romantic notions of love, notions built up from Aristophanes's speech in the *Symposium*. But even so, Blanchot's approach to alienation links him to the Greek. It also sinks him into the predicament Deleuze claims has wrecked the efforts of nearly every thinker after Socrates to think difference: they always reach out from identity; difference is always a product of identity, difference is envisioned in the terms and forms identity allows. Deleuze's project in *Difference and Repetition* was to think difference first. Identity and its accompanying forces of thought—representation, Socratic recollection, innate correspondence—follow. They are products. Now, possession has shifted the dynamic from identity and difference to community and alienation. Thinking community before alienation ruins alienation by reducing it to a simple negative, a reaction to its opposite. Above all, the solitude Deleuze's philosophy allows cannot be thought through the tradition's stubborn categories. Those categories, and even community, may appear, but they must come subsequent to alienation; they must exist in alienation's service as the ironic way alienation manifests itself.

Duras wrote the following near the end of her story, after you have met the woman, perhaps paid her, spent days and nights watching, touching her, sleeping with your head squeezed safely between her legs. You wake one drizzling morning to find her gone. You go out searching.

> Soon you give up, don't look for her anymore, either in the town or at night or in the daytime.
> Even so, you have managed to live that love in the only way possible for you. Losing it before it happened.[3]

Remember the sentence Erickson wrote for Michel-Lauren:

> . . . he could not have predicted the decisions she'd made, since she hadn't yet made them.

And she didn't make them until after the episode passed, she made them as an after-effect of her own action. So too Duras's lover. The decision that he loved her came only after she left, after she took her remoteness and her indifference away. In both cases, an identity follows difference. For Erickson's characters, identity takes the form of a conscious and delineable reason coming after a difference manifested as possession. For Duras's characters, identity takes the form of a phantom community of lovers coming after difference manifested as impregnable solitude.

This section is dedicated to following Deleuze as he reaches to where you can see and touch someone you cannot see and touch, to where you can come close to someone and sense only that nothing will be there ever.

Platonism will reverse decisively on the subject of alienation. For Platonism, our rational souls put us on a continuum of knowledge hanging from clean Truth at the top to right opinion near the bottom, or, even lower, to flawed opinion. But no lower than that. We all have something of the capable philosopher in us. But, in Deleuze's own words, difference has inaugurated a time where:

There is no longer even right opinion, but rather a sort of ironic encounter which takes the place of a mode of knowledge, an art of encounter that is outside of knowledge and opinion.[4]

We have lost our grip. Falling away

. . . implies huge dimensions, depths, and distances that the observer cannot master.[5]

These huge distances hang between the continuum from truth to opinion on one side and difference's products on the other. Difference leaves us perfectly alienated from the line knowledge and opinion string through philosophy.

The question of huge distances and the continuum translates into one of similarity. Hanging on the rope between truth and right opinion means enjoying a similarity, even a possible identity with the highest reaches. Socrates wants us all on the rope so he defines the world in terms of resemblance. And the rebellious becoming intrinsic to difference, the becoming in experience which implies huge distances, distances beyond similarity? According to Deleuze, Platonism attempts

To impose a limit on this becoming, to order it according to the same, to render it similar—and, for that part which remains rebellious, to repress it as deeply as possible, to shut it up in a cavern at the bottom of the ocean.[6]

Socrates was an inflexible tyrant. Everything and everybody twists into the continuum. The incorrigible he cuts away and shuts away. All the world will be rectified as similar or gone

—such is the aim of Platonism in its will to bring about the triumph of icons. . . .[7]

Icons are everything Platonic, they are laws, acts, people, thoughts, and things marching up and down similarity's continuum.

In breaking away from similarity, in generating limitless distances, in staking out a huge field for solitude, in discovering shameless alienation, with all these things, difference enters experiences Socrates cannot. The process: in Chapter 8, difference manifests itself as huge distances Socrates needs to, but cannot, master nor measure. In Chapter 9, I follow Deleuze in naming the gateway to distance without measure, and in characterizing it. The name: the simulacrum. The character: rancor. Finally, in Chapter 10, I reverse Platonism irreparably by going to the desert to find the kind of lonesome wanderer Socrates wanted to shut up in a cavern at the bottom of the ocean.

8

DISTANCE WITHOUT MEASURE

. . . a sort of ironic encounter which takes the place of a mode of knowledge. . . . huge dimensions, depths, and distances that the observer cannot master.

—Gilles Deleuze, *Logic of Sense*

Two distances: one with a measure, like "within reach" or "about as far away as that street light." The other without measure, not infinite distance, but distance without quantifiability. You indicate it not by exceeding all limits, but by avoiding characterizations like near and far. The distance attached to measure belongs to Socrates and his pupil Augustine. The distance without measure belongs to Deleuze.

Distance with Measures

Deleuze's idea develops against (though it finally breaks away from) the background of St. Augustine's theological dedication to measured distance. Augustine's prime example: the pear stealing episode from the *Confessions*. He and friends ally to steal the ripening fruit from a neighbor's tree. If Augustine steals the pears to eat, a shred of goodness infects the act insofar as it fulfills a divinely sanctioned bodily need; the length between the theft and perfect devotion would be great, but not infinite. Even better, had a penniless Augustine stolen the pears to feed a starving family member, the distance would shrink considerably. But the pears were stolen and thrown to pigs. Nothing good came from the crime, so it could not have been invested with even the thinnest slice of divine inspiration. To illuminate the point, Augustine relates that he cannot remember which of the several thieving boys had the idea, he cannot remember who finally said, "Let's steal the pears." The missing individual prompter symbolizes the missing God. Augustine's distance from divine approbation elongates precipitously. But still, the measure is as exact as every other, it is precisely infinite. Augustine called it evil. Though sounding extreme, evil is not radical. For Augustine, no autonomous devil existed, consequently evil held no existence independent of good. The categories and presumptions Augustine used to comprehend evil were picked from those already claimed by goodness. Evil amounted to nothing more than privation of the good; it was bleached good. And just as Augustine comprehended evil in the mode of goodness, so too he comprehends infinite distance in the mode of near and far. Infinity is simply the extreme case or the limiting case of finite measure.

Deleuze's Distance

Instead of judging a deed's worth by pulling out the philosophic yardstick and adding up lengths, Deleuze makes evaluations generate themselves from inside the act, as an effect of the act. Because we don't go anywhere to find a value, we don't quantify any measures of remove from something. Isolated and limited only by an ethical vacuum, action stands on its own: Rousseau's state of nature, Nietzsche's world of noble morality. Discrete, distinguishable acts exist, but the moral degree of their difference does not. The new freedom to forsake an overarching ethical measure in separation allows the concept of distance to split in two: distance and quantifiable, measurable distance. The distinction would be incomprehensible for Augustine. Deleuze invests himself in it.

So did George Bataille when he wrote the *Story of the Eye*. His two adolescent female stars exist in the same place but are separated by measureless space. Marcelle practices Christianity fervidly and understands life roughly within the framework Augustine sketched. Simone personifies difference: she produces without reference to institutions and traditions. Just by living, Simone limits her own acts, fabricates her own meanings, and constructs her own values. She never refers to the morality of her society or even to the morality of her friends. Like a child, she does what she wants. Unfortunately for Marcelle, what Simone usually wants is ostentatious and savage copulation. Even Sade would blush at Simone's indiscretions. Not surprisingly, the raunchy sex overwhelms the angelic Marcelle—her sanity shrieks and flees. Importantly, the cause is not exactly Simone's licentious behavior because Marcelle can still steel her consciousness against any blasphemous carnal acts Platonic morality will not sanction. Even in the extreme case, when Simone forces Marcelle to watch a performance of debasement beyond any the world has seen, Marcelle can resist with the Augustinian failsafe: she can explain that what she sees is ethically zero, but only zero as defined by a lack of God. In a desperate attempt to protect herself, Marcelle tries to keep her antagonist on the divine continuum; she imagines Simone caught at the far end, a dime-store rebel struggling to throw off the tenacious deity. In fact, however, Simone has fallen over the spectrum's edge—she does not spurn God, she ignores His presence and His absence. A new, satanic void spreads. It dilates without negating. On theory's level, no negation because the good has vanished. And empirically, no negation because Simone never pauses before doing. No hesitation, no response here, only untainted autonomy in the name of sodomy.

To compound Marcelle's problems, the void also expresses the free-standing emptiness and the sovereign evil Augustine's philosophy explicitly denies; it expresses them positively and tangibly because Simone's body can be touched and heard and tasted and smelled. And as a final, crushing proof of her heretical freedom, Simone feels no guilt, no remorse, and no disgust as Augustine did in reviewing his relatively trivial malefactions. When Marcelle finally accepts this frigid reality, when she faces a sex not just infinitely removed from God but having nothing whatever to do with Him, when she realizes Simone has reached beyond all recoverable heresy, her mind bends alarmingly.

Because Marcelle understands the world exclusively as relative distances from the Divine, she has nowhere to put Simone, no way to reconcile Simone with the rest of God's creation. How can the casually unrepentant debaucher exist? The earth itself should suck her up. But there Simone is. Smug and impertinent, she stands right in front. She whispers, she stares. She tries luring Marcelle into acts beyond the traditional moral purview. The distance without measure gapes: oblivious Simone on the one side, panic-stricken Marcelle on the other. In the story, Marcelle snaps and retires to the asylum.

By defining "reality" the way Nietzsche did in *How the Real World Became a Myth*,[1] as the stubborn vestiges of Socrates's and Augustine's idealism on our earth, Marcelle can be effectively diagnosed as psychotically delusional because she insists she sees Simone, but Simone cannot exist in God's reality. So, in Augustine's world, Marcelle's disconcerting vision can only be accepted as a dreadful hallucination. Appropriately enough, it is as a delusion that Marcelle can begin to sense Simone's true distance. Marcelle should ask herself, "how far away is a delusion?" Is it near, right in front of your face like a wondering ghost? Is it far, like the ghost's material inspiration now buried six feet under and half the country away? Is it immediate, like emotional shellshock? Is it removed, like the distant childhood trauma a psychologist might summon to explain it? None of the above, the delusion is only out there, somewhere.

Phantom Connections

Separation by distance without measure is heterogeneity. It begins as neutrality. Not neutrality as seen from an encompassing vantage point (from outside, difference practices remorseless aggression, think of Titus Andronicus), but the impenetrable neutrality resulting from the end of third-party mediators. No more Gods, Forms, customs. Deleuze's laissez-faire rule of ontology drops relations between people into free fall. Still, Simone and Marcelle must relate in some sense, even an antagonistic one, because Simone drives Marcelle into an asylum. I grant that for Deleuze's individuals, like Augustine's, some connection runs between. But Deleuze breaks away from Augustine by insisting that associations between individuals do not precede every encounter like divinity precedes every Augustinian congregation. For Deleuze, connections between people come subsequent to their meetings and mask an original and ineffaceable disparity. When Simone and Marcelle relate, they form a dubious community empty of everything except the ironic message of their own alienation. Properly speaking, it is that message, not Simone, that left Marcelle a haggard wreck.

Speaking

When Deleuze's subjects come together, the results cannot be predicted because no regulating third term guides their exchange.

Therefore, the way into the juxtaposition of difference's people does not lie, at first, in a comprehensive theoretical discussion because the theory would become the third term just excluded. The way in runs through a corridor of increasingly particular and concrete instantiation. In what follows, I characterize both kinds of juxtaposition—Augustine's and Deleuze's—in the specific mode of speech communication.

First, idealism's communication sounds everywhere. It postulates a generic structure linking us even before the first word passes. We speak through the structure. It could be a generic "person" that links us all. A more palpable idealism explains that a shared language precedes us. A metaphysician would have several suggestions. A theologian understands our human words as a form of community decayed from the revelatory experience between humanity and the divine.[2] In each case, there is always a functional ideal out there. And since idealism only works through measured distance, our conversation should follow. It does. I say: I am closer to my brother than I am to the cashier at Ballard's. Or: I am very close to Susan, not so close to my first wife. When communication works, we say, "We're getting closer." When it stumbles, we admit, "We're drifting apart."

Next, Deleuze's communication. My example comes from the ten o'clock news. The anchorman introduces the next story and cues the tape. We are out at the scene early in the afternoon. A reporter recounts little eight-year-old Katie Beers's ordeal. She was kidnapped and held for sixteen days in John Esposito's secret basement dungeon. Authorities are now digging up the concrete room for use as evidence in the upcoming trial. A neighbor watches the excavation from her kitchen window. The reporter sees her, hurries over. The tape splices. Next, we see the woman close-up. She says:

"I think its just so unbelievable, you know, it's like a side show, it's just amazing that this was all going on here."[3]

We never heard the reporter's question. Even without it, her response seems readily comprehensible. But the meaning blurs. One phrase, "it seems like a sideshow," is clear enough. But take the sentence's two other key parts, "it's just so unbelievable," and, "it's just amazing." What do they mean? Imprecise adjectives like "unbelievable" and "amazing" multiply in our culture. Because their use has so proliferated, the fact that we exchange them can no longer guarantee we understand what we are saying. Undoubtedly, we understand what we speak, but what about our listeners? Admittedly, an uncertainty like this infects every word in every language. But the words thrown out to the WPIX reporter and then forwarded to everyone watching TV go beyond that usually marginal worry.

Levi-Strauss refers to a set of French words corresponding in some ways to the American phenomenon. He called them "floating signifiers." Examples include *quelque chose* and *truc*. But these French words share more with the American 'thing' or 'watchyamacallit' than they do with 'amazing' or 'unbelievable.' 'Thing, *truc*, watchyamacallit' all explicitly admit their emptiness. They claim no more than to be general terms serving in a stopgap role for a speaker who can't find the word or for a language without the necessary vocabulary. By contrast, words like 'amazing' claim to be full of meaning. Look at the speaker's faces, they are sure, they are confident. But then look at the word, it is tenuous, it disappears.

Words like 'unbelievable' and 'amazing' are special for two connected reasons. First, they carry no meaning. Second, they conceal their emptiness. Both speakers and listeners are lured into filling the words up themselves and then into the natural supposition—a supposition following from the words' proliferation—that everybody else fills them the same way. The supposition becomes explicit in a phrase regularly accompanying empty locutions: you know. Listen to her again: "I think its just so unbelievable, you know . . ." No, we don't know. But what we do know, or, at least what we learn, is that sometimes words get meaning while no pervasive connection exists between what the words mean for the speaker and what they mean for the listener.

Now return to the reporter and his story on Katie Beers. When he edited the footage of his interview with the observer, he dropped out his own question. All we got was her response. We can see why. It didn't matter what the question was. It could have been anything and this answer would suffice. Implicitly or explicitly, the reporter understands that. He uses it, ironically, to approach his audience. By leaving the question out, he proves he sympathizes with the viewers, he proves he shares their concerns. Why? Because he asked this witness exactly what each viewer wanted him to ask. Does he really sympathize, did he really ask what each one wanted, whatever it was? No, but that awkward detail is easily sliced away in the editing room. The reporter has a secret. He knows that any one of his viewers could have been at the scene, could have seen this observer, could have asked her any question and she could have answered with the same sentence dotted with "amazings" and "unbelievables" and the whole exchange would have seemed to make perfect sense. The TV personality has counterfeited intimacy.

The observing woman has become half of a phantom exchange. She thinks she is conveying ideas with meaning, and as we hear her, we understand a meaning. But the precise measure of our misunderstanding has dropped out. Nonetheless, she talks and we listen. A strange connection, it begins only after the words are spoken and as a product of our various attempts to invest them with meaning. Nothing precedes the exchange. We act as though something does, and for that reason it does, but no guarantees, nothing certain except irony. Marcelle saw this clearly, that's why she resides in an asylum.

And more pointedly on the question of distance—how far away is this woman on TV? The seven feet between my eyes and the screen? The two hundred and thirty miles between me in Pennsylvania and her in New York? Should the distance be measured between where she was when she actually spoke to the reporter and where I was at that time, or between where I am as I watch TV and where she is at that later moment? Or, between where I am as I watch TV that night and where she was when speaking this afternoon? The question is neither difficult nor insoluble, it simply doesn't work. It doesn't work because the object—quantifiable distance—doesn't exist.

Allowing Heterogeneity

How do people in Deleuze's world form even a weak connection for vacuous talk? More generally, how do heterogeneous entities come together? In *Anti-Oedipus*, Deleuze casts the question in terms of "alliance" and "filliation." Heterogeneity is alliance, and it does not mean, as we customarily understand it, two individuals or groups fighting for the same goal. Instead, alliance names an only apparent unity hung between radically distinct interests. Filliation, on the other hand, implies a natural bond, a blood bond.

How do people come together? For filliation, the answer is easy, explaining means explaining Augustine's idealism. Explaining alliance ruins the point by collapsing its formative, internal disparity. So, instead of explaining, Deleuze asks his readers to start by using. As usual, Deleuze is reversing the tradition. Instead of starting with theory and the bulwark of its justification, and then letting second-rate, hacking philosophers bring the theory into the world as applying engineers, Deleuze leaves the obsession with abstraction for technocrats. He respects beginnings from the concrete. From there, theoretical answers will eventually emerge. Deleuze's general rule: no matter what form the theoretical question takes, keep stepping into vital examples.

The issues surrounding pornography provide applications for alliance as well as filliation. The National Organization for Women works against pornography. In this battle the membership stands united, even referring to each other as "sisters." The appellation indicates filliative conjoining. Even though backgrounds, educations, social and economic situations may differ, the shared cause, the protest march, the signature drive, and the legislative action all reflect the sisters' ineffaceable, primordial identity.

Pornography also draws other protestors. Jerry Falwell's moral majority continues railing against explicit magazines and the furtive distribution of scandalous VCR tapes. Sundry conservative and religious organizations donate time and energy. Church groups picket in circles around adult theater doors. Clerics lobby the governor for prohibitions on explicit merchandise sales. In front of the peep show and on petitions, these conservative societies find themselves juxtaposed and allied with the decidedly less traditional women of NOW whose current head, Patricia Ireland, claims bisexuality and publicly revels in her adultery.[4] No filliation here, the Christian men are surely not sisters to the members of NOW, and the relationship between the two groups of women remains in serious doubt. Their adjacency at the protest is an oxymoron, a scene of heterogeneity. They are both there, but paradoxically share nothing in common. Pornography seems to form a solid ground on which the two groups locate a small piece of ineradicable unity and the seed of a filliative relation. But the liberal women stand against pornography because it reduces females to caricatures of their own bodies. The conservative groups fight pornography because it incites prurient interests in society. So, even while members of both groups march before the same theater, they are not combatting the same thing. One woman peeks inside and sees pictures reducing her to the letters of a cup size and the numbers of a hip measurement. One man peeks inside and sees magazines tempting his son, encouraging his sin. In a last-ditch effort to find filliation, it could be suggested that the very sidewalk the protestors share provides a common ground. But then one needs to explain why segments of pavement don't themselves hoist signs and join the march.

Only alliance lets philosophy onto the scene. Jean Baudrillard suggests that allied or heterogeneous groups connect in hyperreality.[5] Deleuze's early book on Proust[6] dips into the same scheme. Both authors take exception to the (ironically simple) argument in Plato's *Republic* starting from Socrates holding up two fingers. One is shorter than the other and their shape differs; they are different. Nevertheless, we should know that they are fingers because we have the idea finger stamped into our soul's memory.[7] Deleuze reckons differently. True, the fingers are, in a sense, copies. But instead of each referring upward to the metaphysical case, they refer to themselves, they copy from themselves, they produce and limit themselves. Only after this original self-copying-defining do fingers commence a second kind of copying, one referring across to each other and then to every other. Recognizing two examples as fingers is seeing each finger replicating another itself replicated from some other itself replicated; the regress never ends, neither horizontally nor vertically. When we move from side to side, from one example to another, we just find more copies and more copies; and when we go vertical, when we plumb ontological depths, all we find is no depth, again just more copying, this time internalized. No matter which vector we follow—the horizontal or the truncated vertical—we never get to a solid foundation: the uncopied original drops out. Or, the self-copying original is everywhere. Either way, instead of implying metaphysics, we recognize the twin fingers as fingers as a secondary effect of multiple internal differentiations, as a copying effect of internal copying. This community is like patchwork, sewn together from results. If we find in our consciousnesses an abstract idea of a finger, then we should think of it as woven from the fingers already in the world, not as the stamp of an original intellectual minting.

Deleuze objects to Platonism on two counts. First, by denying any metaphysical and prior finger. Second, by denying the negative connotations Socrates attached to copies without an original (what Socrates called "phantasms," what Baudrillard calls a "simulation"). Socrates thought phantasms could aspire to nothing more than egregious and intellectually poisonous imperfection. But if we think of fingers along with Deleuze, then copying means copying from copies without uncopied originals, not copying from copies as betrayal of the original. Copies lose their inferiority because there is no longer anything superior. Or, everything is superior. Regardless, Socrates's metaphor is dual and vertical: every earthly thing refers upward toward the first one. The metaphor for alliance is horizontal and multiple: every earthly existent refers to itself, to a self without hidden depths, then it refers sideways to other earthly existents, themselves without Socratic depth. Each finger generates itself and subsequently the motion of copying between. Wherever the motion flows, fingers are formed, not vice-versa.

For Socrates, the copying which formed patterns in the world transpired at the ontological level as the way a necessarily imperfect and impermanent physical earth came into existence. Copying was the condition of material experience. For Deleuze, the copying between things (though not internal copying) transpires after ontology and within experience. Copying creates contingent connections between people and things which have previously generated themselves from disparate locations on the ontological plane. This copying plays only an adjunct role in experience.

On a second front Socrates has been reversed. Mundane and ignoble fingers have replaced the grand and dignified exemplars Socrates always favored: Beauty, Justice, Truth. In an important sense, the distance between Deleuze and Platonism can be refined into a distance between examples. Plato himself sets up the contrast in the *Parmenides* where the young Socrates wonders whether there might be Forms of hair and dirt. When hair and dirt become as philosophically relevant as justice and beauty, idealism totters. When Deleuze uses the finger to introduce a metaphysical discussion, the traditional hierarchy dropping from metaphysical nobility down to sensuous baseness begins spinning.

William Gass's example of the horizontal-copying genealogy is the clear plastic cup, the kind you take to picnics or find stacked beside a punch bowl.[8] Each plastic cup is a replication, but a replication of what, and in which direction? Does this cup copy the one stamped out just before it? Does it attempt to copy the one stamped out next? Does it copy the cup sitting on the foreman's desk? They are all the same. Nothing indicates a degeneration from an original. How about the mold, is that the original? No, if it breaks, another can easily be formed, and formed from any one of the existing cups, no Socratic intellectual intuition required, no reference to a metaphysical or original ideal needed. Use this cup or that one or any other, it doesn't matter. Here, Augustine can gauge no distances.

Deleuze writes that we are ". . . faced with a positive difference of different elements: no longer to identify two contraries with the same, but to affirm their distance as that which relates one to the other insofar as they are different."[9] Elements start from alienation. Unities arise as ironic expressions of impenetrable separation. Impenetrable because the separating distance is not near and not far. It is measureless.

The title for the ironic unities rising from impenetrable separation is the simulacrum.

9

RANK WEEDS AND FAIR APPEARANCES

... the simulacrum implies huge dimensions, depths, and distances that the observer cannot master. It is precisely because he cannot master them that he experiences an impression of resemblance.

—Gilles Deleuze, *Logic of Sense*

Simulacra create the illusion of measurable distances by spanning impossible breaches. Because we have the simulacrum, we comprehend a distance.

The simulacrum's distance is always imaginary; scrutinize it and it's gone. On the other hand, while it stakes out its territory and works effectively, it makes us understand that two experiences have something in common intrinsically. It insists that there was a can of Campbell's Soup in Warhol's studio, it hums that we all have soul mates (Aristophanes's lovers), or, by extension, that we all are each other's soul mates. Because of simulacra, we can seemingly hierarchize different actions, sensations, experiences, ideas, accomplishments, and people with regard to each other. Simulacra do socially useful work.

They do so shamelessly. Like Plato's noble lie, the simulacrum marches through experience without contrition and without repenting its deceit. Its confidence, teamed with its salutary social effects, inures it against all but the most skeptical and cynical. It took a sick, bitter philologist like Nietzsche to diagnose our civilization as corrupted by the simulacrum's illusions. Socrates, a patrician despite his humble demeanor, lived too comfortably. He collided with simulacra in his own *Sophist*, but felt only contempt. He went on to blissfully propose that entire lives and even entire cultures be rallied around the true certainty that every important distance can me measured, that every significant act can be evaluated correctly, and that every citizen can get the timeless rules well enough to define their place (king, warrior, laborer) and their particular excellence (philosophy, well grounded discipline, right opinion) in the philosophically planned republic.

Because of its persuasion, the simulacrum successfully creates and then occupies the softest spot in Platonism. It stations itself between possessed beings and stitches them into Socrates's plan. But what if simulacra failed, what would be the answer to the question about links between various productions of difference, do they have anything in common? No. And no in a very specific sense, in a sense that can only become clear by working back through the simulacrum.

What the simulacrum is: the comprehensible and reasonable manifestation of existence that breathes from original difference, of existence that differentiates itself while remaining blind to everything beyond it, of existence that sets questions of relations aside in producing a unique degree of alienation that is alien without being removed from anybody just like it produces a distance that stretches away without measuring a remove from anything. And in the middle of all this generation, the simulacrum claims and appears to be: that moment of revealed convergence between things in a world that emerges from a single origin and heads for a common destiny (the city ruled by philosophy). In other words, the simulacrum hides difference right out in the open, right in the middle of Platonism.

Undercover

As if protecting its very existence, difference throws up simulacra as a defensive measure. Only under its cover can difference carry out its sharply restricted operations. Thinkers dedicated to great, democratic conversations and multiculturalists spellbound by the vision of a harmonious world, neither can tolerate values imposed by the careless power and frequently cruel force of internal differentiation. If philosophy gets out of hand, these political activists can muster outraged editorials and noisy protests in the name of egalitarian decency and antifascistic progressiveness. This is neither a conspiracy against difference nor some new monster stalking over the horizon of literary and philosophic thought. It is simply the latest set of exigencies philosophy must deal with. In ancient Greece, Plato layered his dialogues with levels of teachings. The dialogue form, as a literary version of the noble lie, protected his thought from strangulation in the hands of inappropriate readers. In the *Confessions*, Augustine knew he could not openly admit his experimentation with homosexuality, so he presents his lover, an unnamed young man in book IV, as a cherished, extraordinarily close—but always platonic—friend. For Augustine, friendship is protecting love. These camouflages, dialogue form and friendship, are intentionally imperfect, however. Socrates's clue: he propounds his ideas to adolescents. And of Augustine's book, sensitive, sympathetic readers like Foucault can easily read between the lines. Now, like Socrates's esoteric philosophy and Augustine's homosexuality, difference wants to enter the world. It too needs protection. Thus, the simulacrum.

To Approach Simulacra

Simulacra generate their own safe territory and their own rules for analysis. This leads to the simulacra's first irony: they are blatantly deceitful but undeniably positive. Socrates disdainfully equated deception with the ethereal and impermanence, as though those qualifications themselves sufficed to debunk the subject in question. Deleuze responds that the simulacra may well be ethereal and transient, but they retain a claim on being insofar as they attach to difference. So, to Socrates's chagrin, even while indulging in illusion, simulacra edge us toward the real, difference's real.

In the discursive world, in language and philosophy, the simulacrum alone determines what theories can be applied to it, the rest are beaten aside. Thus, to approach simulacra, we cannot begin by opposing them or interrogating them; we must be sensitive to invitations. The appropriate hermeneutic procedure, the approach the simulacrum itself endorses, starts from perfidious guile. The simulacrum invites duplicity by taking ragged worlds of difference and transforming them into the kinds of civil, coherent experiences Socrates advocated. No playful relationship exists in the process. If there is anything supporting the ceiling and walls of this passage, say there is bitterness, bitterness induced by the simulacrum's impenitent lies.

Plato

The corrosion and duplicity began in the ancient world. Socrates envisioned philosopher-kings harnessing perfect justice into specific discursive regulations. The project makes philosophy transliteration—thinking reduces to glorified secretarial work. But Homer wrote justice, as the Eleatic stranger constructed the statesman[1], from his own inspiration. Homer lived in the productive style of autonomous difference. The danger is obvious. Homer and like-minded thinkers must be spitefully, bitterly cast outside the walls. Listen to the seething under Socrates indignantly demanding to know, "What city gives [Homer] credit for having proved a good lawgiver and benefitted them." And, "Well, is any war in Homer's time remembered that was well fought with his ruling or advice?"[2]

But even with Homer gone, the rancor goes on because the friction is not just between Platonism and Homer, though it is most obviously and prosaically there. It also comes up within Socrates himself, it comes up just as Homer comes up within Plato's own dialogues. Why does Plato even include Homer, why not excise him utterly from the text as he must be excluded from the city? Homer's appearance in Plato's writing leads to an impossible predicament. As Plato presents him, Socrates busily maintains a theoretical stance that refuses to admit the possibility of Homer in the world, because—as Homer is defined by his actions—he is ontologically impossible. Socrates, when in his undiluted mode, postulates no pure production; everything that comes to be must come to be as dependent on the precedent idea beyond it. Even if Homer the simulacrum-poet stands right before him, Socrates must refuse to see, just like in Bataille's story Marcelle had to consign her vision of Simone to the realm of dementia. At the same time, this same Socrates is convincing Adeimantus, Glaucon, and the rest that efforts must be made to separate them, and the entire city, from what can be nothing more than a puppet master and his misleading chimeras. There is, accordingly, a practical Socrates that grudgingly concedes Homer exists and a principled Socrates that cannot admit seeing him. What comes between these two? Surely not cooperation, the myopic Socrates cannot open his eyes to witness his pragmatic and strategic Siamese twin without having his dream sullied by Homer's smirking reality. The sour rancor gurgles up between the Socrates disowning Homer completely and the Socrates taking responsibility for getting the poet out of the city. The reasonable solution is Deleuzean; there is not one but two Socrateses, each ushers from a separate spring of difference and both possess a body and a literary character that pass as the same. But the blind Socrates cannot accept possession and multiple personality, so something else must reconcile the contradiction. Simulacrum is the answer. It steps in and creates the illusion of a community between the Socrateses; they share the same name and the same body, so they must be one. The tremulous certainty suppresses contradiction. Thus falsely united, Socrates manages to forget the bitter discrepancy in his soul and go on, schizophrenically.

But what if he can't forget? Mercifully, Plato is a beneficent author, he never directly casts his hero into his own contradiction. But if Plato had lured Socrates into his own suppressed rancor, if Socrates had realized his theory's, and his own, internal malice, what would it have sounded like, what would the experience be? Nietzsche encourages his readers to find out, he writes: "Would anyone like to look into the secret of how *ideals are made* on earth? Who has the courage?"[3] For those who continue reading, the gates leading to simulacra open:

> Very well! Here is a point we can see through into this dark workshop, but wait a moment or two Mr. Rash and Curious: your eyes must first get used to this false iridescent light.—All right! Now speak! What is going on down there? Say what you see, man of the most perilous kind of inquisitiveness. . . .
> —"They are miserable, no doubt of it, all these mutterers and nook counterfeiters . . ."
> —Go on!
> —". . . . But enough! enough! I can't take anymore. Bad air! Bad air! This workshop where *ideals are manufactured*—it seems to me it stinks of so many lies."[4]

The rancor intrinsic to the simulacrum stinks. Take Nietzsche seriously. Understand difference, possession, and simulacra through the senses. What constitutes legitimate philosophy momentarily shifts from reason (*logos*) to sensation, from the brain to the nose. We smell difference. This is the wafting scent of falsely sweet air that conjured summer itself for Socrates in the *Phaedrus*,[5] it is the sights and sounds that Proust rode directly back to earlier scenes in his life, it is the sensation of a masseur's hands kneading your body. All these things make unities that reason will not condone, unities born from strident, incorrigible disparities, disparities between a scent and a season, between a current sight and a time past, between hands and a back. Simulacra ring disparities and forge sensible coherences from rational and real differences. We sense these differential productions, but we cannot rationalize them.

The critical moment in thinking simulacra arrives when philosophy jumps the tracks of reason. When that happens, Nietzsche teaches us to reach immediately for our bodies, for carnal experiences. No longer does the mind try to escape the body's material infection, the mind now learns the most important things secondhand, from its mortal part.

The simulacrum's internal rancor manifests itself again, in this case entirely within Homer, or within the Homer we understand when reading his myths. Under the Socratic model, imitating a narrative assumes an indelible first narrative. But in the Homeric mode of simulacrum and unlicensed production (which we have seen in Pierre Menard), each retelling becomes itself the myth created. The retelling is the true original, the original without attached copies. Then, in a fit of backward causality, the retelling creates the simulacrum-original myth, original with copies called retellings. We come to think the repetitions refer to the original, and they do, but only after the simulacrum's deviltry. Neither the simulacrum-original nor the simulacrum-copy truly originate. At the fundamental level, as the myths are repeated, what recurs is the act of generating notions of courage and justice in a fertile vacuum. Next comes the fabrication of a counterfeit original that existed only after the creative retelling. The counterfeit original existed after the creative retelling but before the retelling understood as a copy.

Literary generation happens on a field cleared of first stories demanding imitation. And from that field to the reasonable, stratified, measured Socratic field of unblemished originals and deteriorating copies, nothing can reach except the frustrated bitterness of never resolved, never even joined competition: who's number one? Just as effectively as any city's walls, the simulacrum keeps the originals apart; it keeps them apart by artificially dividing first from second, from third, from fourth. At the same time, the simulacrum keeps the story's versions together, it gathers them all under the name of Homer. And if Homer is AWOL, if historians cannot trace back to an actual poet living on or near the Greek peninsula during a certain historical period, then the simulacrum compensates by creating something just as good, a specific, impersonal oral tradition, for example. With this black box, all the various renderings and texts of Homer's myths can be safely stockpiled in one place and with the certainty that one right, uncorrupted myth or kind of myth does exist somewhere. Or at least it did once.

Augustine

Augustine uses simulacra to dismiss a bothersome aspect of experience. His theology postulates a final community, heaven, composed of discrete, spiritualized individuals. It follows that communal living here in the world bears a special significance: it palpably, though imperfectly, manifests God's eternal reality on earth.[6]

Problem: if earthly communities spring from God's seed, then what can be made of the community of criminals, most pointedly, the extreme criminals like the *Confessions'* pear stealers who rob for no good whatever? Assuming the criminals' teaming to steal lacks all good, one of two routes must immediately be taken: either community is not necessarily good, which impinges upon God's omnipotence because he cannot enforce his own metaphysics, or, the pack of Godless thieves is not really a community. Augustine takes the second. He reasons in literary terms through the polymorphously important memory lapse, the failure to remember who finally said, "Let's steal the pears." This thieving community has no origin, it has no one that Augustine can remember in the physical world, and, symbolically, nothing that can possibly exist in the metaphysical world. Thus, the band of thieves floats free from divine Community and from the earthly communities Augustine enshrines in his *Confessions*. Nonetheless, the criminals appear to be a team. Therefore, the thieves together must be a simulacrum. Augustine seemed to suspect as much. But here things become murky, just as they did for Socrates at the same juncture because of their mutual reluctance to admit such metaphysically originless things exist. Despite the reluctance, in the end Augustine cannot allow social unity, a divine gift, to be sullied by criminals. He has no choice but to accept the pear-stealing community as an image without an origin.

Why doesn't Augustine pursue in the *Confessions'* last chapters the theoretical ramifications of the simulacrum-community just as he investigates time and memory? Because of his sourness at having to accept simulacra at all. Regardless, Augustine needs the simulacrum. So it waits there, waits in his book, waits to be used as a handy editing tool for cutting out the little difficulties in life that interrupt his Platonism.

And what is the character of this simulacrum? Looking back across his life, Augustine felt shame and annoyance with the false groups he participated in as a youth, the same annoyance always rising from a world governed by identity when pushed up against difference. He tells us about it and thus transmits the virulence. "This was friendship of a most unfriendly sort, bewitching my mind in an inexplicable way. Can anyone unravel this twisted tangle of knots? I shudder to look at it or think of such abomination."[7] These are Augustine's words, and reason's words, and identity's words, all of them good words for the subject: bewitching, twisted, inexplicable, abomination. At the heart of the rancor is Augustine's realization that the thieves were not really friends. What Deleuze would have him do next is broaden this critique. Widen it all the way.

Kant

A less foreseeable manifestation of the simulacrum's two facedness emerges from Kant; he uses it cleverly to make his philosophy palatable. In his first *Critique*, Kant theorized the physical subject in the phenomenal realm. In his second *Critique*, Kant explored rational being in the ethical realm. The simulacrum comes between.

On the physical side, uniform, regulative categories make the possibility of Kantian sensory experience. The uniformity implies natural necessity (physical determinism). On the other side, ethics requires choices and a meaningful process of decision making. It requires its own perspective, one removed from determinism: ". . . natural necessity . . . attaches merely to the determinations of a thing which stands under the conditions of time. . . . But the same subject . . . views his existence so far as it does not stand under temporal conditions, and . . . [sees] himself as determinable only by laws which he gives himself through [ethical] reason."[8] Kant has split ethical existence from the physical along time's line. Ethics finds and occupies its own dimension, one free from temporality's severe conditions. But now Kant runs up against a staggering difficulty. What does ethics work on? Following the insistence on complete autonomy from the pollution (in Kant's language: heterogeneity) intrinsic to physical life, we should say itself; ethical being generates both the rules for conduct and the choice for the obedience which defines freedom in this realm without time (whatever that means and however action might be possible in it). Hegel picked up on just this when he criticized Kantian ethics as wholly formal and totally futile in the real world. Hegel was right. But Kant would have been unmoved. Physical existence did not concern Kant because corporeality's moribund determinism only belittled human dignity. Kant's interest and human value clove to the ethical field where the rational will and its intentions function unfettered. On this level, Kant postulates the existence of God and the immortality of the soul and an escape from our humiliating, infinite debt to physical causation. Nonetheless, there is a problem. Kant may be satisfied with quasi-mystical reveries, but not everyone else is. What can Kant tell his students looking for moral guidance? What can he tell his book publisher? "My ethics constitutes a mythical state of pure rationality and it offers a way of being without orthodox time." That won't help the undergraduates and it won't sell books. Kant had to reconnect ethics to the lived physical world. Thus, the occasion for freedom's exercise as morality must come from something at least related to the physical experience which seems to birth our concrete and conventional moral dilemmas. Enter "lawfulness."

According to Kant, for physical reality to exist as meaningfully experienced, a law of determination must precede it. On the other side, in the ethical world, freedom exists in accordance with strict rules (the categorical imperative) conditioning the possibility of moral action. So, there is a lawfulness which both ethical and physical reality have in common. Kant writes: "We are therefore allowed to use the nature of the sensuous world as the type of an intelligible nature, so long as we . . . only apply it to the form of lawfulness in general."[9] Now, what is lawfulness? First, the answer to the demand that a practical philosophy have some relation with the regular world. Lawfulness brings the physical over to the ethical, but without physical reality's troubling aspect, its material particularity: an edge of physics crosses into ethics without ruining it. Kant's ethics is rescued from empty formalism.

But this is just a claim—one nearly impossible to defend. Kant is simply shifting the difficulty, the irreducible difference, from the slot between ethics and physics to the slot between physical material and physical law. In reality, a common lawfulness is not intrinsic to both ethics and physics; this lawfulness is something Kant set up subsequent to his two autonomous *Critiques* and his two autonomous worlds. It plays a stopgap role, it plugs up questions about the applicability of ethics to conventional experience. Because pragmatic exigencies precluded the propounding of an authentically pure ethics, Kant needed to invent a term that could carry the weight of pragmatic concern. He did and called it 'lawfulness.' Lawfulness is deceitful, it is two-faced, it makes its living denying itself. It insists that ethics and physics can touch, it insists that a purely rational ethics can have meaning and import in a world of physical people. Yet, lawfulness is only here because the abstract ethics cannot have meaning and cannot have importance for physical beings. So, what stretches between physics and ethics? Nothing except a distance that cannot be measured and then a string of duplicity associated with the law.

In Kant's own words, hidden deep in the *Critique of Pure Reason*'s back pages:

> There is in human nature a certain disingenuousness, which, like everything that comes from nature, must finally contribute to good ends, namely, a disposition to conceal our real sentiments, and to make a show of certain assumed sentiments which are regarded as good or creditable. This tendency to conceal ourselves and to assume the appearance of what contributes to our advantage, has, undoubtedly not only *civilized* us, but gradually, in a certain measure, *moralized* us.[10]

To Socrates's dismay, even the greatest rationalists are conceding that a certain disingenuousness is natural, the simulacrum is natural. Certain lies—like the connection between Kant's rational ethics and material experience—can both civilize and moralize us. Of course, Socrates said the same thing, but he said it to bury the issue, not perpetuate it. No matter what anybody says or does, however, the simulacrum keeps seeping back in, importing its rancor and its churning, corrosive differences. Consequently, and not surprisingly, Kant himself cannot help immediately falling into caustic self-denial. The simulacrum tears people as easily as it tears the world. The now-broken Kant continues:

> But later, when true principles have been developed, and have become part of our way of thought, this duplicity must be more and more earnestly combatted; otherwise it corrupts the heart, and checks the growth of good sentiments with the rank weeds of fair appearances.[11]

The ugly conflict rears its head again on the subsequent page:

> When the common people are of opinion that those who indulge in subtle questionings aim at nothing less than to shake the very foundations of public welfare, it may, indeed, seem not only prudent but permissible, and indeed even commendable, to further the good cause through sophistical arguments. . . . I cannot, however, but think that nothing is so entirely incompatible with the purpose of maintaining a good cause as deceit, hypocrisy, and fraud.[12]

Deceit, hypocrisy and fraud: no better words to end a section on the simulacrum.

Deleuze

In *Difference and Repetition,* Deleuze examines counterfeit linkages under the title of repetition. He starts from David Hume's thesis: "Repetition changes nothing in the object which repeats, but it changes something in the mind which contemplates it."[13] Just something simple, like AB AB AB A . . . , why do you expect a B instead of an A or an M? What is the distinction, within the AB, between an AB that exists only once and a succession of ABs? According to Deleuze's Hume, nothing. It is not something in the AB itself which leads to the right answer—it is something in the way we subsequently synthesize the passing examples. The contrast being drawn is not only a hermeneutic one between a synthesis in the ABs versus a synthesis in the viewing subject. It is also an ontological contrast between something in the ABs as they come into existence, conditioning their existence, versus something pro-

duced after the ABs exist, as an effect of their chain. Deleuze rushes
to add that it cannot be a third party, like successive instants of
time, which link the various ABs, and thus do the hard compiling
work for our experience. Successive instants that bring a next
example into the present moment simultaneously drop a previous
example into the past.[14] In its eager attempt to create repetition,
passing instants, which let only one AB in at a time, defeat themselves. This meshes with Hume's thesis; each AB maintains an
autonomous existence in its own temporal box. Linking patterns
are generated, or, in the technical terminology Deleuze sometimes
adopts, synthesized passively.[15]

You can object, you can respond that there is a connection,
that AB shares something intrinsic with AB. Now, Deleuze's
Humean position and the objection form two irreconcilable readings of the world. Deleuze's sees patterns and generalizations as
the product of artificial and gratuitous synthesis, the other side
accepts the notion of a synthesis, but insists it is an act of understanding going out to a world that intrinsically begs to be understood in certain ways: AB AB leads to AB AB AB, and not AB AB
AM. Between these two readings, rancor, not calm debate. Parti-
sans take their stands and go from there. On the Socratic side,
philosophic work must be done to explain how a world of intrinsic
pattern can break into pieces, how it is that some patterns go unrec-
ognized, how it is that sometimes people don't understand each
other, how it is that a man and a woman can be in love and then
married for years, and then both agree a divorce is inevitable and
necessary because all their time together, everything they shared
and thought they knew of each other was a misunderstanding. Or,
it was an understanding that was produced and could equally well
not have been produced and now is not. On the other side,
Deleuze's side, he needs to explain how it is that in a world of difference patterns develop, and serious people everywhere every
time agree that Shakespeare demands reading, and causal systems
hold together and social progress seems to be made, and people
love like it was meant to be, like they always knew each other even
before they met. Deleuze's answer: the simulacrum. Or, as he says
occasionally, the sign.

Signs link heterogeneous elements. Deleuze gives the example of the thirsty forest animal: the causes that lead it to water are
not really causes, they have nothing to do with the thirst itself. A

clearing for instance, or the sound of a flowing river, or a scent leads an animal to drink even though these signs share nothing intrinsically with the biological or physiological phenomenon called thirst.[16] Signs are like Hume's causes or the passive synthesis of patterns, signs bind objects together, signs make them coherent, signs epistemologically follow the objects they condition. Signs mold heterogeneous things into somethings. Signs become simulacra when the fabricated coherency pushes itself to the next level, when the created connections assume the disguise of an immanent connection, of an essence. Here, Kant situates the term "lawfulness," and people speak using empty, hackneyed phrases like "it's unbelievable, you know," and identical picnic cups pile up all claiming to be the same as the next one and the last one, and feminist zealots join religious zealots in front of porno houses, and the world works.

Characterizing Simulacrum

Deleuze's essay *Michel Tournier and the World without Others*[17] obliquely elaborates the simulacrum and the way it constructs experience to conceal a differential origin. Most importantly, simulacra add to experience, they add two specific qualities with one certain effect. The qualities: contiguity and resemblance. The effect: depth. Simulacra build these onto the world of difference, they make them then claim to have naively found them. Deleuze sharpens his focus by defining a principal location of the simulacrum's invasion: other people. The simulacrum will project its lie of depth by deploying a subject misrepresented with contiguity and resemblance.

By contiguity, Deleuze means a certain regulation for connection. Take time, within the simulacrum's experience, how do I know my world did not skip into some foreign time zone while I slept? Because somewhere in my city a security guard stayed up all night watching for irregularities of whatever sort. And a radio personality was up too, faithfully announcing the clock's turn past each quarter hour.

Next, the simulacrum adds resemblance. Literally, contiguity indicates only a neutral adjacency, but with resemblance, it comes to mean more. Resemblance fortifies contiguity. I see someone at work today and I link him with the same person I saw yesterday.

Time's smooth run during my sleep ties each second into continuity with the preceding and the ensuing. Tomorrow he will talk about similar things, react in the same way to the same kind of joke. If he doesn't, I call it a bad mood or Monday. The simulacrum industriously recommends that when things are contiguous with others, changes within them be marginalized. Dr. Bliss followed the recommendation when confronted with Emily. The personality break was staggering: the patient lost consciousness and something else stormed through to turn the body into a violence machine. But Bliss found a way to keep everything together, he supposed that the violence—Emily—came from nowhere but the patient's own past. Somehow, despite all evidence to the contrary, Emily was part of the patient, she was contiguous with her, and even resembled her well enough to be melded back together with her. The simulacrum's power becomes active; under its dazzling spell, if we can get things side by side—like Emily and the patient side by side in time though otherwise thoroughly dissimilar—then we can make them pervasively similar. Thus, with enough right treatment, we can be certain that multiple personalities will eventually blend. Or, a different example: an ambulance and the hospital may not have been expected today, but the rules of contiguity and resemblance insure us that the possibility was unobtrusively latent and indubitably, if enigmatically, anticipated in the continuous hours, weeks, and years before. Perhaps it was the increasingly frequent heartburn or too much butter on your toast every morning. Regardless, when you think back about a jarring event, you can always find warnings and foreshadowings. This is the mark of similarity's control over juxtaposition. In human terms, similarity's control means there will always be some sign preceding change, at least a sign can always be found subsequently and read retroactively, like a horoscope read the next day frequently seems to have been right. In theoretical terms, similarity's control means a dissimilarity blown up to pure difference does not exist.

From here, we can see why Deleuze chose depth as the metaphor for considering the simulacrum's version of experience. Flowing connections on the existential level become theoretical continuums running from similarity to identity. This immediately feeds into a hierarchy of vertical organization; the lowest levels of the vertical scale mark only faint similarity. Progress up the scale by refining the copy. Socrates crawls up and out of his cave.

Back in the social realm, Deleuze illustrates with the example of a man appearing from around a corner, his face stricken with horror. I take his visage as a warning, something terrible has transpired: a gunman is shooting randomly or an auto has crashed onto a crowded sidewalk. The closer his face comes to representing, to resembling the terror he has just seen, the better his expression. In the extreme case, his expression is enough to scare me, I don't even need to peak around the corner to be terrorized. The proof lies in my quickly turning and walking a different route. Or, in my hurrying to look for myself. Either way, the simulacrum has been exercised. It uses a man to create continuity out of heterogeneity; it turns a facial expression into the direction I walk.

At the start, I wrote that simulacra create the illusion of a measurable distance by spanning a measureless breach; because we have the simulacrum, we comprehend a distance. Now, I can add that those measures are guaranteed by the people that share my world. I can also add by implication what Deleuze thinks of these social people, at least insofar as they participate in the simulacrum: they—we—are noxious, fraudulent creatures.

Surface

Packing so much into our relationships with others is Deleuze pulling back a slingshot aimed for the other extreme: a world without others and an existence without odious depth. He simply needs a field for his experiment, and he sets himself up to find one in Tournier's remake of *Robinson Crusoe*. Deleuze's strategy is straightforward. By suspending other people, by imagining himself robbed of the experience of others, like Robinson trapped on an almost deserted island, Deleuze can effectively suspend the simulacra which operate through others. It follows that he can peel off the protective layer of coherence and vertical measure that difference usually builds around itself. As a result, existence will be seen clearly in the light of, and as a product of, its differential origin. This is the simulacrum's less obvious power: while it works feverishly to keep the world together, to keep my experience flowing, and to keep society ordered, it also lines the way toward (but not all the way to) a coherent elaboration of original disparity and discontinuity. Deleuze calls it the pure surface.

Deleuze: "The pure surface is perhaps what Others were hiding from us."[18] All alone on his island and on Deleuze's surface, Robinson is no longer free to conveniently ignore what others are hiding from us all, almost all the time. Now every distinction becomes just a distance between things, not a measurable distance. Robinson must remake contiguity in conformity with his own law. Instead of understanding resembling seconds following one after the other, he can link events together into different series: along one line, every night may fall into contiguity with the previous, dreams continue without interruption. Along another sequence the days run. And the days may themselves break into different lines: the eating line, the swimming line, the sunning line. When Robinson lies out, his skin immediately tightens under the sun's rays like returning to the state it was in yesterday before he sat up and slid into the shade; when Robinson dives into the water his body automatically switches to the jerking motions of swimming he adopted the afternoon before. Multiple processions of time (sunning, swimming, eating) periodically interrupted by radical breaks (the switch from one activity to the other) replace a single, resembling contiguity strung through public time. And the transformation is not simply temporal contiguity broken into pieces; before Robinson creates sequences, the previous sequences and even the idea of a meaningful sequence vanishes. This is the ramification of the others' abolition, the whole elimination of resemblance-bound contiguity precedes any juxtapositions you line up. Then, sequences arranged by freshly generated rules make their way into the world. Or, possibly no new sequences appear. Robinson alone may produce each new day from nothing, he may always start over with a morning unrelated to the night and the day preceding. Remember that Rousseau's noble savage sold his bed each day only to discover he needed it again because a night he had no reason to suspect ceaselessly reappeared.

Rousseau's savage, like Robinson, lived on the surface. Both Rousseau and Deleuze's Tournier sense a common fate in human isolation. Both push past the ordinary categories dispatched to explain solitude. Ordinarily, when the lonely Robinson or the noble savage acts in ways society cannot condone, when they hide out in pitch black caves for days or refuse to see any pattern developing between the repetition of day and night, we explain them as antisocial and abnormal. We see their situation as demanding more social interaction, more familiarity with our norms. Under this diagnosis, Robinson and the savage suffer alienation, but not radical alienation, their isolation comes shrouded in a community they are being denied or deprived of. This alienation only means insufficient community, a lack. But Rousseau and Deleuze want to understand an alienation that defines itself, that begins without reference to friends or society, that no longer negates or challenges a precedent family or state. It shoots into solitude, or, better yet, as with Tournier's Robinson, it starts over alone after a major wreck. Above all, at its formative stage, this alienation remains immune to community.

Further down the line, alienation may birth its own version of a society, one like Robinson constructed on his island, a subsequent and hollow and absurd social reality, one with laws even though no one is there to break them, one with strict decorum even though no one is there to be appalled, one with form even though no content exists to fill it. This public realm exists as a negative reaction to earlier solitude. But it always remains that at the beginning there was only one man. Robinson's society exists only to the slim degree that original alienation is abridged.

Any community stemming from pure alienation invokes Marguerite Duras's lovers. Her community comes subsequent to alienation and as a negative remove from it, as a loss, as something it no longer has. The message of Duras's *Malady of Death* is not that there really was a love, one discovered too late by the protagonist. The message is that every love circles around prior and inextinguishable solitude. Duras's love succeeds by using passing time to obscure and misrepresent that solitude. Again, her articulation:

> Soon you give up, don't look for her anymore, either in the town or at night or in the daytime.
> Even so, you have managed to live that love in the only way possible for you. Losing it before it happened.

Only when he stops looking for her, when he can never be with her again, does it become possible to believe he loved her. Love means being deprived of tangible isolation.

With the simulacrum stripped away, we can see that in difference every social union—every love—is lost before it happens, not for the frailty of its participants, not because I always want to move too fast or because she can never quite get over Jason or because I don't realize what I have until it's too late. Instead, lost because of the order of the world: difference, later identity: solitude, later community.

Alienation and Community

There are two communities and two alienations, the simulacrum waits at the crossroads. The first community is Socratic, or, better, Augustinian; it begins from something everybody must have in common, and hopefully that thing is the best thing. Here, alienation means being a lost sheep, it means drifting away from the group, it defines itself by strings of nots: not sharing the same beliefs, not practicing the same rites, not participating in the same habits. The other alienation defines itself positively as an irrefutable and inescapable result of its own possession, its differential origin, its unique production and accompanying, signature limitation. Like two people facing each other across a measureless distance, the community following from this alienation positively expresses irony and corrosion and simulacra.

So which is it, which community and which alienation are we? If we are the first, if we really did all spring from the symbolic father Augustine wrote his *Confessions* for, then alienation to the extreme degree Rousseau and Deleuze envision should not, cannot, be. By contrast, if we are the latter, if Augustine wrote in vain, then what passes for authentic public unity decays into a forgery printed by the simulacrum, the simulacrum which generates a counterfeit world of depth and which Socrates despised because it almost intentionally fails to make the claim pervasively; someone like Homer or Rousseau or Nietzsche or Deleuze always escapes. The problem with simulacra is not that they give the world depth artificially. Socrates was a liar, he might have been tempted to accept a conspiracy of depth if it came with the assurance that no one would ever suspect. The problem with simulacra is the grinding rancor. It gives just enough to give itself away; outside city walls and on the back pages of purely rational critiques and on deserted islands, recalcitrant cases of difference and possession intrigue philosophers and lead them apart from Platonism. Socrates's distaste for Deleuze heightens: the rancor must finally and completely be suppressed. There can be no radical alienation. Every case of difference and possession must be snuffed out. No one can face another person or even herself across a distance without measure because everything is measurable. But if a life can be found, a real life, that displays true alienation, then Platonism can no longer hold.

The linchpin of fully developed idealism is pervasiveness, especially pervasive resemblance. Pervasive resemblance can push you and me into the cave, but only if we never doubt its power. As soon as resemblance functions with anything short of perfection, the entire Socratic philosophy comes under suspicion because Socrates is working so obstinately for a reality where nothing important exists except his metaphysics and its copies. Unlike difference, mature Platonism abhors functioning in restricted experience; it applies to everything or considers resignation. In literary terms, Socrates's cave lacks tunnels to an underworld, all of our imperfect experience can only come as a resembling distance from the one sun above. Everything on earth should be an icon. Icons differ from simulacra in two ways: they honestly resemble the metaphysical form from which they draw their nourishment and they do not grossly overstate their proximity to the ideal. Thus, they orient us toward truth while reminding us we have some distance to cover. Socrates himself serves as an icon, he leads the philosophic life but admits at his death that physical embodiment stymies him. Thus, he pushes forward while also admitting his limitations and every physical thing's limitations. Socrates greedily wants everything to aspire to be like him—not necessarily in philosophic ability, we need guardians and laborers as well as thinkers—but everything earthly should aim to correspond directly or indirectly with its pre-ordained destiny. No exceptions or recalcitrance. Ultimately, hopefully, there is only inside the cave and outside, icons and their sources. Again, the last and climaxing wager inherent to ideologically driven Platonism: all or nothing. If an author brings her work into the cave, and it is inspired by something besides the sun-drenched outside, the city's founders must do more than rebuke her. They must coldly banish her until she gives in and writes exclusively in the name of blue sky Platonism.

When Deleuze wrote that the task of contemporary philosophy was to reverse Platonism, he gave himself and his students one central charge: find experiences beyond the pervasive resemblance undergirding Socrates's metaphysics. The demand is simple: locate an example. In the end, Deleuze's project, as set up in his keystone texts, *Nietzsche and Philosophy, Difference and Repetition, Logic of Sense*, stands or falls on the basis of an example, actually a counter-example, a single counter-example. And Socrates's project too, though he already knew that. I need to convince you that there exists at least one substantial case of alienation. If I succeed, then we can claim that Platonism has been again reversed, reversed this time on the subject of community and isolation.

Or, more specifically and dramatically, reversed on the subject of Socrates's cherished *eros*. In the *Symposium*, it was the erotic form of love that made us desire beautiful bodies and then the abstract beauty of finely hewn thought and finally universal Beauty. Eros was the compelling force attracting us to each other and then dragging us up to what we all have in common. But for Deleuze, eros as love is vain and illusory because in both palpable experience and rarified ontological theory, love only arrives after someone has left. For Deleuze, love's value rests entirely in its powerful manifestation of the simulacrum. Love tells me I share something essential with her, but it also leads me to where I might see the futility of the effort. For Socrates, no erotic effort is completely futile because eros necessarily drives us toward our ultimate unity. For Deleuze, love is a cheap lie because it extends from alienation. So, the question of isolated experiences can be translated into this: does someone deny Socrates's eros?

10

LOVE IS FOR OTHER PEOPLE

... and, for that part which remains rebellious, to repress it as deeply as possible, to shut it up in a cavern at the bottom of the ocean—such is the aim of Platonism in its will to bring about the triumph of icons over simulacra.

—Gilles Deleuze, *Logic of Sense*

Isabelle Eberhardt: born, Geneva, 1877, died twenty-seven years later, Algeria. She filled the years between with a wretched existence of malnutrition and aimless travel across desert, Arabic culture. Through it all, she wrote. Her notes, journals, newspaper and magazine articles, short stories, and unfinished novels provide historians with elaborate accounts of North Africa during French colonialism. They also exemplify existence on Deleuze's surface. Her life slips into the transience of insubstantial being. Her temporality denies continuity. The localities she establishes diverge in bursts. Alienation invests her relations to others and herself. This chapter documents those alienations, alienations that exist solely in Deleuze's world, alienations that put the lie to Socrates.

Women of the Scar

At the age of twenty-three Eberhardt wrote this imperative into her journal: "Lead two lives, one that ... belongs to the desert, and one, calm and restful, devoted to thought and far from all that might interfere with it."[1] This resonates with her kind of time. Moments divorce each other. One minute no longer needs to stick with the previous. Her short story *Blue Jacket* carries the same temporal structure. The protagonist, a young Arab conscript guarded with pride the scars cut across his powerful chest and biceps—scars made by knives and stones, and even by firearms—the result of women he no longer remembered.[2]

The conscript cannot remember. But if time runs straight through in the mode of depth—as a chain of resembling moments—then the scars never escape their physical origin. This kind of time disallows the conscript's forgetting, or allows it in only a limited sense because forgetting cannot mean cutting an episode clean away; pervasive resemblance cannot be interrupted. This forgetting operates only imperfectly by erecting a mental boundary to enclose the section marked for oblivion. The boundary remains as its own scar of the deletion: you may not remember, but you vaguely remember something you are not remembering. Reading the way Eberhardt demands, however, for her own life and her own writings—reading on the surface and through a time absolved of continuity from one moment to the next—these scars cease all memorial functioning. The past is no longer covered over, it is sliced away. Forgetting succeeds. It succeeds absolutely, just as it did for Rousseau's savage erasing every past night so completely that he sold his bed every morning. The story *Blue Jacket* requires this wild forgetting, one incompatible with resembling moments. Consequently, Socrates cannot fully appreciate Eberhardt's story. But Deleuze can.

How does the forgetting Eberhardt invokes succeed? Or, to pose the same question indirectly and within the confines of her short story, there is still a woman with each scar, who is she? A biographer would answer by examining the soldier's bodily marks and tracing them to specific past conflicts and their causes. As Eberhardt writes it, however, each scar, when it slides from underneath a sleeve or flashes in the mirror, invokes a current self-glorification disjointed from the biographer's subject. A new female occupies each of the scars, one composed of pride, not flesh, one discovered by an emotion, not an historian. Because the displacement and the soldier's rough vanity require an unblemished forgetting, another production at first unrelated to the physical women must stir up and remake the soldier's past in accord with its omnipotent whim. The forgetting then sweeps over the scene as that production's after-effect. The locus of Eberhardt's churning production: the scar. The medium: time. In Eberhardt's time, wounds work forward instead of referring backward, they project themselves as soldier's medals of bravado and female admirers. More than that, they become the bravado and the lovers. Each scar locates its own origin and cause by insisting it be understood as a badge worthy of pride and as a memory worthy of sentiment. Each scar exclaims a meaning for now and only then for the past. The scar didn't happen in the past, the scar made the past. It made the past in accord with its own story and without reference to the actual, physical women who so completely controlled the protagonist years ago.

Two times and two women. One past time from depth's world fills with a physical person, her love and the scar she caused. On Deleuze's side and Eberhardt's side, the present, surface time fills with the scar and a woman the scar causes, a woman cast back through time and encased in the illusion of precedence. If, by chance, the woman Eberhardt envisions resembles the actual physical woman of years past, then the similarity is a freak accident and only a counterfeit. The two women have entirely different origins, they function according to wholly different rules: the woman from the past is born from flesh and blood parents, the woman of the scar is born from tarnished skin. The woman of the past gained definition by conjuring infatuation from two men, by setting them against each other, by winding their desire around her and throwing them together in violence. The grandiose woman of the scar gained definition by possessing a wound, by flashing it at compatriots, by brandishing it before rivals, and always by parlaying it into exuberant pride. Critically, these two women, the woman of the past and the woman of the scar, delineate irreconcilable times. One runs forward as physical causation. The other cuts apart into the reverse narratives of swarthy romance Eberhardt instills in the simple, coarse men of Arabia. Alienated temporalities.[3]

And there is another alienation at this scene: the Arab conscript from himself. Scars that produce their own time and their own women finish by producing their own men. Eberhardt's hero can be understood to have lived a conventional life, each day piling up on the one preceding. But when he proudly unbuttons his shirt to reveal a band of repaired skin, and when the skin produces its own time and woman, where does this man stand with respect to the other who actually fought and lost? Nowhere.

Surface Love

Alienation pushes into the danger zone for Socrates when Eberhardt leaves fiction to record her occasional foreignness from herself. The first medium is romance, romances separating through her various unorthodox loves, and consequently separating Eberhardt herself as the lover.

At twenty-four she married Slimene Ehnni, a Muslim with French nationality. Before the union, she reflected in her journal on him and on those who came before. She wrote:

> Incontestably, I love Taste . . . the man who sensually attracted me the least, at least physically. . . .
>
> [But] all that is so distant! More so in that the memory of these men creates no emotion in me: she who believed to love them, these distant ghosts, *is dead*. And she who lives is so different she is no longer responsible for past wanderings [*errements*].[4]

How can this be sensible? Eberhardt writes she loves Taste and within a few sentences insists her love for all those coming before Slimene, including Taste, has died. She loves Taste, she loves only Slimene. Psychologists are paid to frown on contradictions like these; they diagnose Eberhardt as suffering cognitive dissonance. Eberhardt's biographers follow their general lead. Under Freud's influence, they struggle to explain her incoherent writing by emphasizing that always reliable culprit, childhood familial difficulties.[5] They assume traumatic episodes from her formative years linger in her psyche and unsettle it now. I will propose a different explanation for the conflicting loves, but I admit Eberhardt ushered from a traumatized, bizarre family. Her mother left an aristocratic husband in Russia to run off with her children's deranged tutor. After reaching Switzerland, the two conceived and raised Isabelle in reclusiveness. She was educated in her dilapidated home, mainly in post-apocalypse survival skills and foreign languages. She slept outside with the animals. For all its discomfort and eccentricity, her literary upbringing and bestial habits would prove invaluable for her traveling life in North Africa. Another childhood habit she picked up was drugs. Following her older brother's inglorious lead, she quickly became addicted and sank into a cycle of manic depression. During one bout, she expressed a wish to die. Her nihilistic father hurried to retrieve a loaded pistol. Happily, she refused his mad charity. Surreal episodes like this fill page after page of the biographies. Taken together, or even in part, they can explain away nearly any inconsistency in her memory or writings. The strategy is simple and effective: whenever she writes or does something contradictory, say she was addled.

Underneath this psychological strategy lies the assumption of resemblance-dominated temporality running along its unbroken line. Psychologist-readers assume Eberhardt's past is important because they assume she cannot escape it. And it is because Eberhardt cannot escape her traumatic past that she suffers cognitive dissonance and thus writes contradictory things in the present. But what makes her writing contradictory? Nothing more than the assumption of an unbroken temporal line tying the Eberhardt who writes she loves Taste to the Eberhardt who moments later writes that she loves only Slimene. Let the certainty of that unity go and the contradiction in Eberhardt's diary disappears. The Eberhardt running along one time line loves Taste while another, unrelated Eberhardt on another, unrelated line loves Slimene. The two appear contiguously in Eberhardt's writing, but the separating distance between them voids similarity. So, the problem with the journal entry is not the logical incompatibility of the two loves, but the notion of temporality Eberhardt's readers stamp on it. Because the problem is us, not her, no one will solve it by digging around in her childhood.

Still, we can safely assume there will be persistent readers digging, trying to solve contradictions while implicitly buttressing the assumptions underneath. But again, the assumptions cause the contradiction. This choking situation exemplifies a Deleuzean teaching: "The aim is not to answer questions, it's to get out, to get out of it. Many people think that it is only by going back over the question that it's possible to get out of it. . . . But getting out never happens like that. Movement always happens behind the thinker's back, or in the moment when he blinks."[6] The solution to questions, especially the solution to the question of Eberhardt's contradictory loves, comes by getting out, it comes like forgetting. You cannot forget by heading back into the episode you want to annihilate, you forget by heading in an unrelated direction by producing fresh memories which simply preclude the others. Solve problems by avoidance, not by obsessing. The imperative: diverge and separate. Eberhardt's journal presents a psychological conflict that can be solved by heading away from psychology and toward a time strung from alien moments. The problem dissolves when times generate themselves in accordance with difference's rule of production and limitation. A past episode of loving Taste generates its own codes of passion without conflicting with the ardor burning Isabelle and Slimene. Instead of rushing to compare these two flames, surface temporality lets them both continue separately.

In his *Confessions*, Rousseau, too, functions alternately along divergent times: "I gave myself over entirely, as you might say, to these young ladies, so completely in fact that when I was with either of them I never thought of the other."[7] Eberhardt is like Rousseau when she says she can no longer be responsible for her past wanderings because she means just that; she bears no responsibility for them. The time filled with Slimene never converges with the time Taste occupies. These are alien loves.

Diverging Locality and Surface Desires

On Deleuze's surface, Eberhardt's loves are no longer a single story, but multiple. Contiguity no longer assures similarity, time breaks apart. Other things break too. Eberhardt alienates from herself in three ways. First, her body and dress split. Then, her body splinters. Finally, her sexuality multiplies. I will take them in order.

In a world of depth, people's bodies and their dress go together; the continuity should hold even to the degree that their material clothing partially communicates their immaterial ideas. As an ostensible believer in pervasive resemblance, Plato continually finds ways to describe Socrates's attire. This is not just literary ornamentation, it is a necessary consequence of idealism. So, in the *Symposium*, Alcibiades tells the story of Socrates wandering barefoot across icy planes.[8] His point: Socrates arrogantly dismisses sensual, earthbound existence. How a person dresses reveals them. But not on the surface and not for Eberhardt. Her break from pervasive resemblance is immediately evident: she dressed as a man. In Africa, the burnouses, turbans, and fezes she donned were men's and were worn in their style. She was not a woman with a proclivity for feminine variations on male stalwart articles; she didn't choose men's clothes because she liked the way they hung across her body. Much stronger than that, she dressed as though her body were male.

Practical considerations played a role, as she spent her active life travelling through remote regions of the Algerian desert, she was prudent to find commodious outfits—gender design meant little when weighed against survival necessities. Also, as she was frequently the only woman in trains of camels, horses, and men, she may have had good reason for disguise. Nonetheless, she goes further. In her own writings, Eberhardt refers to herself as a "man of action".[9] And she wrote in French, so her adjectives were either masculine or feminine. When she describes herself, she feels free to choose the masculine version.[10] Thus, Eberhardt understood her clothing not just as a convenience or a deception, but as a positive expression. She was not just a woman in disguise, a woman fitted to female categories with male auxiliary parts. She was a man. Nonetheless, her genitals irresistibly tell us she was a woman. Whatever the case, wherever she travelled, she herself presented the paradox of simultaneous woman and man. Between her body and her clothes: alienation.

Also, the actual body underneath splits up. An approximately stereotypical female aspect functioned with Slimene. She married him, became a wife. Simultaneously, Eberhardt's body engaged itself physically in a process of becoming male. Rana Kabbani reports that Isabelle was completely flat-chested, had an abundance of bodily hair and no periods.[11] But even after listing this jolting empirical evidence, Kabbani jealously guards Eberhardt's orthodox femininity by insisting these removals from the traditionally feminine arose from that consummate female malady, anorexia. According to Kabbani's reasoning, the cause of Eberhardt's becoming male is her being a woman. But Eberhardt was hardly capable of indulging in the denial of food. She suffered first from maladies both women and men suffer: poverty and drug addiction. Eberhardt's problems were not psychological misapprehensions about her body but an ineradicable craving for marijuana which consumed any little funds she may have had. At night she frequently slept outdoors in public squares, wrapped only in her burnous, clutching her papers and few other possessions. Her almost toothless jaws chomped and swallowed little more than the dried bread other Muslims offered. She visited her friends at meal time so she could eat.[12] Anorexia would have been a luxury. Eberhardt's body, like her body and clothes, was generating difference—male and female, not resemblance—female and female malady.

The intellectual system catching Kabbani as she reviews Eberhardt's existence is one of simple duality: woman/man. If Eberhardt were simply a woman or simply a man, then it might be reasonable to try and connect all her habits underneath one of the two rubrics while rejecting the other. We could explain her clothing choices as practical matters, her mentality as so wholly feminine her anorexic body grew hair. But why reduce her like that? Instead of imposing exterior, dialectical categories onto Eberhardt's every act and then twisting them into a single line of actions all explained by a single, gendered motivation, let her generate her own rules, let her produce multiple sets of categories governed by logics alien to each other. This stance will work far better in explaining Eberhardt. The sexes winding through her existence fire in different directions. They explain different practices, they produce different writings. She is male. She is female. She was born, like all of us during our first months and years, essentially genderless. She is destined, like all of us in our old age, for the life of a eunuch. These differences are not measured in degrees. They are not measured. How far apart are lines with disparate trajectories? Is Eberhardt a woman or a man? There are no answers to these questions.

In his own writing, Deleuze takes up multiple-sexed bodies as a call to arms. He rallies us in insisting there are "not one or even two sexes, but *n* sexes."[13] And the "slogan of the desiring revolution will be first of all: to each its own sexes."[14] Eberhardt and Deleuze have the same sexed body.

Even more than her clothes and her sexed body, Eberhardt's various and uncommon sexual appetites demand a multiplicity only available on Deleuze's surface. Conventionally, we understand sex as heterosexual, all our encounters become varieties of that core act. Homosexuality, for example, frequently amounts to nothing more than repositioned heterosexuality; it participates in the procedures, fantasies, and seductive techniques previously regularized by its more popular partner. Thus, within this traditional framework, in evaluating Eberhardt's libido, we should limit ourselves to defining her particular brand of heterosexuality. The commentator Paul Bowles leads the way.[15] He reports Eberhardt spent evenings wrestling incognito as a male with soldiers in the barracks. Later, she would slip off with one, surprising him with her revelation. These encounters could be labeled deviantly homosexual or transvestisms. But either way, the categories of standard heterosexuality organize the action.

Eberhardt's journals, however, are filled with much more than heterosexuality and its monotonous cousins. With Slimene, the man who finally became her husband, physical love does seem prosaic. But about another lover, Eberhardt confides:

> Certainly [Taste's] eroticism, sometimes brutal and violent, sometimes neurotically subtle, was not without pleasure. To him I said things no one else has heard me say.[16]

And she pithily describes still another sex with still another man, Toulat, like this:

> There is something savage in the way he loves. . . .[17]

For Eberhardt's sexuality, we have Toulat with his savagery. Beside that, we have Taste employing a certain masochism and Slimene with his straight heterosexuality and Bowles relating a heterosexuality as bizarre homosexuality practiced in the military barracks. On the surface, no single system unites these practices. Eberhardt lists them and leaves them there. A cogent evaluation begins by taking each practice on its own terms and releasing it from commitments to the others. Eberhardt's acts become perverse in the Bataillian sense. Not perverse as a sex act mutating from convention, stretching away from it by variation or exchange. Instead, perverse as a sexuality operating independent of the rules normally governing sex acts. Perversity names a carnal desire which in turn defines the acts and their sexual regulation. Simply breaking the rules, which means engaging in deviations prohibited by morality or tradition, is puerile. Teenagers do that. Eberhardt makes rules. The effect is an abandonment of formerly imposed, public structures. Since public categories and public mechanisms like language fall away, Eberhardt has little choice but to convey her perversions with Toulat in largely negative terms: "There is something savage in the way he loves, something un-French and un-modern . . ."[18] His love is un-French and un-modern because it is unlike them, it takes nothing from them.

Because of Eberhardt's perversity, her practices are impenetrably private. She needs no closed doors, she doesn't worry about others peeking through windows or paging through her journal— the rules for understanding what she does and what she writes generate from the scene and are thus unavailable to general society. Even if we look, we cannot see.

Eberhardt sometimes claims a standard love for traditional objects—several French soldiers and Arab desert traders for example. And sometimes she constructs her own sex with men like Toulat and Taste. And sometimes she goes further. She also insists she loves Algiers and myriad small desert towns. Sexuality ruled by normal desires pulls up short of these claims. But in multiplying and divorcing from herself, Eberhardt throws off the rules of regularized carnality. She wrote this:

> . . . there, in the early dusk, was Africa vanishing from sight, the ardently beloved soil that harbors both the glorious Sahara and Slimene.[19]

She associates "ardently beloved soil" with the Sahara and her husband Slimene. Undoubtedly Isabelle exercised and consummated a passion with Slimene, but her love did not stop there. She shoves the Sahara right next to Slimene. Her desire stretches right into the desert soil. The Sahara attracts her body. Starting down this line, Eberhardt's biographer, Annette Kobak, writes that Isabelle was tormented during her evening walks by what she took to be the moans and sighs of lovers emerging from behind every roll of earth and every dune. Kobak writes under the auspices of heterosexuality where moans and sighs mean men and women diving into each other. But Eberhardt was further down than Kobak thought of going. In *The Vagabond* Eberhardt writes this of a man who could be her:

> His old desire for the former, tyrannical mistress, drunk with sun, had returned.
> Again, he belonged to her with all the fibers of his being.[20]

The subject of this love is the desert. And the passage should be evaluated with a literal sexual component. Eberhardt means exactly what she writes, including the carnal implications, including the moans and sighs of a human body rubbing hard against the countryside.

Here is Deleuze on the same subject: "The truth is that sex is everywhere: The way a bureaucrat fondles his records, a judge administers justice, a businessman causes money to circulate. . . . Hitler got the fascists sexually aroused. Flags, nations, armies, banks get a lot of people aroused."[21] Sexually, the surface is noisy and prolific. All these sexes generate. They each generate their own reasons and their own regulations and their own satisfactions.

The surface brings alien desires into relief: it grants sexualities endless locked rooms; it leaves the people practicing them alone. It turns the practitioners into localized machines of erotic production, an erotic production that flows nowhere but back into itself. Socrates is scandalized.

Alienation

Eberhardt wallows in the solitude of difference. Legion autobiographical sentences exemplify. This one begins her first journal: "I sit here all by myself, looking at the grey expanse of murmuring sea . . . I am utterly *alone* on earth, and always will be in this Universe. . . ."[22] Not a bright start. But not burdensomely sad either. Eberhardt abides in a very particular seclusion. It is not physical isolation. Her life generally teems with people. She had a family, large numbers of friends and a constant willingness to set off in travel with acquaintances freshly made. So, her solitude was not literal. Why is she utterly alone? The explanation runs through a short story, one including this brief description of a woman and her travelling lover: "They don't speak, for they comprehend each other better in silence."[23] Reading the sentence, you might first be struck by the romantic notion of a love so pure no words need exchanging. If Eberhardt understood this as her lover's state, then her short story should immediately end. There would be nothing more to tell except the constant reconfirmation in silence of an understanding so wide it eludes every word. But the story does not end. Eventually, Eberhardt's vagabond leaves, leaves and returns to the rigor of solitary desert wandering.

On the heels of the split, a second meaning for Eberhardt's silence comes forward. This silence conforms to Deleuze's surface, it emanates from the two comprehending nothing of each other. More, it is not just that they do not understand each other, but they cannot even grasp how the other would organize the very process of understanding. Icons, deities, transcendental structures, common linguistic regulations, everything over-arching, all of it gives out. What had seemed a Socratic resemblance between two individuals heightened to identity and confirmed by perfect companionship now falls back past imperfection and disintegrates altogether into Deleuzean futility. No dreamy compassion under this lovers' silence, instead, the inexplicable and jarring realization of difference juxtaposing two identities. A human oxymoron, the vagabond and his lover are the unique products of separate generations. They share only a comprehension of mutual, independent existence on Deleuze's surface; they share only the barest resemblance, one empty of everything but irony. So they are silent.

The lover's ironic realization allows the term 'alienation' to occupy a remarkable place in the vocabulary evolving from Deleuze's work. Like the simulacrum, it can come between two people without linking them. Unlike the simulacrum, alienation tells the truth, it comes between to show there is nothing there. When we challenge the simulacrum, when we chisel away its Socratic facade, what we find is alienation, just as when we chisel away at romance what we find is Isabelle Eberhardt.

For Deleuze, individuals generate in a swirl of possession. The rules extended in understanding and valuing remain intrinsically foreign to everything beyond. Identity projects imperviousness. This does not forbid people from joining, they do it all the time: camel trains, armies, lovers, new friends and enemies. But according to difference's rule, when we do really join others we are emancipated from ourselves. It is not that I go out to another while holding something of myself back. Instead, in inaugurating community, individuals are dismissed from previous responsibilities. When we join another in becoming enemies we are not two people agreeing to dislike, we are two people possessed by a charge of enmity which generates us and so razes everything we antagonists used to be before hating. To express itself, enmity needs people so it makes us and knocks us together. Only after the actual conflict does the process reflect backwards to manufacture subjects with the causes for their antipathy, the scattered disagreements, the slowly brewing resentment, the critical moment. In terms of concrete experience, it happens that sometimes people are just going to fight. It doesn't matter who or why. It happens in bars every weekend. It isn't until the mess is being cleared away that anybody gets around to stitching together presumptive reasons and chains of events. The same with a new love. I can go back and say it was her wide eyes or her careless voice or her violent gestures or the way she made me laugh at stupid things or her selfish poses. But it wasn't any of those things. It has nothing to do with what I saw or heard. It has nothing to do with what I saw or heard because people who see or hear do not come together. If they are in love, they are produced as lovers all at once with the present production including an element of rationalization cast out behind two freshly constructed subjects. First comes the love, then the subjects in love, then their rationalizations. Only now is it her voice, her gestures. Is this true every time, for every love and every hate? No, but it's true sometimes.

On the question of a Deleuzean community—one without founding members because the active community makes the members—there are two points of view. From the misleading perspective of stable, orthodox identities, Deleuze means that unions form from people with their pasts sliced off. On the other side, on Deleuze's own reading, generation in accord with infinitive-based possession happens, and the discrete entities requisite to its manifestation are taken up and abandoned indiscriminately. Abandoned indiscriminately because of their irrelevance, like the irrelevance of noun arrangement in verb-centered language. Both views amount to the same thing, but with distinct stresses. The first, narrow perspective understands the transformation in Deleuzean community as a loss: I am severed from my previous life, from my memories, from my comfortable habits, from my certainties, from my guideposts. I lose control. Deleuze understands the transformation generously as another force positively defining itself in the world, as liberated from the encumbrances and accretions of a stolid identity. Deleuze proposes a voracious philosophy; it wants more energy, more experience, more identities. And for the selves that fall away in the midst of difference's productive cutting? No pity. Socrates mourns a loss. Deleuze doesn't care. He is Nietzschean here.

And during times without cutting, during the days and weeks Eberhardt lingered in a world without merging, without Slimene and Toulat and Taste? During those times she ended with herself and her own produced borders. The further she reached out for something social she could stir into, the deeper she drove back into her own productions because every effort, every reach took its impetus from internal difference. Socrates said impetus grows from *eros*, from desiring lack stretching out to that one thing out there we all have in common. Deleuze says the best lacks are those we construct. For Deleuze, the process of reaching out for others becomes manic: intensifying the effort fuels the engine of internal difference making lacks, which increases the irresistible vacuum sucking us each back through ourselves. Escape is impossible. Anyway, there is nowhere to escape to. Experience on the surface leaves solitude as a formative condition. Not an achievement, not a liability, not active reclusiveness, not an imperfect understanding but a tenuous realization. Above all, Eberhardt's solitude is not a loss, it is not a condition of being denied a real love or a real other. True, sometimes she had no real love or real other, but those facts made no sense to her. Because of her origin in difference, Eberhardt recognized no state of existence and no existence beyond her own self-imposed limits. For her, every separation from everybody else becomes a measureless distance.

When Eberhardt writes that she is utterly alone, she documents a perfect alienation she can't explain except by practice and she can't justify except by being. When Eberhardt writes *I am utterly alone on earth, and always will be in this Universe*, Platonism comes undone.

She died in a flash flood at the base of the Atlas mountains. The scant evidence indicates suicide. If it was that, it would be misdirected to assert a sadness born from loneliness as the cause. Instead, it was the final throes of a life that had recklessly defined itself at the expense of others. Martin Heidegger once believed that being and life began with death, a death that came from elsewhere. Anxiety rising from its inexorable approach intruded to give us our unmistakable limits and our best chance for discovering authentic, sober meaning in the world. For Eberhardt, meaning and being are fabricated as the expression of existence. She has no need for limits imposed from beyond, she has no need for intrusive death, she has no need. Even the simplest things cannot trap her. In her life, she did not need food, her body was constantly dogged by malnutrition, but she hardly noticed. She did not need money, one of the few times she came into it she immediately threw the bills out her window (incidentally setting in motion the very false rumor that she was rich). She did not need beds, she did not need homes, she did not need truth. I could go on. But the point is not to list everything and then claim she did not need it; the point is to undercut that entire line of reasoning by claiming she produced her own needs and her own limits. The final step to renouncing everything beyond her, to insisting she and she alone controls the world, and even stronger that nothing exists in the world except herself, the final stage of alienation lies in controlling her own end. Imposed and necessary death, like everybody and everything, slides off the impermeable outer shell of possessed subjects. If possessed subjects die, they must commit suicide because they can pass from their earth in no other way. There is no more compelling demonstration than this. The ultimate scene of Eberhardt's possession, and the highest display of her alienation from any need in common, from any shared world, and finally, from any other, is her sinking herself in rushing flood waters.

She left her writings. But they attempted no communication because no community penetrated her. Read them and say: that's not me.

NOTES

Introduction

1. If I needed to adopt technical terminology at this point, I would write that this book is a collection of philosophic narratives. A philosophic narrative is the concretization of a localized theory. Philosophic narratives have strictly and intentionally restrained applicabilities. They explain particular experiences and terminate. They incorporate both literary and philosophic modes.

2. Making this case would be a book in itself. The book might start by considering Plato's claim in the seventh letter that, even if he could, Plato would not venture to put into words an account of the world in general. Socrates, on the other hand, does seem to want to, at least metaphorically, account for the world. Another point of departure could be the discussion of writing in the *Phaedrus*, where Plato has Socrates say that writing will be a kind of intellectual hobby for the very gifted, something to do while lesser intellects amuse themselves at banquets. Socrates, of course, never wrote anything and is presented as amusing himself at a banquet in the *Symposium*. Anne Bowery's forthcoming book on Plato's *Symposium* investigates in greater depth the possibility of Plato's negatively critiquing Socrates in the dialogues.

3. Deleuze, Gilles, *Difference et repetition* (Paris: Presses Universitaires de France, 1968), p. 82. My italics. Translations my own unless otherwise noted.

4. In Deleuze's words, experiences under the yoke of Platonism are "like the animal in the midst of being trained, its movements in final crisis best witness the state of natural liberty about to be lost." [Deleuze, Gilles, *Difference et repetition*, p. 83.] So, it is not just that Platonism serves as a guide to limited philosophizing, more, Platonism's failures indicate the most fecund ground for it.

Introduction to Part I: Difference

1. Deleuze, Gilles, *Logic of Sense*, trans. Lester (New York: Columbia University Press, 1990), p. 52.

1. Difference as Production and Limitation

1. Deleuze, Gilles, *Difference et repetition* (Paris: Presses Universitaires de France, 1968), p. 43.

2. Man, Paul de, *Allegories of Reading* (New Haven: Yale University Press, 1979).

3. Deleuze, Gilles, *Difference et repetition* (Paris: Presses Universitaires de France, 1968), p. 286.

4. This translation from Deleuze's *Difference et repetition* comes via Descombes, Vincent, *Modern French Philosophy*, trans. Scott-Fox, Harding (Cambridge): University of Cambridge Press, 1980), 156. The reference seems to be to *C'est l'etre qui est Difference* . . . Another, more literal, translation is: It is being which is Difference.

5. Plato, *Symposium*, trans. Hamilton (London: Penguin, 1951), 216d.

6. This is like infinity as against the unlimited. The unlimited must cover everything. The infinite, on the other hand, can partake in some of the radicality of the unlimited without spilling everywhere. Think of a point tracing a circle, its movement will be infinite but still confined to the perimeter it travels. The unlimited, by contrast, would crudely wipe out every shape and distinction in its chaotic free-flow. In a way, difference coincides with the point tracing the circle: infinite in persuasive motion but restricted in applicability.

7. Fitzgerald, F. Scott, *The Crack-Up* (New York: New Directions, 1956), p. 69.

8. Deleuze, Gilles, *Difference et repetition* (Paris: Presses Universitaires de France, 1968), p. 48. In his later work, Deleuze talks favorably of concepts; he understands philosophy as charged to produce concepts. What remains true, however, is that concepts are to be mustered to explain experience, and not to constrain it with implicit conditions of conceptualization that ruin the effort to think constructively.

9. Deleuze gives a brief example in one of his footnotes. Difference explains the experience of certain nomadic communities in the Homeric era. [Deleuze, Gilles, *Difference et repetition*, p. 54.] These nomadic tribes occupied fields and mountainsides without any formative idea of staking out a claim or possessing a region. Still, these tribes did have territories, even if they were only ambiguously defined and shifting with each season. Deleuze spots difference working to create these transient delin-

eations. The nomads would move to a new locality, then set out to explore their surroundings. Because no other tribes contested them for control of the barren space, the only force limiting the size of their new region was their own tiredness with walking and exploring. That is, the same walking exploration which created the interior of their territory also produced fatigue and therefore the territory's limit. The process of expanding over the land itself generated the border which gave the land palpable definition as particular and defined. This is difference: the territory's definition is produced from within the nascent territory. The territory produces itself.

2. The Eternal Return Does Difference: Production

1. The title is a sentence from: Deleuze, Gilles, *Différence et repetition* (Paris: Presses Universitaires de France, 1968), p. 77. Translation of: *L'eternel retour "fait" la différence.* . . .

2. Genet, Jean, from *The Selected Writings of Jean Genet*, edited by E. White (New Jersey: The Ecco Press, 1993), p. 333.

3. Nietzsche, Friedrich, *The Gay Science*, trans. Kaufmann (New York: Vintage, 1974), p. 274.

4. See Nietzsche, Friedrich, *Thus Spoke Zarathustra*, trans. Hollingdale (New York: Penguin, 1961), Book III, p. 191.

5. Even the least shade of reaction disallows Nietzsche's will. Jacques Derrida demonstrated his sensitivity to this point with his work on the "supplement." Derrida insists that the seemingly gratuitous, exterior, and largely irrelevant parts of a textual scheme magnify themselves under close examination. In the end, the text cannot resist its own minor adjunct. You can easily move the same point off the text and into the real world. Take an alcoholic now sober. What difference can one finger of bourbon make? Seemingly none after having gulped several bottles worth each week for fifteen years. But if you haven't had a drink in months, one shot can mean as much as cases.

6. Throughout this section I rely heavily on Michael Hardt's recent book *Gilles Deleuze* (Minneapolis: University of Minnesota Press, 1993). My contribution lies in shaping Hardt's accomplished review of Deleuze's debate with Hegel's defenders around Deleuze's actual philosophic practice.

7. With which philosophic figures should this dialectic be associated? Deleuze begins by mooring his notion of the dialectic to Hegel's phi-

losophy. But philosophers chronicling the history of Deleuze's development, like Michael Hardt in *Gilles Deleuze*, have noted that Deleuze could
not have entirely separated Hegel from Kojeve's appropriation and presentation during the famous lectures Kojeve delivered in Paris (Hardt, p.
33). So, Deleuze's concept of the dialectic mixes into Kojeve as well as
Hegel. Hardt goes on to argue that the principal Hegel Deleuze actually
rails against exists in the *Science of Logic* (Hardt, p. 33). Thus, we have the
Hegel of master/slave dialectic as presented in the *Phenomenology*, the
Hegel of the *Science of Logic*, and Kojeve's appropriation. Judith Butler, a
thoughtful defender of Hegel, also contributes to the discussion by elaborating how Deleuze works against the master/slave dialectic not so much
as Hegel presented it but as it emerges from Nietzsche's hyper-critical
evaluation in the *Genealogy of Morals* [Butler, Judith, *Subjects of Desire* (New
York: Columbia University Press, 1989) p. 207 and following]. That makes
two different Hegels, a Kojeve, and a Nietzsche. In the end, it would be
impossible to define exactly what Deleuze has in mind when he invokes
the dialectic under the symbolism of the master/slave dialectic or in the
name of Hegel. What he means probably bounces about somewhat freely
between and in the midst of the various inspirations I have listed.

8. Deleuze, Gilles, *Nietzsche and Philosophy*, trans. Tomlinson (New
York: Columbia University Press, 1983), p. 195.

9. Houlgate, Stephen, *Hegel, Nietzsche, and the Criticism of Metaphysics* (Cambridge: Cambridge University Press, 1986), p. 7.

10. Wahl, Jean, "Nietzsche et la philosophie," *Revue de metaphysic et
de morale*, 1963, p. 352.

11. Wahl, Jean, "Nietzsche et la philosophie," p. 364.

12. Deleuze, Gilles, *Dialogues*, trans. Tomlinson, Habberjam (London:
Athlone Press, 1987), p. 1.

13. Hardt, Michael, *Gilles Deleuze* (Minneapolis: University of Minnesota Press, 1993), p. 52.

14. Hardt, Michael, *Gilles Deleuze*, p. 53.

15. de Man wrote: "Moreover, the reversal from denial to assertion
implicit in deconstructive discourse never reaches the symmetrical coun-
terpart of what it denies." Man, Paul de., *Allegories of Reading* (New Haven:
Yale University Press, 1979), p. 125. He imagined the struggle of deconstructive discourse to move like an imbalanced pendulum between one
denial, an assertion, a second denial, a second assertion, etc. The pairs constantly changed, but the structure of the relation remained.

16. Deleuze, Gilles, *Nietzsche and Philosophy*, trans. Tomlinson (New York: Columbia University Press 1983), p. 10.

17. Deleuze, Gilles, *Nietzsche and Philosophy*, p. 195.

18. Deleuze, Gilles, *Nietzsche and Philosophy*, p. 188.

19. Of course, spontaneity can still exist, just never in the shadow of a command. The same is true of the eternal return.

20. Nietzsche, Friedrich, *The Gay Science*, trans. Kaufmann (New York: Vintage, 1974), p. 273.

21. Deleuze, Gilles, *Nietzsche and Philosophy*, trans. Tomlinson (New York: Columbia University Press, 1983), p. 69.

22. Deleuze, Gilles, *Nietzsche and Philosophy*, p. 104.

23. They split apart elsewhere, however. First, for Socrates, the immanent connection between the individual and the intuition is actually a bridge leading out of the self and up toward understanding the Truth. For Deleuze, the immanent nature of the intuition leads only back to itself, the intuition gets produced by the individual will, not discovered beyond it. Second, for Socrates, the moment of revelation is a recognition. In the *Phaedrus*, Socrates portrays his intuition as a return trip to a state the philosophic soul once had. For Deleuze, Socratic recognition plays no foundational role because the intuition gets generated, not discovered, by the individual. Third, for Socrates, the community of the Good would owe a debt to the Good. The metaphysical ideal draws its dependents together and manifests itself as a destiny there all the time, attracting its members inexorably. For Deleuze, the community of the second affirmation would be accidental. It is a contingent juxtaposition of individuals having already produced the eternal return. It could have happened or it might not have. No destiny. Fourth, for Socrates the earthly version of the community of the Good was a community in the strongest sense, they were bound by something overriding that they had in common. For Deleuze, the eternal return provides the barest of linkages because each volition takes responsibility for acting and producing its own revelation. If anything, Deleuze's community is the community of those with nothing in common. Fifth, Socrates believed intuition was a natural augmentation of the rational mind. Crafts, arts, the sciences, and finally mathematics prepare the way for an interpretive revelation that caps and seals them; a certain intellectual method leads to intuition. Deleuze's Nietzsche spurns any particular method and method generally. [see Deleuze, Gilles, *Nietzsche and Philosophy*, trans. Tomlinson (New York: Columbia University Press, 1983), p. 103.] The truths we deserve are not at the end of an instruction manual,

and intuition is not necessarily allied with the intellect. Sixth, Socrates spoke to draw people toward, and finally reveal to them, his Good. Socrates was a leader. Deleuze writes for people who have already realized the eternal return. Deleuze is a Nietzschean. Seventh, Socrates clearly claimed that one truth, his truth, was preferable to all the others. Deleuze's Nietzsche stops short of that. We all get the truths we deserve. Not we all or at least some of us deserve the high and privileged truth. Here, Nietzsche's readers could object. Does not Nietzsche proclaim the Overman? Yes, and Nietzsche certainly can bend into a reading demanding that as the model. But elitist positions like this find more footholds in Nietzsche than Deleuze's Nietzsche. Or, to put the point differently, a Deleuzean truth is privileged, but only from within the truth's action. Finally, Socrates insists his intuition exists for all time. When you get it, you reach beyond the dimension of passing moments. Deleuze's philosophy stresses relentless partiality and restriction. Reaching the eternal return for all time is not the goal. Deleuze despises goals and attributes no special significance to the category "all time." Both goals and eternities impinge upon the will. The way some wills have sometimes already acted intrigues Deleuze.

24. Deleuze, Gilles, *Nietzsche et la philosophie* (Paris: Presses Universitaires de France, 1963), p. 80.

25. Deleuze, Gilles, *Nietzsche et la philosophie*, p. 55.

26. Deleuze, Gilles, *Nietzsche and Philosophy*, trans. Tomlinson (New York: Columbia University Press, 1983), p. 48.

27. Ironically, Rousseau chronicled his retreats in his *Reveries of a Solitary Walker*.

28. Shakespeare, *Titus Andronicus*, Act V, scene ii.

29. Deleuze, Gilles, *Nietzsche and Philosophy*, trans. Tomlinson (New York: Columbia University Press, 1983), p. 111.

30. Deleuze, Gilles, *Nietzsche et la philosophie* (Paris: Presses Universitaires de France, 1962), p. 206.

31. Shakespeare, *Titus Andronicus*, Act V, scene iii.

32. Deleuze, Gilles, *Nietzsche et la philosophie* (Paris: Presses Universitaires de France, 1962), p. 206.

33. In *The Accursed Share* Georges Bataille takes up the human condition of production. He postulates that humanity must produce an excess over what is needed to survive. He then studies the ways humans have

developed to vent this excess, everything from festival dances to festival slayings (ritual sacrifice), from mad economic growth (capitalism) to mad world wars. Bataille creatively develops the curse of this state of production, he indicates the tragedy intrinsic to it.

34. All the groundwork has here been laid for understanding Nietzsche ironically as a protector from the radically productive forces he espouses and claims to promote, because by citing them and theorizing them he blocks our way to them. Thanks to Nietzsche, we can recognize Titus's character, how it works, where it came from. But because of Nietzsche, it has become almost impossible for philosophers to reach Titus, to walk beside him, to act like him.

3. See with My Own Eyes: Limitation

1. In *Gilles Deleuze*, Michael Hardt locates the book where Deleuze develops the idea of a produced limitation: *Expressionism in Philosophy*. According to Hardt, Deleuze realized that determination cannot be Hegelian in the sense of the negative, so he had been flirting with the idea of indetermination, but that still left him trapped in Hegel's dialectic system: in his frantic attempt to escape the negative limitation intrinsic to Hegel, Deleuze simply fell off the other edge. With the idea of a positive, affirmed limitation, Deleuze regains his balance and stakes out a position independent of Hegel. Hardt's discussion can be found on pages 67 and 68.

2. Foucault, Michel, "A Preface to Transgression," in *Language, Counter-Memory, Practice*, edited by D. Bouchard, trans. Bouchard, Simon (Ithaca: Cornell University Press, 1977).

3. Foucault, Michel, "A Preface to Transgression," p. 32.

4. Foucault, Michel, "A Preface to Transgression," p. 35.

5. Foucault, Michel, "A Preface to Transgression," p. 35.

6. Foucault, Michel, "A Preface to Transgression," p. 30.

7. For a graphic illustration of why Bataille can understand the family in terms of opposition, see his memories of his own family in the back of Neugroschal's translation of the *Story of the Eye*.

8. Bataille, Georges, *Story of the Eye*, trans. Neugroschal (San Francisco: City Lights, 1984), p. 11.

9. The Greeks understood that our vision gives us form. Their word *eidos*, which we translate as idea in the sense of metaphysical ideals, means literally, "the look of."

10. Bataille, Georges, *Story of the Eye*, trans. Neugroschal (San Francisco: City Lights, 1984), p. 82.

11. Bataille, Georges, *Story of the Eye*, pp. 83–84.

Introduction to Part II: Possession

1. Laing, R.D., *The Divided Self* (New York: Pantheon, 1969).

4. Verbs and Nouns

1. Milford, Nancy, *Zelda* (New York: Avon, 1970), pp. 306–7.

2. This doubling is not the ramification of a shared essence between the series. Rather, it is a mark of the series' differentiation. Instead of thinking, as Socrates taught us, to assume that an original and now corrupted identity lies at the bottom of every resemblance, think that every resemblance masks an original disparity with the counterfeit of a fundamental resemblance. Deleuze postulates that series begin from difference and come into relation as an expression of that difference. The name he applies to this counterfeit community is "resonance." The series' characterization as parallel and analogous arises from a preliminary distance across which the two series resonate without coming into contact and thus without reducing into each other. Again, the two series share no *a priori* essence, though their resonance subsequently produces what appears to be an identity or essence between them. From this premise of an ersatz community growing from primary and unconquerable difference, Deleuze can talk about experience while he talks about language without fearing that the one will cave into or undercut the other. In brief, language and experience belong to different logics. In *Logic of Sense*, when Deleuze writes on one, he also writes on the other, but he does so without sacrificing each series' autonomy. Deleuze's voice literally doubles.

If I were going to push this further, I would begin by noting that the doubling of Deleuze's voice marks the end of Deleuze as a single identity. He transforms from being the original, single character linking the two voices into a production of the voices. It is no longer Deleuze who speaks, and speaks twice, it is two voices responsible for creating a false sense of similarity that we call Gilles Deleuze. This Deleuze comes subsequent to his own voice, as a resonance.

3. Deleuze, Gilles, *Logic of Sense*, trans. Lester (New York: Columbia University Press, 1990), p. 63.

4. Deleuze, Gilles, *Logic of Sense*, p. 5.

5. Deleuze's infinitive in some ways complements Levinas's "there is" (*Il y a*). For Levinas, there is a thing, a particular noun, and separate from that, there exists the general thinghood of the thing. Similarly in speech, there is what is said, and then there is a distinguishable "to say" which attaches to no particular words but acts underneath every utterance. The infinitive is a special linguistic case in some ways like "the saying." It acts without particularity. It attaches everywhere, but constantly escapes to return again attached to new bodies and new particularities.

It should also be noted that the restricted analogy between Deleuze and Levinas should not be extended to Heidegger. Heidegger discusses the infinitive in several important pages of *An Introduction to Metaphysics*, [trans. Manheim (New Haven: Yale University Press, 1959), pp. 54–70.] Here, Heidegger relegates the infinitive to a derivative position. For him, the infinitive comes after—both ontologically and historically—the particular inflected forms. The infinitive is only an empty grammatical tool invented by staid academics to organize language. In fact, for Heidegger, the infinitive even functions negatively, its empty generality covers up the specific, material, temporal moment of a particular person doing a particular thing at a particular time. Instead of seeing the infinitive overflowing into "I do," "he does," etc., Heidegger sees the infinitive as deficient to the degree that it effaces particularity and thus denies being, which for Heidegger is above all situated concretely in history. Heidegger's infinitive does not lead us to the root of being as it does for Deleuze. For Heidegger, the infinitive obscures being-in-the-world.

6. Deleuze, Gilles, *Logic of Sense*, trans. Lester (New York: Columbia University Press, 1990), p. 75. Common sense also insists upon a unidirectional sequence for states of affairs. For example, Titus Andronicus's production defies common sense.

7. Deleuze, Gilles, *Logic of Sense*, p. 33.

8. Deleuze, Gilles, *Logic of Sense*, p. 33. For Plato's consideration of the paradoxes of becoming, see his *Parmenides*.

9. Deleuze, Gilles, *Logic of Sense*, p. 52. The quote actually belongs to Deleuze's simultaneous discussion of the (pure) event and what he calls "singularity." But the thrust of the ideas apply equally to the infinitive, and they fit in there naturally in accordance with the twin series of discussion Deleuze has already set up, the first running from events to things to states of affairs and the second running from infinitives to substantives

to propositions. The notion of "singularity" fits into both these series at the first step, in the event and the infinitive. It is something like the defining force acting in both. Deleuze is careful to note in the sentences preceding the cited passage that his idea of singularity should not be confused with a specific personality or the individuality of a state of affairs. In other words, singularity does not mean singular in the sense of a metaphysical boundary. Rather, singularity is the name for the active force in series of being that begin from events and a discourse (or logos) that begins with infinitives.

10. For Deleuze's discussion of this term, see Deleuze, Gilles, *Logic of Sense*, pp. 4–7.

11. For a discussion of this structure of transformation, one which is, in Deleuze's language, not arboresque but rhizomatic, see the section entitled Rhizome in Deleuze, Gilles, and Felix Guattari, *One Thousand Plateaus*, trans. Massumi (Minneapolis: University of Minnesota Press, 1987), pp. 3–25.

12. Hemingway, Ernest, *A Moveable Feast* (New York: Charles Scribner's Sons, 1987), pp. 155–156. Readers should keep in mind that Hemingway's relationship with Fitzgerald was complex. Hemingway respected Fitzgerald's work and owed the latter a debt of thanks for intervening to help Hemingway publish his first book. On the other hand, Hemingway disdained Fitzgerald's zealous and sometimes uncritical respect for wealth. Hemingway also disliked Zelda Fitzgerald; he believed that she threatened Scott Fitzgerald's equilibrium. Further, Hemingway and Fitzgerald naturally saw themselves to be in competition for book sales and literary respect. These tensions sometimes manifested themselves bitterly, and they certainly colored any words either author wrote concerning the other.

13. For an extended and clear consideration of this argument, especially as it pertains to Stoic philosophy, which Deleuze valorizes, see Deleuze, Gilles, *Logic of Sense*, trans. Lester (New York: Columbia University Press, 1990), pp.4–7.

14. Hemingway, Ernest, *A Moveable Feast* (New York: Charles Scribner's Sons, 1987), p. 154.

15. Hemingway, Ernest, *A Moveable Feast*, p. 147.

16. Deleuze, Gilles, *Logic of Sense*, trans. Lester (New York: Columbia University Press, 1990), pp. 210, following.

17. Deleuze, Gilles, *Logic of Sense*, p. 33.

18. Fitzgerald, F. Scott, *The Great Gatsby* (New York: Collier Books, 1992), pp. 137–138.

19. I am using the term 'quasi' in accordance with Deleuze's practice in *Logic of Sense* where he writes about the "quasi-causality" of the infinitive's dimension.

20. Fitzgerald, F. Scott, *The Great Gatsby* (New York: Collier Books, 1992), p. 189.

21. Fitzgerald, F. Scott, *The Great Gatsby*, p. 157.

5. Emily, the Patient, Bliss, Deleuze

1. Bliss, E.L., "Multiple Personalities," *Archives of General Psychiatry* 37 (1980), p. 1392. Copyright 1980, American Medical Association.

2. Bliss, E.L., "Multiple Personalities," p. 1392

3. The principal debate swirling around multiple personality disorder concerns the reality of the state. Much of the medical profession believes multiple personalities are not authentically multiple, but rather patients play acting. This skeptical group insists that patients who appear to have multiplied actually pick up cues unwittingly given by the doctors as to how they should act in order to be multiple or confirm their multiplicity. Other doctors belive that their patients have authentically independent personalities. But this independence is always conditioned by a common past. That is, even though the specific personality now appears to be autonomous, it shares some part of its history with the main identity from which it split. Dr. Bliss is in this camp. I am pushing further by denying the metaphor of the split and seeing the alien personality as originating entirely from beyond the patient.

4. Bliss, E.L., "Multiple Personalities," *Archives of General Psychiatry* 37 (1980), p. 1393. Copyright 1980, American Medical Association.

5. This mimics Deleuze and Guattari's discussion of desiring machines on the body without organs in *Anti-Oedipus*.

6. Deleuze suggests that in capitalistic society, mores, habits, and desires change as often as Sony invents musical devices or the USA Today publishes a new poll or the next Newsweek hits the newsstands. Lines of perversion and acceptability, of revulsion and normalcy, evaporate and slide atop wavering markets. There can be no stability and no enduring identity in this commercial society of constant transformation. One week

the television news is ruled by concern for economic well-being, the next environmental concerns fill every channel. Bliss's family sculpts immutable lines variant society cannot. The family defines the child, it gives the child a sustaining identity by sectioning him or her in terms of specific sexual frivolities and degradations.

7. Bliss, E.L., "Multiple Personalities," *Archives of General Psychiatry* 37 (1980), p. 1392. Copyright 1980, American Medical Association.

8. Bliss, E.L., "Multiple Personalities," p. 1392.

9. Guattari certainly plays a major role in the development of Deleuze's thought on this topic and others, and I do not mean to dismiss his importance by mentioning him only in passing. But because I am concentrating on Deleuze's thought and the ideas Deleuze brought with him to his collaboration with Guattari, I have largely left Guattari's name out.

10. This does not imply that all strategies for treating multiple personality disorder can be wedged into the model Bliss exemplifies. Perhaps only some can, but Deleuze would maintain that elements of Bliss's approach infiltrate much of contemporary psychology.

11. Deleuze, Gilles, and Felix Guattari, *Anti-Oedipus*, trans. Hurley, Seem, Lane (Minneapolis: University of Minnesota Press, 1983), p. 55.

12. Bliss, E.L., "Multiple Personalities," *Archives of General Psychiatry* 37 (1980), p. 1393. Copyright 1980, American Medical Association.

13. Bliss, E.L., "Multiple Personalities," p. 1393.

14. Many doctors dismiss multiple personality disorder as a misdiagnosis of a patient who is actually quite adept at role playing. The actual physiological effects of multiple personality disorder (sometimes one personality needs glasses while another does not, sometimes one has diabetes while another does not) argue against this cynicism. There is, however, a point in most standard treatments where role playing does enter in. It is right here, at the point where doctors insist that patients be cured while giving them tools that can only drive them further away from unity. Thus, role playing enters into multiple personality, but it does not enter because there is no authentic multiple personality. It enters because the misguided efforts doctors exert to cure multiples actually force them to begin role playing. All the while, the divergent personality remains outside the system.

15. Bliss, E.L., "Multiple Personalities," *Archives of General Psychiatry* 37 (1980), p. 1393. Copyright 1980, American Medical Association.

16. This is the reactive force Nietzsche located in his *Genealogy* as slave morality.

17. See Rorty, Richard, *Contingency, Irony, and Solidarity* (Cambridge: Cambridge University Press, 1989).

18. Conway, Daniel, "Thus Spoke Rorty: The Perils of Narrative Self-Creation," *Philosophy and Literature* 15 (1991), pp. 103–110.

19. Deleuze, Gilles, *Difference et repetition* (Paris: Presses Universitaires de France, 1968), p. 44.

6. Desire, Not Want

1. Locke, J., *Essay Concerning Human Understanding* [1690], Book II, chapter xxvii, paragraph 11; vol. i, pp. 448–49.

2. Satten, Joseph, et al., "Murder Without Apparent Motive—A Study in Personality Disorganization," *The American Journal of Psychiatry* (July 1960).

3. Deleuze, Gilles, and Felix Guattari, *A Thousand Plateaus*, trans. Massumi (Minneapolis: University of Minnesota Press, 1988), p. 3.

4. For example, see Bliss, Jonathan, and Eugene Bliss, *Prism* (New York: Stein and Day, 1985).

5. Ferry, Luc, and Alain Renaut, *French Philosophy of the Sixties*, trans. Cattani of *La pensee 68* (Amherst: University of Massachusetts Press, 1990), p.26.

6. Bliss, Jonathan, and Eugene Bliss, *Prism* (New York: Stein and Day, 1985), p. 215.

7. Deleuze, Gilles, and Claire Parnet, *Dialogues*, trans. Tomlinson, Habberjam (London: Athlone Press, 1987), p. 96.

8. Deleuze, Gilles, *Proust and Signs*, trans. Howard (New York: Braziller, 1972), p. 149.

9. Mallarme claimed the end of the world would be marked by the perfect book.

10. Likewise for injustice and imperfection generally. These things flow out of desiring action. They are not categories in place before experience and programmed to evaluate experience, but one of many results. Productive desire constructs evaluations like unjust and imperfect just like

everything else: afterward, contingently, temporarily. See Deleuze, Gilles, *Proust and Signs*, trans. Howard (New York: Braziller, 1972), pp. 166–67: In Socrates, the intelligence still comes before the encounters; it . . . organizes them. [For Deleuze] the intelligence always comes after. . . . To think is therefore to interpret. . . .

11. See Deleuze, Gilles, and Felix Guattari, *Anti-Oedipus*, trans. Hurley, Seem, Lane (Minneapolis: University of Minnesota Press, 1983).

12. Books in the early twentieth century came with the pages folded together in the binding, so the reader needed to cut the pages apart before beginning.

13. Wilkes, Kathleen V., *Real People* (New York: Oxford University Press, 1988), p. 129.

14. Wilkes, Kathleen V., *Real People*, p. 129.

15. Art historians, classicists, and cultural anthropologists have developed and written extensively on this Greek conception of the fractured body under the title of "parataxis."

16. Erickson, Steve, *Days Between Stations* (New York: Vintage Books, 1986), p. 49.

17. Erickson, Steve, *Days Between Stations*, p. 49.

18. Erickson, Steve, *Days Between Stations*, pp. 51–52.

19. Erickson, Steve, *Days Between Stations*, p. 51.

20. Erickson, Steve, *Days Between Stations*, p. 52.

21. Erickson, Steve, *Days Between Stations*, p. 180.

22. The world of coherent entities now forms a continuum from the smallest things ceaselessly splitting off to the giant combinations that stretch the limits of the imagination: the world, the solar system, the universe. Every subject falls somewhere on this line, somewhere between the extremes which themselves never exist.

23. Deleuze, Gilles, and Felix Guattari, *A Thousand Plateaus*, trans. Massumi (Minneapolis: University of Minnesota Press, 1988), p. 3.

7. Invitation to Possession

1. Capote, Truman, from his preface to *Other Voices, Other Rooms* (New York: Random House, 1948), p. xiv.

2. Bukowski, Charles, *Notes of a Dirty Old Man* (San Francisco: City Lights, 1969), p. 8.

3. Fishburn, Evelyn, and Psiche Hughes, *A Dictionary of Borges* (London: Duckworth, 1990).

4. Menard, Pierre, *L'Ecriture et le subconscient: Psychanalyse et graphologie* (Paris: Librairie Felix Alcan, 1931).

5. Borges, Jorge, *Borges, A Reader*, Monegal and Reid, eds. (New York: Dutton, 1981), p. 99.

6. Borges, Jorge, *Borges, A Reader*, p. 99.

7. The space for the new Quixote has not always been out there waiting for someone like Menard to appear and try to fill it, the space comes subsequent to Menard and his intention. The intention creates the space for the project just as it creates Menard to carry the project through.

8. Borges, Jorge, *Borges, A Reader*, Monegal and Reid, eds. (New York: Dutton, 1981), p. 100.

9. Nietzsche, Friedrich, *On the Genealogy of Morals*, trans. Kaufmann (New York: Vintage, 1979), p. 84.

10. Barthes, Roland, "From Work to Text," in *Textual Strategies* (Ithaca: Cornell University Press, 1979), pp. 73–81.

11. Fitzgerald, F. Scott, *The Last Tycoon* (New York: Charles Scribner's Sons, 1941), p. 163.

Introduction to Part III: Alienation

1. Blanchot, Maurice, *The Unavowable Community*, trans. Joris (Barrytown: Station Hill Press, 1988), p. 54.

2. Blanchot, Maurice, *The Unavowable Community*, p. 43.

3. Duras, Marguerite, *The Malady of Death*, trans. Bray (New York: Grove Weidenfeld, 1988), p. 55.

4. Deleuze, Gilles, *Logic of Sense*, trans. Lester (New York: Columbia University Press, 1990), p. 258.

5. Deleuze, Gilles, *Logic of Sense*, p. 258.

6. Deleuze, Gilles, *Logic of Sense*, pp. 258–59.

7. Deleuze, Gilles, *Logic of Sense*, p. 259.

8. Distance without Measure

1. Nietzsche, Friedrich, *Twilight of the Idols*, trans. Hollingdale (London: Penguin, 1988), pp. 40–41.

2. Augustine's third conversion in the *Confessions* claims to move from human conversation to a divinely sanctioned, revelatory conversation.

3. 10 o'clock news, WPIX Television, New York, January 17, 1993.

4. The current (1992) leader of the National Organization for Women, Patricia Ireland, is married and openly states that she has a female lover. Whether her homosexual activity constitutes adultery is, I concede, an open question.

5. See Baudrillard, Jean, *Selected Writings*, edited by Mark Poster (Stanford: Stanford University Press, 1988).

6. Deleuze, Gilles, *Proust and Signs*, trans. Howard (New York: Braziller, 1972).

7. Plato, *Republic*, 523d.

8. Gass, William, *Fiction and the Figures of Life* (New York: Vintage, 1958), p. 255.

9. Deleuze, Gilles, *Logic of Sense*, trans. Lester (New York: Columbia University Press, 1990), p. 173.

9. Rank Weeds and Fair Appearances

1. The Eleatic stranger employs a constructivist method to define the statesman. This is especially clear in his method of division, where we conclude that the statesman is essentially of the same class as the pig. The point Plato is making is that constructivist epistemologies can make anything. The world can be cut into whatever form the stranger chooses to make it. Of course, Plato sows the dialogue with the stranger's absurdity and in this way argues against radical construction in philosophy.

2. Plato, *Republic*, trans. Bloom (New York: Basic Books, 1968), 599d–e.

3. Nietzsche, Friedrich, *Genealogy of Morals*, trans. Kaufmann (New York: Vintage, 1989), p. 46.

4. Nietzsche, Friedrich, *Genealogy of Morals*, pp. 46–47.

5. See Plato, *Phaedrus*, 230b.

6. The best single example of right community would be the one Augustine forms with his mother Monica. She was a persistent, if simple Christian, devoted to bringing Augustine to the Faith. At the end, after Augustine has caroused, made money in Rome, aged, and finally converted, it is with Monica that he chooses to display the sanctity of his new belief. The episode is appropriately surreal: "And while we spoke of the eternal wisdom, longing for it and straining for it with all the strength of our hearts, for one fleeting instant we reached out and touched it. Then with a sigh, leaving our spiritual harvest bound to it, we returned to the sound of our own speech, in which each word has a beginning and an ending. . . ." Augustine, *Confessions*, trans. Pine-Coffin (London: Penguin, 1961), Book 9, Chapter 10, p. 197. This community of Monica and Augustine is erotically real, it has a common ground: God's beneficence. And it shares a common destiny: eternal blessedness. We hear its authenticity in exchanges of those enigmatic words that do not need beginnings and endings.

7. Augustine, *Confessions*, p. 52.

8. Kant, Immanuel, *Critique of Practical Reason*, trans. Beck (Indianapolis: Bobbs-Merrill, 1983), p. 101.

9. Kant, Immanuel, *Critique of Practical Reason*, pp. 72–73.

10. Kant, Immanuel, *Critique of Pure Reason*, trans. Smith (New York: St. Martin's, 1965), p. 599.

11. Kant, Immanuel, *Critique of Pure Reason*, p. 599.

12. Kant, Immanuel, *Critique of Pure Reason*, p. 600.

13. Deleuze himself does not cite this reference, so I myself have simply translated his French articulation back into English. Deleuze, Gilles, *Différence et répetition* (Paris: Presses Universitaires de France, 1968), p. 96.

14. See Deleuze, Gilles, *Différence et répetition*, p. 97.

15. Passive synthesis differs from active synthesis in a way similar to realization. The succession of items in a pattern may not be recognized as a pattern, but they still have been constructed passively by the understanding in such a way that the pattern can be discerned. Then, a teacher or simple speculation will lead you to see the pattern that was latent—this recognition is active synthesis. In either case, the pattern is constructed— first as a possibility, then as a realization—by forces external to the repeating items. In brief, the repetition is produced.

16. Deleuze, Gilles, *Difference et repetition* (Paris: Presses Universitaires de France, 1968), p. 100.

17. Located as an appendix to the English translation of Deleuze, Gilles, *Logic of Sense*, trans. Lester (New York: Columbia University Press, 1990).

18. Deleuze, Gilles, *Logic of Sense*, p. 315. The term 'Other' is capitalized because Deleuze is referring to what he calls the "structure-Other." The structure-Other is the specific other person insofar as he or she imposes resemblance through contiguity through the world. The structure-Other is the transcendental plane of Platonism made specific as other people.

10. Love Is for Other People

1. Eberhardt, Isabelle, *The Passionate Nomad: The Diary of Isabelle Eberhardt*, trans. de Voogd (Boston: Beacon Press, 1987), p. 11.

2. Eberhardt, Isabelle, *Ecrits sur le sable*, Vol. 2 (Paris: Bernard Grasset, 1988), p. 297. Translation after Bowles.

3. These two times are not poles of a single time line. They do not, like Carroll's "bats eat cats" and "cats eat bats," mark opposite bounds of a single event called eating. Instead, these two times separate like experience flowing from two dissonant infinitives, or what Deleuze calls two different senses. *Logic of Sense* and *Difference and Repetition* (pp. 153–64 of the Patton translation) painfully distinguish sense in general from non-sense. Sense, which in French also means "direction," composes an entire field of separate but common directions, directions understood here in terms of time as the various trajectories an event has followed. For instance, the physical, Socratic woman may be recalled as having intentionally incited the fight between her suitors, she may be recalled as having attempted to intervene on one side, she may be recalled as having tried to pacify them. These paths of memory conflict with each other, but all carry the same sense, all flow in the same general direction: an orderly march through history from past to present. Reaching another sense of time requires dipping through non-sense, through murky difference. From that passage, a distinct temporal orientation may be cast out, one again open to various related trajectories, but unrelated to the trajectories of other senses. For instance, the Deleuzean woman of the scar may be rendered as a shrill, energetic creature or as a reserved and calculating beauty. These two are not the same but they relate intimately; they have the same sense insofar as both flow out of a time travelling from the present scar into the past. But

for the women and times participating in independent senses, they separate through pure difference which translates existentially as unquantifiable distance. No vertical measure, only a flat surface of experience allows space for alienated temporalities like these.

4. Eberhardt, Isabelle, *Ecrits sur le sable*, Vol. 1 (Paris: Bernard Grasset, 1988), p. 425.

5. See, for example, Kobak, Annette, *Isabelle* (New York: Knopf, 1989).

6. Deleuze, Gilles, and Claire Parnot, *Dialogues*, trans. Tomlinson, Habberjam (London: Athlone Press, 1977), p. 1.

7. Rousseau, Jean-Jacques, *Confessions*, trans. Cohen (London: Penguin, 1953), p. 36.

8. Plato, *Symposium*, 220b.

9. Eberhardt, Isabelle, *The Passionate Nomad: The Diary of Isabelle Eberhardt*, trans. de Voogd (Boston: Beacon Press, 1987), p. 10.

10. Eberhardt, Isabelle, *Ecrits sur le sable*, Vol. 1 (Paris: Bernard Grasset, 1988), p. 303: Je suis seul. . . .

11. From Rana Kabbani's introduction, Eberhardt, Isabelle, *The Passionate Nomad: The Diary of Isabelle Eberhardt*, trans. de Voogd (Boston: Beacon Press, 1987).

12. See Kobak, Annette, *Isabelle* (New York: Knopf, 1989).

13. Deleuze, Gilles, and Felix Guattari, *Anti-Oedipus*, trans. Hurley, Seem, Lane (Minneapolis: University of Minnesota Press, 1983), p. 296.

14. Deleuze, Gilles, and Felix Guattari, *Anti-Oedipus*, p. 296.

15. See Bowles's introduction, Eberhardt, Isabelle, *The Oblivion Seekers*, trans. Bowles (San Francisco: City Lights, 1982).

16. Eberhardt, Isabelle, *Ecrits sur le sable*, Vol. 1 (Paris: Bernard Grasset 1988), p. 425.

17. Eberhardt, Isabelle, *The Passionate Nomad: The Diary of Isabelle Eberhardt*, trans. de Voogd (Boston: Beacon Press, 1987), p. 79.

18. Eberhardt, Isabelle, *The Passionate Nomad: The Diary of Isabelle Eberhardt*, p. 79.

19. Eberhardt, Isabelle, *The Passionate Nomad: The Diary of Isabelle Eberhardt*, pp. 48–49.

20. Eberhardt, Isabelle, *Ecrits sur le sable*, Vol. 2 (Paris: Bernard Grasset, 1988), p. 377.

21. Deleuze, Gilles, and Felix Guattari, *Anti-Oedipus*, trans. Hurley, Seem, Lane (Minneapolis: University of Minnesota Press, 1983), p. 293.

22. Eberhardt, Isabelle, *The Passionate Nomad: The Diary of Isabelle Eberhardt*, trans. de Voogd (Boston: Beacon Press, 1987), p. 1. Also, compare Eberhardt with the first lines of Rousseau's spirited declaration of paranoid alienation, his *Reveries of a Solitary*: "Here am I, then, alone upon the earth, having no brother, or neighbor, or friend, or society but myself." [Rousseau, Jean, *Reveries of a Solitary*, trans. Fletcher (New York: Burt Franklin, 1927), p. 31.]

23. Eberhardt, Isabelle, *Ecrits sur le sable*, Vol. 2 (Paris: Bernard Grasset, 1988), p. 376.

BIBLIOGRAPHY

Augustine. *Confessions*. Pine-Coffin, trans. London: Penguin Books, 1961.

Barthes, Roland. "From Work to Text," in *Textual Strategies*. Ithaca: Cornell University Press, 1979, pp. 73–81.

Bataille, Georges. *Story of the Eye*. J. Neugroschal, trans. San Francisco: City Lights, 1984.

———. *The Accursed Share*. R. Hurley, trans. New York: Zone Books, 1988.

———. *Erotism*. M. Dalwood, trans. San Francisco: City Lights Books, 1986.

———. *On Nietzsche*. B. Boone, trans. New York: Paragon House, 1992.

Baudrillard, Jean. *Selected Writings*. M. Poster, ed. Stanford: Stanford University Press, 1988.

———. *Simulacra and Simulations*. Foss, Patton, Beitchman, trans. New York: Semiotext(e), 1983.

Blanchot, Maurice. *The Unavowable Community*. Joris, trans. Barrytown: Station Hill Press, 1988.

Bliss, Eugene. "Multiple Personalities." *Archives of General Psychiatry*, 1980. Copyright 1980, American Medical Association.

Bliss, Jonathan, and Eugene Bliss. *Prism*. New York: Stein and Day, 1985.

Borges, Jorge. *Borges, A Reader*. Monegal and Reid, eds. New York: Dutton, 1981.

Bowles, Paul. Introduction to Eberhardt, Isabelle, *The Oblivion Seekers*. Bowles, trans. San Francisco: City Lights, 1982.

Bukowski, Charles. *Notes of a Dirty Old Man*. San Francisco: City Lights, 1969.

Burroughs, William. "Wouldn't You," in *Naked Lunch*. New York: Grove Press, 1992.

Butler, Judith. *Subjects of Desire*. New York: Columbia University Press, 1989.

Capote, Truman. *In Cold Blood*. New York: Signet Books, 1965.

———. *Other Voices, Other Rooms*. New York: Random House, 1948.

Deleuze, Gilles. *Difference et repetition*. Paris: Presses Universitaires de France, 1968.

———. *Difference and Repetition*. P. Patton, trans. New York: Columbia, 1994.

———. *Expressionism in Philosophy*. M. Joughin, trans. New York: Zone Books, 1990.

———. *Logic of Sense*. M. Lester, trans. New York: Columbia University Press, 1990.

———. *Masochism*. J. McNeil, trans. New York: Braziller, 1971.

———. *Nietzsche and Philosophy*. Tomlinson, trans. New York: Columbia University Press, 1983.

———. *Nietzsche et la philosophie*. Paris: Presses Universitaires de France, 1963.

———. *Proust and Signs*. R. Howard, trans. New York: Braziller 1972.

Deleuze, Gilles, and Felix Guattari. *A Thousand Plateaus*. Massumi, trans. Minneapolis: University of Minnesota Press, 1988.

———. *Anti-Oedipus*. Hurley, Seem, Lane, trans. Minneapolis: University of Minnesota Press, 1983.

Deleuze, Gilles, and Claire Parnot. *Dialogues*. Tomlinson, Habberjam, trans. London: Athlone Press, 1977.

Descombes, Vincent. *Modern French Philosophy*. L. Scott-Fox, J. Harding, trans. Cambridge: University of Cambridge Press, 1980.

Duras, Marguerite. *The Malady of Death*. B. Bray, trans. New York: Grove Weidenfeld, 1988.

Eberhardt, Isabelle. *Ecrits sur le sable*. Vols. 1 and 2. Paris: Bernard Grasset, 1988.

———. *The Oblivion Seekers*. Bowles, trans. San Francisco: City Lights, 1982.

———. *The Passionate Nomad: The Diary of Isabelle Eberhardt*. de Voogd, trans. Boston: Beacon Press, 1987.

Erickson, Steve. *Days Between Stations*. New York: Vintage Books, 1986.

Ferry, Luc, and Alain Renaut. *French Philosophy of the Sixties*. Cattani, trans. Amherst: University of Massachusetts Press, 1990.

Fitzgerald, F. Scott. *The Last Tycoon*. New York: Charles Scribner's Sons, 1941.

———. *The Crack-Up*. New York: New Directions Books, 1956.

———. *The Great Gatsby*. New York: Collier Books, 1992.

Foucault, Michel. "A Preface to Transgression," in *Language, Counter-Memory, Practice*. D. Bouchard, ed. D. Bouchard, S. Simon, trans. Ithaca: Cornell University Press, 1977.

Gass, William. *Fiction and the Figures of Life*. New York: Vintage, 1958.

Genet, Jean. *The Selected Writings of Jean Genet*. E. White, ed. New Jersey: The Ecco Press, 1993.

Hardt, Michael. *Gilles Deleuze*. Minneapolis: University of Minnesota Press, 1993.

Heidegger, Martin. *An Introduction to Metaphysics*. Manheim, trans. New Haven: Yale University Press, 1959.

Hemingway, Ernest. *A Moveable Feast*. New York: Charles Scribner's Sons, 1987.

Houlgate, Stephen. *Hegel, Nietzsche, and the Criticism of Metaphysics*. Cambridge: Cambridge University Press, 1986.

Kabbani, Rana. Introduction to Eberhardt, Isabelle. *The Passionate Nomad: The Diary of Isabelle Eberhardt*. de Voogd, trans. Boston: Beacon Press, 1987.

Kant, Immanuel. *Critique of Pure Reason*. N.K. Smith, trans. New York: St. Martin's, 1965.

Kobak, Annette. *Isabelle*. New York: Knopf, 1989.

Laing, R.D. *The Divided Self*. New York: Pantheon, 1969.

Man, Paul de. *Allegories of Reading*. New Haven: Yale University Press, 1979.

Milford, Nancy. *Zelda*. New York: Avon, 1970.

Nietzsche, Friedrich. *The Gay Science*. W. Kaufmann, trans. New York: Vintage, 1974.

———. *On the Genealogy of Morals*. W. Kaufmann, trans. New York: Vintage, 1979.

———. *Thus Spoke Zarathustra*. R. Hollingdale, trans. New York: Penguin, 1961.

———. *Twilight of the Idols*. R. Hollingdale, trans. London: Penguin, 1988.

Plato. *Phaedrus*.

———. *Republic*.

———. *Symposium*.

Rorty, Richard. *Contingency, Irony, and Solidarity*. Cambridge: Cambridge University Press, 1989.

Rousseau, Jean-Jacques. *Confessions*. J.M. Cohen, trans. London: Penguin, 1953.

———. *The First and Second Discourses*. Masters, trans. New York: St. Martin's Press, 1964.

———. *Reveries of a Solitary*. Fletcher, trans. New York: Burt Franklin, 1927.

Satten, Joseph, et al. "Murder Without Apparent Motive—A Study in Personality Disorganization," *The American Journal of Psychiatry*, July, 1960.

Shakespeare, William. *Titus Andronicus*.

Wahl, Jean. "Nietzsche et la philosophie," *Revue de metaphysic et de morale*, 1963.

Wilkes, Kathleen. *Real People*. New York: Oxford University Press, 1988.

INDEX